Justice as a Basic Human Need

JUSTICE AS A BASIC HUMAN NEED

ANTHONY TAYLOR
EDITOR

Nova Science Publishers, Inc.
New York

For permission to use material from this book please contact us:
Telephone 631-231-7269; Fax 631-231-8175
Web Site: http://www.novapublishers.com

LIBRARY OF CONGRESS CATALOGING-IN-PUBLICATION DATA

Justice as a basic human need / Antony Taylor (editor).
p. cm.
Includes index.
ISBN 1-59454-915-X
1. Justice--Psychological aspects. 2. Social justice. 3. Criminal justice, Administration of. I. Taylor, A. J. W. (Antony James William)
BF789.J8J87 2006
172'.2--dc22 2005034940

Published by Nova Science Publishers, Inc. ✦ New York

CONTENTS

BRIEF CURRICULA VITAE OF CONTRIBUTORS

Paul Burns studied Clinical Psychology at Victoria University of Wellington (VUW) New Zealand, followed by Human Resource and Change Management in the UK. After a varied career he now works in London as a psychotherapist and an Organisation Development Consultant. In 2000 he became a volunteer Caseworker/Counsellor at the Medical Foundation Caring for Victims of Torture and, later, a Group Psychotherapist there. He was a founding member of the Neuro-linguistic Psychotherapy and Counselling Association and promoted the first UK, NLP based psychotherapy training. He is a member of the European Society for Traumatic Stress Studies and edits the *Cooperative Online Dictionary of Trauma* www.codt.org. Paul acknowledges the contribution of John Schlapobersky to his chapter - John has insights as a political refugee after being tortured by the Apartheid regime in South Africa, he helped set up the Medical Foundation, is one of its most experienced psychotherapists, and with Paul developed informal assessment scales for group work and survivors of torture.

Lynne Eccleston gained her PhD at the University of Melbourne, where she.is now the Course Convener of the Forensic Psychology Program Previously she worked as a clinician with male and female offenders in various forensic/psychiatric institutional environments including community settings, in-patient secure facilities and maximum security prisons. She has experience in individual and group therapy with offenders displaying a wide range of issues and dysfunctional behaviours associated with their offending behaviour, and has delivered workshops to other psychologists and prison officers. Her publications include journal articles and book chapters on prediction of risk and dangerous behaviour in violent offenders; assessment, treatment and rehabilitation of offenders; treatment and prevention of suicide and self-harming behaviour in offenders; and female offenders. She also consults to Corrections Victoria and Victoria Police in relation to violent and sexual offenders.

Ronald Fischer gained his DPhil from the University of Sussex, UK, working with Peter B. Smith on cross-cultural aspects of distributive justice before joining the School of Psychology at Victoria University of Wellington, NZ. His main research is in cross-cultural aspects of organizational behaviour and organizational justice, as well as research methodology, and statistics. He is actively involved in various projects that focus on reward allocation across continents and cultures, cultural values and work performance, social justice perceptions and political violence in the Middle East, paternalistic leadership styles, social and processes of leadership. He is also the international co-ordinator of a ten-country study on effects of national culture on organizational practices and employee behaviour.

Paul Jose received his Ph.D. in Developmental Psychology from Yale University in 1980. Then after holding two post-doctoral fellowship positions at the University of Illinois, Champaign-Urbana, he took his first position at Loyola University Chicago in 1985. Recently he relocated to Victoria University of Wellington with the rank of Senior Lecturer. His research encompasses topics in moral development, sex role socialization, adolescent wellbeing, stress and coping, and early literacy. He has published over 35 articles in journals of developmental, social, and clinical psychology.

Andrew Ladley is a lawyer specialising in human rights who earned his PhD at the London School of Economics and worked extensively as a Legal Adviser for a number of international missions, including the United Nations (Cambodia 1993; East Timor 1999/2000), the Commonwealth (South Africa 1994; The Gambia 1996), and the United Nations Development Programme (Jamaica 2002). He conducted research missions for the International Commission of Jurists (Malaysia 1987), and for Amnesty International (Samoa 1995, Bosnia 1996), in between teaching law in the National University of Singapore and Victoria University of Wellington. For four years he was Chief of Staff and Coalition Manager in the Office of Deputy Prime Minister/ Minister of Economic Development, Government of New Zealand. Currently he is the Director of the Institute for Policy Studies at VUW - a non-partisan umbrella body in the VUW School of Government, described recently as 'New Zealand's most influential think tank' that brings together a wide range of thinkers to discuss and publish views on social and political policy. In 2000 he received the Inaugural UNESCO 'Peacebuilders' award for his work in East Timor, and in 2001 he was made an Officer of the New Zealand Order of Merit.

Chris Marshall holds a Ph.D in New Testament Studies from King's College, the University of London, England, and an MA in Peace Studies from the Associated Mennonite Biblical Seminary in Indiana, USA. After 19 years of teaching New Testament at the Tyndale Graduate School of Theology in Auckland, New Zealand, he was appointed to the St John's Senior Lecturership in Christian Theology at VUW. He has an extensive list of publications on biblical and ethical themes, including a book *Beyond retribution: A New Testament vision for justice, crime and punishment* (Eerdmans, 2001) that was named in the 2002 outstanding academic titles list produced annually by the leading American book review journal *Choice.* The same book was also listed in the top ten books for parish ministry by the American Academy of Parish Clergy, and was nominated for the coveted 2003 (and again for the 2005) *Grawemeyer Award in religion* administered by the University of Louisville, Kentucky Press and the S/Herald Press, 2001).

Gabrielle Maxwell is currently a consultant to the School of Government at VUW and to the emerging restorative justice programmes in a number of countries around the world. Until she retired in 2003, she was the Director for the Crime and Justice Research Centre at VUW. Before that she was Senior Researcher at the Office of the Commissioner for Children, Research Fellow in the Department of Justice, and a Senior lecturer in Psychology at the University of Otago. Her current research focuses on youth justice, crime prevention, children and family violence, human rights, legal services and court systems. With Allison Morris and other colleagues, she has an extensive list of publications in the areas of restorative justice and youth justice – their most recent book being *Restorative justice for juveniles: Conferencing, and mediation circles* (2001). Her latest research report, *Achieving effective Outcomes in New Zealand* (Maxwell, G.M., Kingi, V., Robertson, J., Morris, A., and

Cunningham, C., 2004) provides an in depth analysis of the effectiveness of the country's recently transformed youth justice system.

Allison Morris is a consultant for the Crime and Justice Research Centre at VUW and an independent researcher. Previously she was Professor of Criminology and the Director of the Institute of Criminology at VUW from 1993 until 2001. Previously she was a Reader in Criminal Justice at the Institute of Criminology in the University of Cambridge. In recent years, much of her research has focused on restorative justice in general, and on the New Zealand youth justice system in particular. Apart from her joint publications with Gabrielle Maxwell, she completed the *Second New Zealand National Survey of Crime Victims,* and currently, with others, is carrying out the evaluation of the pilot of court referred restorative justice conferences in four courts in New Zealand.

Palmer Reg Orovwuje is the Professional Advisor (Social Work Mental Health) for Capital and Coast District Health Board, and a Consultant Social Worker at the Central Regional Forensic Mental Health, Rehabilitation, and Intellectual Disability Services in Wellington, New Zealand. A Nigerian by birth, he did his post-graduate studies at the London School of Economics and Political Science and the University of Birmingham in the UK, before working as a grass-roots social worker and an academic. He has participated in the development and implementation of several innovative service programmes in the mental health field, and has published papers on mental health, social versus business models of health, problems faced by refugees and minority ethnic groups, and cross-cultural issues.

Linda J Skitka gained her PhD from the University of California at Berkeley, and is a Professor at the University of Illinois at Chicago. She has an active research program broadly devoted to investigating the decision making calculus that leads people to decide whether to support various social policies, and to suggest why political liberals and political conservatives differ so fundamentally on such issues as spending on the poor. She is concerned about the ways people decide whether a policy is just or unjust, and with the part that moral convictions play in comparison with other kinds of strong attitudes in determining their positions.

Jeffrey Sluka earned his PhD from the University of California at Berkeley, and is an Associate Professor in the Social Anthropology Programme at Massey University of Palmerston North, New Zealand. A political anthropologist, his research interest lies in political violence and the cultural dynamics of armed conflicts involving ethnonationalist movements and indigenous peoples. He is the author of *Hearts and minds, Water and fish: Popular support for the IRA and INLA in a Northern Irish Ghetto* (JAI Press, 1989), and he edited *Death squad: The anthropology of state terror* (University of Pennsylvania Press, 2000).

Tony (A.J.W.) Taylor is Emeritus Professor of Psychology at VUW, having previously held a Chair in Clinical Psychology there. He studied at the London School of Economics before becoming a Probation Officer, and then at VUW before becoming a Prison Psychologist, Head of a University Student Counselling Service, and an honorary Consultant in the Department of Psychiatry at Wellington Hospital. In retirement he worked part-time in the West Coast Health Forensic Psychiatric Unit, and he began a stress/trauma practice. In his research he was concerned initially with the reactions of people of all sorts to long-term captivity and isolation – and in that connection he was an adviser to NZ Volunteer Service Abroad, NZ Antarctic Division, and Greenpeace Antarctica. Later he came to focus on different groups that had been exposed to different kinds of disaster. He has over 260 publications that include the joint editorship of *Deviant behaviour: New Zealand Studies:Antarctic psychology* (Wellington: DSIR, 1987) and of *Man in the Antarctic: The scientific research of the International Biomedical Expedition to Antarctic*(Taylor and Francis, 1988), and authorship of *Disasters and disaster stress* (AMS Press, 1989). He is a Companion of the Royal Societyof New Zealand and a Docteur Honoris Causa of the University of Rheims.

Charles W. Tolman is Professor Emeritus in Psychology at the University of Victoria (UV) in Vancouver Island Canada, where he taught courses in most areas of psychology but especially in the methods, history and theory in psychology. Until recently, he was a Fellow in the Centre for Studies in Religion and Society at UV where he pursued interests in the problems common to religion, psychology, and moral philosophy. He is author of *Problems of theoretical psychology* (Captus Press, 1996); *Psychology, society, and subjectivity* (Routledge, 1994) and editor of several books devoted to philosophical and theoretical problems in psychology, such as *Positivism in psychology* (Springer-Verlag, 1991); *Critical psychology* (Cambridge University Press, 1991).

Tony Ward is a clinical psychologist by training. He has been working in the clinical and forensic field since 1987. He was formerly Director of the Kia Marama Sexual Offenders' Unit at Rolleston Prison in New Zealand, and has taught both clinical and forensic psychology at Victoria, Canterbury, and Melbourne Universities. He is currently the Director of Clinical Training at Victoria University of Wellington. His research interests fall into the five main areas of correctional rehabilitation models and issues; cognition and sex offenders; the problem behaviour process in offenders; the implications of naturalism for theory construction and clinical practice; and the assessment and case formulation in clinical psychology. He has published over 170 journal articles, books, and books chapters. His two most recent books are titled *Theories of sexual offending* (2006), John Wiley & Sons Ltd and *Culture and child protection: Reflexive responses*. (2006) London, UK: Jessica Kingsley.

David B. Wexler is John D. Lyons Professor of Law and Professor of Psychology at the University of Arizona in Tucson, Arizona and Professor of Law and Director of the International Network on Therapeutic Jurisprudence at the University of Puerto Rico in San Juan, Puerto Rico. His outstanding academic career is matched by his contributions to many leading Commissions on different aspects of law and mental disability that earned him a Distinguished Service Award from the National Center for State Courts. He first expounded the therapeutic jurisprudence in a paper written in 1987, and subsequently he and Professor Bruce Winnick of the University of Miami worked together to develop the topic – their latest book being *Judging in a therapeutic key: therapeutic jurisprudence and the courts* (Durham: Academic Press 2003). Their publications have captured the attention of practitioners and academics in many disciplines in many countries.

PREFACE

Psychologists in different tributaries of the discipline have long been preoccupied with aspects of 'Justice', but none previously has addressed the essential question raised in this book – namely of justice being as vital to the essentials of life and to the flowering of the human spirit as other basic needs. The same can be said for academics and practitioners in other fields of social science, including mental health and psychiatry. Except for the groups represented by two contributors in this book, it seems to me that lawyers in the main direct their expertise to the superficial maintenance of systems of justice rather than to the underlying reasons for doing so.

This book, arising from academic, clinical, empirical, and theoretical studies, goes further by giving justice its proper place in the hierarchy of basic human needs. It is designed in accord with a general systems theory in which contributions are welcomed from scholars and researchers in different domains of knowledge. Above all, it is written in the hope of inducing others to share a commitment to maintaining justice and do their utmost to prevent injustice.

The first chapter delineates the strands of justice, defines human needs, and advances the argument for justice to be brought firmly into the classical hierarchy proposed originally by Abraham Maslow. Then, instead of merely regarding justice as a utilitarian procedure for resolving conflict, in the second chapter Charles Tolman advances the philosophical argument that *a priori*, justice is a prerequisite that enables human beings to become fully developed individuals in an orderly society. He comments on the particular and the universal aspects of justice in the sharing of power both to attain common goals and to meet individual and social needs, draws attention to the power that creates injustice to the ultimate detriment of both individuals and society, and explores the dissonance between the sharing and the restriction of justice.

Chris Marshall, a theologian, follows by asserting that justice is not merely the product of social consensus, but it is an intrinsically *religious* notion. He argues that justices can be part and parcel of a larger understanding of the ultimate meaning, values, and obligations of life that are intrinsically the subject matter of religious discourse. Without denying the contributions of other religions, he outlines the key components of a Christian approach. He comments that while the wellsprings of Christian nurture seem to be drying up in the present secular and post-modernist age, the scriptures of the Old and New Testaments still offer profound and distinctive insights into the meaning of justice.

Then Paul Jose gives a review of the major theoretical approaches to moral development, and considers the more recent empirical studies, most of which are concerned with the pragmatics of 'when' and 'how' moral judgments are made rather than their origins and their essential nature. Following Piaget, he argues that moral judgments are the natural outgrowth of cognitive development, combined with the need to access sufficient resources in the environment for survival. He goes on to consider the socio-biological argument of Wilson and others that morality is of necessity hard-wired into the genetic make-up of human beings.

Lynne Eccleston and Tony Ward also regard sensitivity to unfairness or injustice as a biological component - although acknowledging that human beings seek a range of valued outcomes, relationships, autonomy, food, and warmth in order to function in an optimal manner, and accepting that social justice helps to provide the necessary context for their attainment. As clinical psychologists they suggest that its neglect of justice under the conventional punitive system might explain the persistent high rates of recidivism of some offenders. They review a number of alternative proposals on offer, and conclude that a 'good lives model' should be adopted that equips offenders with the necessary internal and external skills for meeting their primary needs in more socially acceptable and personally meaningful ways than by breaking the criminal law.

David Wexler regards the law as a social force that produces behavioural consequences, some of which can be called therapeutic, and others not – hence the title of his chapter. Under the rubric of 'Therapeutic Jurisprudence', he brings to the table some of the procedures and issues that previously have gone unnoticed, to show how they can be factored into law-making, 'lawyering', or judging, while still respecting justice and due process in the detection and determination of guilt. In following the theme, he describes the essential factors that separate 'desisters' from recidivists, and goes on to show how discriminating judges apply therapeutic principles to both kinds of offender. Already his thesis for humanizing the law and the legal process is commanding widespread international attention.

Criminologists Gabrielle Maxwell and Allison Morris are pioneers who present restorative justice as a new approach to conflict resolution between the parties involved in the perpetration of crime. They point out that while conventional western criminal justice systems primarily emphasises due process and punishment for the repair of harm and the prevention of re-offending, the system they developed, firmly recognizes the need to reintegrate both offenders and their victims back into society. They detail the new and necessary processes that directly involve offenders, victims, communities, and representatives of the state in the processes of decision-making about outcomes, and they give the empirical evidence of their studies designed to answer questions of accountability.

Social psychologists Linda Skitka and Ronald Fischer give a theoretical view of the industrial/organizational, interpersonal, and community/political related aspects of justice. In doing so they cover distributive, procedural, and interpersonal aspects to show that justice is strongly related to behaviour and attitudes towards groups and authorities - as well as to individual identity, health and well-being. They review the different self-interest, relational, and moral-normative explanations of justice, and discuss claims that have been made about their universality. They conclude that psychological research has been too pre-occupied with justice in Western industrialised societies at the expense of considering cultural processes and cross-cultural differences.

Reg Orovwuje challenges the practices of patient management and care from the standpoint of an experienced social work consultant who is familiar with institutional and community treatment of both the mentally ill and forensic patients. With Tony Taylor he draws attention to the fearful and deeply held perceptions of health professionals and of the public towards vulnerable groups of mental health consumers. They trace the philosophical and professional origins of that prejudice, and they describe recent attempts that have been made in New Zealand to put matters right and give a lead to the community to improve the part it might play in the recovery of the mentally ill. Together they argue that negative attitudes deny consumers of mental health services the necessary protection of human rights and social justice that most other members of society enjoy. They say that the denial of justice adds substantially to the burdens that the mentally disabled already carry.

Jeffrey Sluka, an anthropologist, regards social justice as a cultural universal and a fundamental necessity for human survival. He finds justice and human rights to be inextricably linked, and holds that their increasing abuse by the authorities is the fundamental cause of growing political violence - including warfare, and terrorism: internecine and international. To this cultural perception he applies the 'relative justice' theory of political violence, and he argues that major injustice - universally experienced as oppression - leads inevitably to conflict and active resistance. He concludes that human rights, social justice, and survival have a common ground, and he considers that all must feature in problem-solving if the unrelenting and bitter chain of action and reaction is ever to be broken asunder. Towards that end he gives a detailed analysis of the functions of terrorism, whether perpetrated by groups or governments for political purposes. In such matters, he argues, anthropologists should not be ethically neutral.

Paul Burns, a psychotherapist, acknowledges the help of psychiatrist John Schlapobersky in approaching justice from a clinical perspective through its abuse in the extreme forms of torture. He outlines the relevant regulatory international conventions relating to torture, gives the incidence and the conditions most likely to encourage politically motivated violence, and offers tentative explanations for the motivation of those who either practice torture or support its use. Like Sluka he documents the abuse of detainees and prisoners in Afghanistan, Iraq, and Guantanamo Bay, Cuba, and raises moral questions about the complicity of governments in such matters. He details the commonly reported practice of physical and mental torture and their sequelae for survivors, and refers to the compounding factors when as so often happens victims are treated simply as refugees. He goes on to illustrate the difficulties that victims of torture have in providing clear-cut evidence for purposes of prosecution about the abuse to which they had been subjected. Finally he introduces the integrated model of Testimony Therapy that the Medical Foundation in London has developed for its entire staff to adopt in the treatment of clients who have been tortured.

Andrew Ladley, an experienced academic lawyer and an international mediator, examines the commonalities in international law relating to justice and human rights, to discover what they tell about the human condition, about rulers and the ruled, about the nature of individuals/societies/states, their shared obligations and expectations, and the fears that all parties in conflict have of each other. He suggests that although the documents from the core provisions of the UN Charter to the latest international instruments present a bleak view of human nature in general and of the group psyche in particular, they also speak of human beings as a normative species optimistically articulating the possibility of curbing a violent and dangerous nature, and trying constantly to learn from the past to avoid the repetition of strife in the future.

The final chapter dwells on the theme of the book as a whole, and considers theories of motivation in which the need for justice might appropriately be lodged. It settles on Abraham Maslow's theory in which justice could be accommodated in the security stratum of hios hierarchy of basic needs, while partly fulfilling the needs for belonging, and also expecting the 'self-actualised' to be active in its promotion. With justice brought into the mainstream of psychology, the outcome could do much to reassert the value of justice in the whole panoply of human affairs. It asserts that psychologists have a major part to play in the proposition - especially if they are wise enough to follow a general systems model for the acquisition of knowledge that broadens the focus of their post-graduate education and includes contributions from other academic disciplines. It leaves open the possibility that other academic disciplines might also restructure their approach by incorporating a concern for justice in their teaching, research, and application of knowledge for the benefit of mankind.

Acknowledgments

Thanks are due to the Editorial Board of *New Ideas in Psychology* for taking the seminal article in November 2003 that led to the preparation of this book, and to President Frank Columbus of Nova Science for supporting the expansion of the theme with an interdisciplinary mixture of international contributors – all of whom were active in various ways in promoting the cause of justice and prepared make time to share their experiences, insights, scholarship, and personal concerns. Finally on a personal note, I thank my partner Denise for the support she has given me as I closeted myself to tinkle away on the electronic keyboard to do my editorial bit with the many manuscripts that came my way.

In: Justice as a Basic Human Need
Editor: Anthony Taylor, pp. 1-12
ISBN 1-59454-915-X

Chapter 1

DOING JUSTICE TO JUSTICE

A. J. W. Taylor
School of Psychology, Victoria University of Wellington
New Zealand

ABSTRACT

Although clinical, community, developmental, forensic, and social psychologists have been concerned for a long time with different aspects of justice - such as the acquisition of conscience, responsibility for unlawful behaviour, fair reward for labour, and the essential rules for the maintenance of communities - none previously has suggested that justice is so fundamental for safety and belonging as to be regarded as one of the basic needs for human development. The case is presented, the manifold concept of justice explored, human needs defined, and the argument advanced for justice to be brought firmly into mainstream psychology.

INTRODUCTION

Applied clinical and social work invariably puts psychologists firmly in touch with questions of morality, legality, and justice, but in general their academic training will have offered them little by way of guidance in such important but abstruse matters. Most of their university teachers will have been emerging behavioural scientists in denial about the real world as they strove to promote the pure methodological paradigm of logical positivism (cf. Israel and Goldstein, 1944). For them objectivity and rationality reigned supreme. They regarded a preoccupation with subjectivity and elusive belief-value systems as indicators of intellectual immaturity. Subsequently the ways of students and staff will have parted, with the one helping the maladjusted either to adapt to the status quo or to challenge the social structures they found unbearable, and the other either making extensive inroads in the laboratory study of psychosensory processes or vigorously debating the language and methods of discourse analysis with which to approach their studies (cf. Parker, 2002).

But the epistemological tension between the opposing psychological schools did give rise to the humanistic movement (Bugenthal, 1967), and eventually to a lone voice for values to be incorporated as a third component of the scientist-practitioner model for clinicians to adopt without tarnishing their reputations (O'Donohue, 1989). In academic psychology the matter of acknowledging human values still remains far from settled – except as they apply to researchers in the course of conducting their experiments and to clinicians when conducting professional practice (cf. Francis and Cameron, 1997, chs. 9 and 10). The hope in presenting this chapter, is that practitioners and purists might enlarge their platform of understanding about human values, come to share their experiential and intellectual concerns, and apply their intellectual and empirical skills to examine justice in its patterns of diversity.

Experience in the South Pacific

For many people the genocide in such places as Bosnia, Cambodia, Nazi Germany, Rwanda, and Somalia prompted a personal reconsideration of justice in its totality *per se* (cf. Ellwood, 2005). But it was a direct encounter with the bewilderment, disappointment, and shock of the Parliamentary hostages and their families in Fiji in May 2000 that brought the issue finally to the boil for me (Taylor, Nailatikau, and Walkey, 2002). There the primary victims (the former hostages) complained that the ideals they had promoted, the policies they had shaped, and the substantial progress they had made towards their attainment, neither 'justified' the armed terrorist assault made against them nor their subsequent detention. Equally the secondary victims (the families of the hostages) thought that the sudden extraction of loved ones from their family circles defied rational explanation. For them, the experience was truly traumatic, and it had adverse consequences on the emotional wellbeing of the young, the middle-aged, and old, with all but the most resolute and resilient withdrawing emotionally for weeks until the military regained control and formed an interim government. Some felt so vulnerable that to gain protection from potential home-invaders they made their houses into caged fortresses, and a few even fled the country to seek sanctuary abroad.

Conceivably the hostage-takers might have had similar 'justification' as the hostages for the actions they took, and their families might also have had some of the same apprehensions and fears as their counterparts. But data is lacking because there was only an invitation from the wife of one of the captors to visit her home to discuss her family situation, where coincidentally a chance opportunity arose to canvass the views of one of her friends in a similar position who happened to be present. However, any such opposing claims for justice would not negate the proposition that justice is a basic human need, but it would simply affirm the importance of having independent tribunals established for the resolution of disputes if not for the restoration of tranquillity.

While the psychological reactions of many in the hostage situation fell within the familiar balance of post- traumatic factors reflecting individual resilience and vulnerability (cf. McFarlane and Yehuda, 1996), the symptoms of shock, horror, disillusionment, and disbelief attributed to the shattering of their legitimate expectations from being members of a community, did not. Rather their expression raised unfamiliar questions for stress/trauma clinicians and researchers about the nature of justice and of inviolable human rights, the attacks on which were perceived as manifest stressors to be brought into the familiar equation when assessing the need for therapeutic intervention.

But at the time, attention could be paid only to the immediate symptomatic clinical demands, leaving the underlying protests to be construed as comparable to some extent with those of victims of crime and other kinds of catastrophe (cf. Young, 2001). Later when the situation eased, fragments of previous experience led sequentially to a consideration of the definitions of justice and morality, a brief foray into jurisprudence and related aspects of clinical/forensic/pastoral/community and social psychology, and finally to a conceptual consideration of basic human needs and schema in which the need for justice could properly be placed (Taylor, 2003a).

Fragments of Earlier Experience

Experience in the criminal courts made clear that the community looks for justice to provide the orderly rules for discourse, the breaches of which if detected might lead to prosecution, or otherwise play on the minds of the perpetrators and induce their confession and remorse. It led me to refute the widely held notion that social scientists should be totally accepting and completely non-judgmental in their work, because I found that most criminals did have a keen sense of justice, even if at times they had chosen to override it. In their Court appearances they had either pleaded guilty or were found guilty of the facts as presented (a few, it is true, quite erroneously - cf. Royal Commission on Criminal Justice 1991-1993: Thorp, 2005), and, having been sentenced, they were under some pressure from the psychologist to reflect on the emotional consequences of their guilt (Taylor, 1959; 1961). In the process it was found helpful to differentiate between legal, moral, neurotic, religious, and social strands of guilt, and to discover the particular combinations that suggested dimensions that might be susceptible to change (Taylor, 1964). Subsequent research showed the sequential phases of group cohesion, group interaction, value change, and group dispersal to be salient when helping offenders to change their attitudes and behaviour for the better (Taylor, 1967).

Later professional experience as an expert witness in the civil courts, if only in relation to the presence or absence of signs and symptoms of occupational stress, opened up the question of civil justice between parties in which the state was concerned to see that fairplay resulted (Taylor, 2002).

Finally, the social injustice that generated the Civil Rights movement and the student revolution of the late 1960's in the United States (Taylor, 1970), together with concerns about the iniquities perpetrated by the early colonisers of New Zealand (Belich, 1998) and the social injustice of free-market policies (Shirley, 1990; Dommen, 2003), completed the triumvirate of situations that induced reflections on justice.

Definition of Terms

The legal, philosophical, and psychological definitions of justice, morality, and needs are many and various, and they could generate endless debate. Without being too pedantic, from the definitions on offer by the OED Online:

- 'justice' was taken to mean 'the exercise of authority or power in maintenance of right; vindication of right by assignment of reward or punishment'
- 'morality' to refer to the 'personal qualities judged to be good' or bad: and
- 'needs' to 'be under a necessity to do something'.

Specifically the offerings on justice relate to the system that sustains laws and procedures rather than to any underlying basic need of individuals for security. But 'the times, they are a-changing' (cf. UN *Handbook on justice for victims*, 1999), and the changes might soon be reflected in the dictionary definition of justice. Towards that end it was thought helpful:

- to regard *justice* as an essential precondition for approximating the good life: in other words, the reciprocal quality of relationships that obtain between people for their mutual wellbeing
- to retain *morality* as the quintessential code by which behaviour might be ordered: the distinction between morality and law resembling the difference between idealism and pragmatism – as Denning (1953, chs. 1 and 5) so succinctly set out, and
- to affirm *basic human needs* as the major motivators for personal and social development – the mainsprings of action that curiously are energised by depletion and tranquillised by repletion.

REFLECTIONS ON THE FUNDAMENTALS OF JUSTICE

Moral philosophers, certainly since Confucius in the East (551-479 B.C: McGreal, 1995) and Plato in the West (428-348 BC: Lindsay trans. 1935), have long emphasised the importance of human rights as being necessary for the fulfilment of the good life, and political philosophers throughout the ages have made attempts to design societies in which the principles could be put into practice. For their part constitutional lawyers framed rules and regulations to provide security to enable people to conduct their lives with minimal disturbance and at the same time fulfil their responsibilities to the wider community (Thompson, 1992).

The origin of such regulatory activity has been traced to the 18th century BC Code of Hammurabi. But without reaching back quite that far, from her extensive fieldwork in Africa, Lindner (2001) described three historic phases in the development and changes in the expression of justice. She associated the first with the primitive hunter-gathering period, the second with the agrarian revolution and the use of slavery, and the third with the creation of 'pyramids of power' necessary for building civilisations. However Robert Wright (2000, 2002), a supremely detached observer and prodigious reporter of historical trends, would not be so specific. Instead he discerned the fluctuating influence of a non-zero-sum force behind human affairs that depends on rules for cooperation being established and maintained to prevent chaos and terrorism. From this, and despite the perpetuation of conflicts within and between communities, it would follow that the law is a somewhat dynamic force in the life of national and international communities.

In fact the preamble to the 1948 *Universal Declaration of Human Rights*, adopted by United Nations to set the heights of human endeavour (Brownlie, 1981: Mullen, 1986), said that:

> 'Whereas recognition of the inherent dignity and of the equal and inalienable rights of all members of the human family is at the foundation of freedom, justice and peace in the world, Whereas disregard and contempt for human rights have resulted in barbarous acts which have outraged the conscience of mankind, and the advent of a world in which human beings shall enjoy freedom of speech and belief and freedom from fear and want has been proclaimed as the highest aspiration of the common people.'(*New Zealand Handbook on International Human Rights*, 1998, p.142).

Subsequently the signatories began to put their houses in order to ensure that their laws and procedures conformed to international expectations, and they also began to shed their colonial obligations. Later, because inevitably in this less than ideal world the processes failed that were intended to fulfil the reasonable expectations of the parties concerned, they gave special attention to the serious breaches of agreement that had occurred (Chowdhury, 1989). As a result it is probably true that most countries, if not all, have policies in place for preventing injustice and procedures ready for dealing with breaches. Certainly Claude B Levinson (2004), the newly appointed United Nations Commissioner for Human Rights, asserts that 'human rights are above all a question of justice'.

Yet justice *per se* received scant attention from mainstream psychologists and the writers of introductory textbooks in psychology. It was completely ignored in a comprehensive review of motivation (Wong, 2000), and it escaped the attention entirely of a galaxy of high-powered researchers that contributed to a recent volume on the same subject (Efklides, Kuhl, and Sorrentino, 2001). An unlimited PsychINFO search on 2nd June 2005 for studies relating justice either to moral development or to basic need also produced no results. But by inference the topic is embedded in theories of personality that pay attention to individual super-ego development, classical conditioning, operant conditioning, moral development, and group norms (cf. Lundin, 1996). In clinical psychology it is also subsumed under the rubric of 'value-conflict stress' in relation to individuals that have become so alienated from their communities as to develop mental illness (Marsella, 1979). In a rare statement of affirmation about the place of environmental forces in the creation and treatment of extreme psychological stress, Summerfield (2000) went so far as to say that

> 'history shows ... social reform is the best medicine, for victims of war and atrocity, this means public recognition and justice. (*He goes on to assert that*) post-traumatic reactions are not just a private problem, with the onus on the individual to recover, but an indictment of the sociopolitical forces that produced them.'

But again, those forces have attracted comparatively little attention in the area of political psychology. There, a search of the journals shows the emphasis to be primarily on studies of conflicting ideologies and voting behaviour that govern systems of power, rather than on the fundamentals of justice and human rights. Similarly in forensic psychology, justice is addressed pragmatically in debates on the causes of crime and their correction without concern for the fundamental moral issues (cf. Muller, Blackman, and Chapman, 1984; Wrightsman, 2001). Certainly the revelations of the indefatigable campaigner Lincoln Steffens (1931) against corporate corruption in the US at the turn of the century have almost passed into oblivion, but the light that Edwin Sutherland (1883-1950) once turned on white-collar criminal corruption (Sutherland, 1949) now shines strongly in corporate law, criminology, and victimology (cf. Comer, 1998; US Department of Justice, 200: Legal Information Institute, 2004), and they feature in a catalogue of man-made disasters (Taylor, 2003b).[1]

Such a turn of events in business and public service would have dismayed Friederich Hayek (1899-1992), the authority who inspired Milton Friedman and others of the Chicago School who provided the ideology for the New Right in politics. Hayek (1944), the Nobel laureate economist with a passing interest in the psychoneurological aspects of impulses, took a narrow individualist stance in management as an extreme reaction to the encroachments of centralised government. He went on to declare 'social justice as nothing more than an empty formula', and to argue that 'individual moral responsibility for one's actions is incompatible with the realisation of any...overall pattern of distribution' (Hayek, 1979, pp. 3-4). As if to justify a return to primitive self-interest rather than to develop from it, he denied completely the continuing importance of social bonds, saying that 'we have all inherited from an earlier different type of society...some now deeply ingrained instincts which are inapplicable to our present society' (p.5). In fact he seems to have spurned all individual needs other than the one of self-interest – and even there he overlooked the dangers of avarice that the medieval monks included in their list of seven deadly sins. He construed the market as a game in which 'the results must be accepted as fair, so long as all obey the same rules, and no one cheats' (p.11) – and although conceding that 'a society in which a few can exert power to which they feel they are entitled to may be highly unpleasant for the others', he thought it would 'at least be viable' (p. 30).

As is well-known, the economics and the rhetoric of competitive individualism came to dominate public policy in the Anglophone countries in the 1980s and 1990s under the banner of a global free-market economy, before being imposed elsewhere. But few social scientists gave it attention. Restrictive monetary policies, financial deregulation, and the virtues of minimal state intervention reigned supreme. The terms 'Thatcherism' (Britain) 'Reganomics' (USA) and 'Rogernomics' (New Zealand) became shorthand descriptions for revolutionary economic reductionism, with society portrayed as a collection of individuals devoid of social and cultural identity, and consequently, responsibility. This doctrine of the Chicago School replaced the traditional working concepts of human groups, institutions, and collectivities of one sort or another by the single abstraction of a world of rational individuals who were

---

[1] Consider for example the recent debacles of the Bank of Credit and Commerce International, the Barings Bank, and the insider trading at Lloyds in the UK, of Elf Acquitaine in France, of LG Card in Korea, of Akold in the Netherlands, of the Parmalat Corporation in Italy, of the Allied Irish Bank, Andersons, Enron Energy, Xerox, Worldcom, Merrill Lynch and a number of big investment banks in the USA, and of Ariadne, Reid Murray, and the HIH Insurance Company in Australia – to say nothing of the celebrated cases of JBL, Equity Corporation, and Ansett NZ plus many other large companies that sailed close to the wind recently in the heady days of global free-market de-regulation.

seeking to maximise their personal wealth. It even reduced the major policy domains of health and education to a range of commodities to be purchased by individuals for their own enhancement and wellbeing, and it expected charitable institutions to do their best to deal with casualties on the wrong side of the deepening and widening divide between the wealthy and the others - with serious consequences for the most disadvantaged (Public Health Advisory Committee to the National Health Committee, 2002).

However, although justice and morality have to be restored in economic affairs, they have always had a firm place in the practice of pastoral psychology (Delaplane and Delaplane, 1966: Young, 1994/2004, ch.10: Kurtz, 1999; Miller, 2002). But the theological explanations advanced to account for adversity need constantly to be revised in the light of advances in the accumulation of knowledge from natural science, as well as from the reappraisal of the existential truths as distinct from the literal interpretations of the scriptures (cf. Spong, 1991). For example, it seemed quite anachronous for the clergy of four different denominations in a small South Pacific island to take turns to berate their followers for their moral transgressions to account for a cyclone, when a simple account of *El Nino* weather patterns was all that was required (Taylor, 1999). To this clinician it would have been more appropriate had the clergy supported the bereaved with compassion and education rather than increase their emotional burdens by imposing *Old Testament* admonitions. But after a tragic fire in a school dormitory on a different South Pacific island shortly afterwards, the clergy there spoke of the power of religious belief in helping the bereaved and the survivors to recover, and they placed commendable emphasis on teachings in the *New Testament* (Taylor, 2001).

The religious have also to make a constant reappraisal of the application of the essential truths they espouse if they are to make amends for the sustained campaigns of atrocities that zealots have perpetrated on their behalf[2]. Similarly they need to account satisfactorily for the bitter conflicts within religions as well as between them. But it is interesting that the World Council of Churches has made justice – economic, political and social, cultural, and racial - one of four themes in its ambitious campaign to overcome violence in the first decade of the present millennium, with religious identity, the use/abuse and misuse of power, and the spirit and logic of violence being the others (Mavunduse and Oxley, 2002).

Justice also held central place in community psychology from its birth in the 1980's as a separate domain of intellectual inquiry. There it was construed as a prominent motivating force in human behaviour, with the primary emphasis on environmental rather than individual factors (Lorion, 1992). According to Newborough (1992a; 1992b), many governments at the time were committed to policies of social change because of the widespread amalgam of violence, inequality, abuse of human rights, and ecological neglect perceived by post-modern global society. As a result, community psychologists adopted the idealistic Princeton World Order project and committed themselves to its associated Quest for the Just Community. But within ten years, as Gregory (2001) commented, 'the lofty spirit, awakening of morals, and arousal of conscience… dimmed, (and) wealth and power (replaced) principles about what is right, or the pursuit of justice for all, or simply the greater good'.

[2] See Reid (2001) for a critical reappraisal of the complex motivations of the Crusaders, and Sells (1996) for a discussion of the attempts made in Bosnia to cloak a basic ethnic war with religious overtones, and Ignatieff (1998) for the same in Afghanistan.

Yet in the narrower interpersonal domain of social psychology, Lerner (1980) championed the concept of a 'just world' that was more realist and pragmatic than idealistic and teleological, and his effort continues to command attention. Initially he restricted the term to what he thought was the tendency of individuals to maintain the status quo after any adverse incident by blaming the victim, unless the magnitude of their distress was substantially disproportional to the action that might have caused it. Subsequently he broadened his focus by addressing the morality of punishment in the treatment of offenders (cf. Lerner and Lerner, 1981), and he went on to establish the International Society for Justice Research, become one of the founding editors of *Social Justice Research* and the Plenum Press series of publications on Critical Issues in Justice, and inspire an international group of researchers to follow in his footsteps (cf. Ross and Miller, 2002). To quote Lerner (2002) in his opening chapter of the Ross and Miller volume, 'at least in Western societies, justice has a special status superseding all other norms and values…(*with*) the power to legitimise and, at times, to demand the sacrifice of liberty, lives, and happiness'. He went on to suggest that justice was a primary or primordial motive of human behaviour that was built into the cognitive structure of the young according to the treatment they receive, rather than by any 'dominant or omnipresent desire to maximise outcomes'.

Finally, in their introduction to another challenging volume of papers on social injustice, the social psychologists Skitka and Crosby (2003) traced the changing emphasis from distributive justice, through procedural justice, and retributive justice, to current concerns with large-scale injustice and, ultimately, to forgiveness. In referring to the 'vitality' of the topic, they drew attention to the models of 'Accessibility Identity' and 'Group Engagement' that offered explanations for individual and collective portrayals of justice, and they pointed to the emotional component in such appraisals that had to be taken into account when trying to understand reactive behaviour.

CONCLUSION

It remains to build on the work of the hardy pioneers by giving due recognition to the concept of justice that engaged their attention. In doing so, it would seem quite appropriate to suggest that justice be regarded as a basic human need on the satisfaction of which depends the development of individuals, their families, their communities, nations, and the whole of mankind. The precise place in any existing theoretical framework of needs in which the concept might be lodged will be deferred until the final chapter of this book. Other contributors will now have their say.

REFERENCES

American Psychological Association. (1992). Ethical principles for psychologists and code of conduct (rev. 1992). *American Psychologist,* 47, 1597-1611.

Belich, J. (1998). *New Zealand Wars and the Victorian interpretation of racial conflict.* Auckland: Penguin.

Brownlie, I. (Ed.). (1981). *Basic documents on human rights.* Oxford: Clarendon Press.

Bugenthal, J. (Ed.). (1967). *Challenges of humanistic psychology.* New York: McGraw-Hill.
Chowdhury, S.R. (1989). *Rule of law in a state of emergency: The Paris minimum standards of human rights norms in a state of emergency.* London: Pinter.
Comer, M.J. (1998). *Corporate fraud.* (3rd edn.). Aldershot UK: Gower.
Delaplane, D. and Delaplane, A. (1966). *Victims of child abuse, domestic violence, elder abuse, rape, robbery, assault and violent death: A manual for clergy and congregations.* Washington DC: US Department of Justice.
Denning, Sir A. (1953). *The changing law.* London: Stevens and Sons.
Dommen, E. (2003). *How just is the market economy?* Geneva: World Council of Churches.
Ellwood, W. (2005) Crime and punishment. *New Internationalist,* December, pp.2-6.
Francis, R.D., and Cameron, C. (1997). *The professional psychology handbook.* Melbourne: Macmillan Education.
Gregory, R.J. (2001). The spirit and substance of community psychology: Reflections. *Journal of Community* Psychology, 29, 4, 473- 485.
Hayek, F.A. (1944). *The road to serfdom.* London: Routledge.
Hayek, F.A. (1979). *Social justice, socialism, and democracy.* Australia: Centre for Independent Studies.
Ingnatieff, M. (1998). The warrior's honor: Ethnic war and the modern conscience. London: Chatto and Windus.
Israel, H., and Goldstein, B. (1944). Operationism in psychology. *Psychological Review,* 5, 1, 177-188.
Kurtz, E. (1999). The historical context. In W.R. Miller. *Integrating spirituality into treatment: Resources for practitioners.* (ch.2). Washington DC: American Psychological Association.
Legal Information Institute. (2004). Law about white-collar crime: An overview -accessed 12 April 2004 from http://www.law.cornell.edu/topics/white_collar.html
Lerner, M.J. (1980). *The belief in a just world. A fundamental delusion.* New York: Plenum.
Lerner, M.J. (2002). Pursuing the justice motive. In M. Ross, and D.T. Miller, (Eds.). (2002). *The justice motive in everyday life.* (ch.1). Cambridge University Press.
Lerner, M.J., and Lerner, S.C. (1981). *The justice motive in social behaviour: Adapting to times of scarcity and change.* New York: Plenum.
Levinson, C.B. (2004). Avant tout, une question de justice. *Le Nouvel Observateur Hebdomaire,* 19 August. – accessed 21 August 2004 from http://www.truthout.org/docs_04/082104H.shtml
Lindner, E.G. (2001). Reports from the field. *Traumatology,* 7, 1, 43-68.
Lindsay, A.D. (trans. 1935). *Plato's Republic.* London: Everyman's Library.
Lorion, R. P. (1 992) Community psychology in the 1990's : Reflections from the editor. *Journal of Community Psychology,* 20, 3-6.
Lundin, R.W. (1996). *Theories and systems of psychology.* (5th edn.). Lexington MA: Heath and Co.
Marsella, A.J. (1979). Cross-cultural studies of mental illness. In A.J. Marsella, R.G. Tharp, and T.J. Ciborowski. (Eds.). *Perspectives on cross-cultural psychology* (ch. 11). New York: Academic Press.
Mavunduse, D., and Oxley, S. (2002). *Why violence not peace?* Geneva: World Council of Churches.

McFarlane, A.C., and Yehuda, R. (1996). Resilience, vulnerability, and the course of posttraumatic reactions. In B. van der Kolk, A.C. McFarlane, and L. Weisaeth. (Eds.). *Traumatic stress: The overwhelming experience on mind, body, and society* (ch. 8). New York. Guilford.

McLelland, D. (Eds.). (1985). *Human motivation.* Cambridge University Press.

McGreal, I.P. (Ed.). (1995). *Great thinkers of the Eastern world.* New York: HarperCollins.

Miller, W.R. (Ed.). (1999). *Integrating spirituality into treatment: Resources for practitioners.* Washington DC: American Psychological Association.

Miller, W.R. (Ed.). (2002). *Integrating spirituality into treatment: Resources for practitioners.* Washington DC: American Psychological Association.

Montada, L. (2002). Doing justice to the justice motive. In M. Ross, and D.T. Miller. (Eds.). (2002). *The justice motive in everyday life.* (ch.2). Cambridge University Press.

Mullen, T. (1986). Constitutional protection of human rights. In T. Campbell, D. Goldberg, S. McLean, and T. Mullen (Eds.). *Human rights: From rhetoric to reality* (ch. 2). Oxford: Blackwell.

Muller, D.J., Blackman, D.E., and Chapman, A.J. (Eds.). (1984). *Psychology and law: Topics from an international conference.* Chichester: Wiley and Sons.

New Zealand Handbook on International Human Rights. (1998). Wellington: Ministry of Foreign Affairs and Trade.

Newborough, J.R. (1992a). Community psychology for the 1990's. *Journal of Community Psychology,* 20, 7-9.

Newborough, J.R. (1992b). Community psychology in the postmodernworld. *Journal of Community Psychology*, 20,10-25.

O'Donohue, W. (1989). The (even) Bolder Model. *American Psychologist*, 44, 12, 1460-1468.

Parker, I. (Ed.). (2002). *Critical discursive psychology.* New York: Palgrave Macmillan.

Public Health Advisory Committee to the National Health Committee. (2004). *The health of people and communities: A way forward: Public policy and the economic determinants of health.* Wellington, Ministry of Health

Read, P.P. (2001). *The Templars.* London: Phoenix.

Ross, M., and Miller, D.T. (Eds.). (2002). *The justice motive in everyday life.* Cambridge University Press.

Royal Commission on Criminal Justice. (1991-1993). London: HMSO.

Sells, M. (1996). *The bridge betrayed: Religion and genocide in Bosnia.* Berkeley: University of California Press.

Shirley, I. (1990). New Zealand: The advance of the New Right. In Ian Taylor. (Ed.). *The social effects of free market policies: An international text.* (Ch.14). Hemel Hempstead, Herts: Harvester/Wheatsheaf.

Skitka, L.J. (2003). (Ed.). *Personality and Social Psychology Review.* Special edition devoted to research and theorizing in justice.

Spong, J.S. (1991). *Rescuing the Bible from fundamentalism: A bishop rethinks the meaning of scripture.* San Francisco: Harper.

Steffens, L. (1931). *The autobiography of Lincoln Steffens.* New York: Harcourt Brace.

Summerfield, D. (2000). Conflict and health: War and mental health: a brief overview. *British Medical Journal,* 321, 232-235.

Taylor, A.J.W. (1959). Psychology and values. *Australian Journal of Psychology,* 1, 2, 149-161.

Taylor, A.J.W. (1961). Ethics and prison psychology. *Australian Journal of Psychology*, 13, 2, 226-230.

Taylor, A.J.W. (1964). The differentiation of guilt patterns in prisoners *American Journal of psychotherapy,* 18, 3, 470-474.

Taylor, A.J.W. (1967). An evaluation of group psychotherapy in a girls' borstal. *International Journal of Group Psychotherapy*, 17, 2, 168-177.

Taylor, A.J.W. (1970). Counselling and student unrest in universities abroad. *New Zealand Journal of Social Work*, 6, 3, 47-55.

Taylor, A.J.W. (1999). Value-conflict arising from a disaster. *Australasian Journal of Disaster and Trauma Studies.* http://www.massey.ac.nz/~trauma/issues/1999-2/taylor.htm

Taylor, A.J.W. (2001). Spirituality and personal values: Neglected components of trauma treatment. *Traumatology*, http://www.fsu.edu/~trauma/v7/Spirituality.pd8

Taylor, A.J.W. (2002). Submission on the Health and Safety in Employment Amendment Bill. *Bulletin of the New Zealand Psychological Society.* 100, 27-29 and 33.

Taylor, A.J.W. (2003a). Justice as a basic human need. *New Ideas in Psychology*, 21, 3, 209-219.

Taylor, A.J.W. (2003b). Bringing 'complex terrorism' and 'corporate malfeasance' into a classification schema for disasters. *Australian Journal of Emergency Management,* 18, 1, 27-34.

Taylor, A.J.W., Nailatikau, E., and Walkey, F.H. (2002). A hostage assignment in Fiji. *Australasian Journal of Disaster and Trauma Studies,* http://www.massey.ac.nz/~trauma/issues/2002-2/taylor.htm

Taylor, I. (Ed.). (1990). *The social effects of free market policies: An international text.* Hemel Hempstead HERTS: Harvester Wheatsheaf.

Thompson, J. (1992). *Justice and world order: A philosophical inquiry.* London: Routledge.

Thorp, Sir T. (2005). *Miscarriages of justice.* Auckland: Legal Research Foundation.

Thrash, T. M., and Elliot, A.J. (2001). Delimiting and integrating achievement motive and goal constructs. In A. Efklides, J. Kuhl, and R.M. Sorrentino. (Eds.). *Trends and prospects in motivation research.* (ch.1). Dordrecht/Boston/London: Kluwer.

United Nations. (2004). Global issues of the twenty-first century: United Nations Challenges: Non-State actor: business, media, NGO, civil society roles. (http://www.global-challenges.org/14extra-state-actors.html - accessed 20 March 2004.

US Department of Justice. (2001). *Roles, rights, and responsibilities: A handbook for frauds victims participating in the federal criminal justice system.* NCJ 172520. Washington DC.

van der Kolk, B. (1994). The body keeps the score: Memory and the evolving psychobiology of posttraumatic stress. *Harvard Review of Psychiatry*, 1, 5, 253-265.

Walter, J. (Ed.). (2002). *World disasters Report: Focus on reducing risks.* Geneva: International Federation of Red Cross and Red Crescent Societies.

Wong, R. (2000). *Motivation: A biobehavioral approach.* Cambridge University Press.

Wright, R. (2000) *Nonzero: The sum of human destiny. London: Little Brown.*

Wright, R. (2002). A real war on terror. – accessed 5 February 2005 from http://slate.msn.com/toolbar.asp?action=printandid=2070210

Wrightsman, L.S. (2001). *Forensic Psychology.* Belmont CA: Wadsworth.
Young, M.A. (1994/2004 update). *The Community Crisis Response Team training manual.* (2nd edn. rev.). Washington DC: National Organization for Victim Assistance.

In: Justice as a Basic Human Need
Editor: Anthony Taylor, pp. 13-23
ISBN 1-59454-915-X

Chapter 2

BEING HUMAN AND THE NEED FOR JUSTICE

Charles W. Tolman

ABSTRACT

The characteristics that distinguish us as human beings from other animals derive from the social relations in which we produce the conditions of life. Central here are the shared meanings, manifest in individuals as intentional action and agency, that can be detached from their objects and manipulated as such. These are the necessary and sufficient conditions for our humanity. We are not human without intentional action and agency; there is no agency or intentional action in the absence of humanity. An important implication of this is that the relations that insure our humanity are not natural but intentional; that is, we must act so as to maintain them. A consequence is that our humanity can range between forms that are merely rudimentary to forms that represent the fullest possible development of individuals as persons in community. Acts that intend community are moral. We can be human and not moral, but we cannot be moral without being human. In the long run, however, immorality is destructive of both individual and society, and ultimately of humanity. Thus morality is a necessary condition for the maintenance of the conditions of our humanity. But we cannot be truly moral unless we are moral respecting all others. Morality is nothing if it is not fairly applied, that is, if the rights of all are not respected. Thus justice, which is fairness, is a necessary condition for our being moral. Justice is the most basic need we have in the maintenance and furtherance of our humanity.

INTRODUCTION

Justice is fundamental to our being human. It is a necessary condition for our humanity in the sense that if there were no justice at all, we could not continue effectively to exercise our distinctly human capacities. But it is not necessary in the sense that humanity would utterly disappear in the face of injustice. We know very well that at least in the short run we retain our humanity in one degree or another despite injustice. Our humanity may be challenged, may be distorted, even threatened by injustice, but humans can be recognizably human and unjust at the same time. After all, only a human can be inhuman. The relationship between our humanity and our need for justice is a complex one that requires special attention. In what follows, I shall sketch some of the connections as I understand them. This will result in an argument – or at least the outline of one – that justice is indeed the most fundamental of *human* needs.

The argument moves through five main steps. The first is to establish that which distinguishes us as human beings. This will turn out to be what we shall call meaningful social practice. At bottom, our humanity is essentially social. It also has an historical dimension, which means, among other things, that as such our humanity exists not as actual but as potential. By our practices we can create conditions that promote the development of that potential, individually and collectively, but we can also create conditions that inhibit or distort it. Second, we shall see that individual participation in social practices takes the form of intentional action. Our sociality, our practices, and our actions are thus all intentional and not merely matters of fact. Third, intentional action implies agency, the power to act according to known interests. But agency takes two forms, one that reflects individual freedom and promotes development, and one that reflects restrictions on that freedom. Fourth, intentional action and agency are inherently subject to moral judgment. Moral is what intends the social relations – that is, the community – upon which our humanity as individuals depends. The good that it intends is the common good. Rights grow out of the common good and are thus also inherently social in nature. Fifth, it is impossible to intend community or exercise moral agency in the absence of fairness or justice. Justice is therefore, in the long run, a necessary condition for the conditions that support our humanity and all that that implies. It is thus the most fundamental of the truly human needs.

BEING HUMAN

Human beings use tools, but because many non-human animals also use tools their use is not the differentia of the species. A recent issue of *National Geographic* (Holland, 2004) shows photos of a brown capuchin monkey (*Cebus apella*) using a stone to break open a nut. A side note reminds us that the Galapagos woodpecker finch uses twigs or cactus spines to retrieve larvae from the holes they make in trees, and that Egyptian vultures hurl stones at ostrich eggs in order to break them open. The literature on animal behaviour provides a long list of similar examples.

Nor is the differentia tool-making, because many non-human animals make at least rudimentary tools. Goodall reported the modification of materials by wild chimpanzees, such as stripping twigs to make them more effective for fishing termites or using crumpled leaves as a sponge to get water from hollows (Woolfson, 1982, p. 38). And some species that are not known to make tools in the course of their natural lives can be induced to do so under special conditions, thus revealing at least the potential capacity for tool-making. Well known in this regard are Köhler's experiments with chimpanzees. Wright (1972) reported a particularly intriguing example of toolmaking by an orangutan. The animal had learned by imitation to use a hammer-stone to strike flakes from a flint core, which it then used to cut string that held a food box closed.

What distinguishes humans is not tool-use or tool-making as such, but the context in which we make and use tools, and the ways in which we do so - in short, the manner in which we produce the conditions of our life.

It is true that all animals produce the conditions of their lives to some extent. Even bacteria secrete substances that make their environments more conducive to their modes of existence, and most animals at all levels of the phylogenetic scale (and indeed many plants) have ways of moving from less congenial to more congenial environments to secure the ecological niche most promoting of their functions and activities. Many insects are well known for their structures of habitation. And many vertebrate species build nests and construct burrows. But these practices are almost always biologically specific, that is, determined by the biological inheritance of the animals.

Human beings are distinguished by the very active and complex ways in which they produce the conditions of their lives. They build houses, roads, and vehicles. They plant and harvest the plants they need, and they breed, raise, and slaughter the animals they eat and use. They devise ingenious means of both producing and distributing the goods they both need and want. Moreover, they construct elaborate systems of social relations within which all this is carried out. Human modes of production are not biologically specific; they are *culturally* specific. The information required by individuals in order to achieve these ends is carried not in their genes but in the cultural practices in which they become participants in the course of their growing up.

There are two interrelated but distinct aspects of what is specifically human here. The first is the separation of actions and objects. Köhler's apes were able to put two sticks together in order to reach an object outside their cages. But this occurred only in the presence of the object. This appears to be the case with all instances of animal toolmaking. The action is immediately linked to its object and does not occur in its absence. Apes, for instance, do not prepare longer sticks, chipped rocks, stripped twigs, or any other tool, unless the object demanding it is present. Humans on the other hand characteristically prepare their tools in the absence of their objects. The implications of this are enormous; I'll return to it in a moment.

The second feature of human making and use of tools is the division of labour. Of course this is linked to the first feature. If toolmaking can be separated from its object, it can be done by someone other than the user of the tool. In other words, the maker and user need not be – indeed usually are not – the same individual. Where the wisest apes fall short, is in being unable themselves to link the tool and its object in the absence of either. That is, they fail to abstract the meaning of each and to link the meanings. It appears that this is a uniquely human capability. Certainly animals are able to grasp the meanings of objects, but they have difficulty manipulating the meanings independent of the objects.

For humans, the abstraction that is taking place in the case of tools is associated with the manipulation of meanings and with the symbolization of those meanings as occurs in the development of language. Again, apes are capable of symbolizing meanings, but their capacity is limited and invariably depends on constant reinforcement from human care-takers. Something resembling 'culture' may be producible in some animals, and indeed basic levels of what might be considered culture are even found among some naturally existing species, such as the washing of food among Japanese macaques or the use of stones among brown capuchins, but culture is not the dominant feature of the life of any non-human species of animal. Culture as such, and as a dominant feature of life, is associated only with humans, because it requires the ability they have to abstract, symbolize, and manipulate meaning. Thus humans have culture as other animals do not, and as a consequence humans have history, as other animals do not.

Humans conduct their lives today in very different ways from the way they did so a century or millennium ago, whereas the habits of most animals today are virtually identical to those that have long been characteristic of the species. The changes that do occur in animal habits in the long run are due either to evolution or, within individual lifetimes, to learning. Animal evolution is slow: human history is rapid. Both reflect alterations in environmental demands. Human habits, however, can and often do change with little or no alteration in the natural environment, because humans make their own demands for change. In animals the information required for evolution is stored in their genes; the information for human history is stored in cultural practices. Indeed cultural practices not only supersede the limits of biological genetics, we now know how those practices can alter the genetic information itself. Whereas biology dominates culture in animal species, culture dominates biology in the human species. Animals can live without culture; humans cannot.

The dominance of culture means that our existence is essentially historical. The cultural conditions upon which we depend are those produced by our cultural practices, and they change constantly. Our humanity is thus more than merely the product of evolution; it is the product of our own activities. As such, it is in a constant state of becoming. As societies, we collectively produce possibilities for ourselves that did not exist for our ancestors, although individually we may have varying access to those very same possibilities. In short, humanity, whether collectively or individually considered, is effectively potential, not actual. Whether and to what extent that potential is developed depends on social and historical conditions.

The essential elements of culture are meaning, practice, and language, and all three reflect the power of consciousness. Being conscious is our ability to grasp, abstract, manipulate, symbolize, and communicate meanings in social practice and language.

Intentional Action

When language (or the abstractive capacity altogether) enters upon the scene, behaviour itself changes in its essential quality. I am not convinced that animal behaviour was ever as simple as psychologists have traditionally treated it, that is, as a collection of responses to sources of external stimulation, but I need not argue this point here. It certainly is the case that human behaviour was never so simple. And the evidence for that is clearly given in our own everyday experiences. When the traffic light turns yellow just in front of us while driving, we may 'reflexively' take our foot off the accelerator and move it gently to the brake. We have the impression of ourselves responding to the stimulus of the light change. But the least amount of reflection reveals that we have other possibilities, the most common being to press harder on the accelerator and get across the intersection before (or just as) the light turns red.

There are two things about this example that are noteworthy. First, it appears that in fact I always have a choice in the matter – either to stop or to speed up – and much of the time I consciously consider the circumstances and make that choice. Second, it is not at all obvious that I am responding to the colour or the change of colours in the light as such. There is nothing about 'yellowness' in and of itself that prompts me to slow down. It may be said that it is not the yellow as such but the change to yellow in the context of a traffic light and intersection and my being at the steering wheel of an automobile moving at 60 kph, etc. But the context as such again makes no difference at all. In fact, the colour change and the context have their effect not through any property belonging to them but only through the *meaning* that they have for me. And I had to learn that meaning as a driver-in-training, that is, as I became a participant in the social practice of driving. It is, in short, not the stimuli to which I respond but to their meanings. This is no mere quibble: that meanings mediate our relationship with the world is central to the way we produce our lives.

But where do these meanings reside? It is not in the objects or stimuli themselves, nor in our responses to them. The traffic light has meaning not in any physical context on either side of the apparent S-R connection, but only in the context of an established and shared cultural practice, and these practices are not anything that we as individuals possess on our own; they are rather complex relations in which we participate.

Language is a cultural practice that exemplifies the meaningful aspects of all other practices. What is important for us to understand about language is that it cannot exist for an isolated individual – unless of course that individual became isolated only after having acquired the language. Languages are by their nature shared entities because meanings are shared entities. There is no private language because there is no private meaning. Wittgenstein's well-known argument against private language applies here (Wittgenstein, 1953, 269ff). Meaning is essentially social.

Thus when we act, we do things like ride a bicycle, go for a walk, build a house, drive a car, wash a window, or till a garden. These are things that we could not in principle do as isolated individuals. Only by engaging the pertinent objects as meanings, only by participating in social practices, can we do these things. They are intentional actions, the intentional aspect of which is the culturally existing meaning.

Can we act unintentionally? Yes, but we would then call it a reflex or behavioural response, not action. We can behave as animals, but what is characteristically *human* about us is intentional action. Intentional action is aimed at achieving ends; it involves choice and is teleological.

If all that we are as human beings depends on meanings and our ability to use them, and meanings and abilities exist only as components of shared cultural practices, then we are, once again, essentially social, cultural beings. Everything that I am, everything that I do or am capable of doing, depends on the cultural context into which I was born. There is much more to being born a human being than biological parturition.

Here it is important to stress the nature of the context that makes intentional action possible. When we say that human beings are essentially social, there are at least two misunderstandings that need to be recognized and rejected. The first is that the society or culture exists independently of individuals such that individuals may or may not take part. What, in contrast, we want to assert is that every individual person is social by his or her very nature and cannot exist outside of society or culture. The individual person is a product of societal existence. Society and the individual exist in a necessarily reciprocal or dialectical relationship to one another.

The second misunderstanding is that humans are social in the same way the other animals are said to be social. That this is not the case is already evident in the fact that humans have history whereas bees or termites, say, do not. Again, it is the dominance of culture in our lives that makes the difference. Animal societies are matters of fact; human societies are matters of intention. Bees can have only one kind of society, one kind of "culture." Humans can have many kinds of societies and cultures; indeed individual humans can share in different societies and cultures simultaneously.

It is of the utmost importance to recognize that we need the society of others both to be human as such and to be the particular humans that we are. But at the same time, society would not exist without us as individuals, we depend on it; it depends on us.

AGENCY

In our inherent sociality there is a complex relationship between dependence and independence. We are clearly dependent on culture for the exercise of our human capabilities. But we are also the creators of our own culture. One way of approaching the matter is to examine claims about independence - such as we hear of children becoming independent as they grow up, or of people in business saying that they have become independent agents. The picture here is one of initial dependence, overcome by maturity or effort and eventuating in independence, a state that is generally more highly valued and regarded. But there is an essential absoluteness beneath the apparent relativity here. We cannot be entirely independent of other human beings without the risk of losing our humanity. In fact, we have no choice in the matter: even fully committed hermits carry their social relations and thus their dependence on others with them. The very decision to become a hermit could not be made outside of a societal context. It may appear that we are independent of our children or that people in business are independent of their workers, but as Hegel's well-known analysis of the lordship-bondage relationship convincingly demonstrated, this is not the case (Hegel, 1807/1977, pp. 111ff). The one exists only in relation to the other; independence is achieved only through dependence.

When we speak of independence, we are often intending something more akin to power – such as growing children gaining power over the things that are important to their existence, and business executives gaining power over their own time. But the exercise of this power is absolutely dependent on the cooperation of other human beings. The powers we have to achieve the things we need and want, are all first acquired, and then continuously supported through our social relations. This power is also called agency, of which two broad forms can be identified: i.e. the generalized and the restricted (Holzkamp, pp. 459ff). Generalized agency is the power that individuals have, in concert with others, to achieve the fullest personal development and satisfaction of needs possible within the limitations of the current state of historical social development. Generalized agency is exercised in one's personal interest as an aspect of the general interest. It pursues individual 'goods' as aspects of the common good. There is an identity here between the particular and the universal. There is no question in the exercise of generalized agency of power to dominate others. The power exercised is common, shared power, the power of working together effectively to achieve common goals that are at the same time individual, personal goals. Justice here is natural; it is so thoroughly characteristic of generalized agency that it, like oxygen, is not noticed until it goes missing. But it is an essential condition for generalized agency and thus a fundamental need, like our need for oxygen.

Restricted agency is the power achieved by individuals through subjection of their own interests to those of others. It is a shared power, but it is purchased at a price. Moreover, in its exercise it tends to require in turn the subjection of others, that is, power over others is central to restricted agency. It contributes little to the full human development of the agent; indeed it more often stunts and deforms that growth. Its benefits are often contrary to the common good, with no identification of the particular and universal. As such, the exercise of restricted agency, in the end, violates both the interests of the agent and of humanity as a whole. Justice is more obviously an issue here, and more visible as a problem, than in the case of generalized agency. Restricted agency is power that both derives from and creates injustice. In the long run, therefore, it undermines itself.

The exercise of agency, as already noted, necessarily depends on the relations between the agent and others. Where there are two forms of agency, there are also two basic forms of social relations: the personal and the instrumental. The correlation between the forms of agency and forms of relation is neither perfect nor necessary, but the personal relations are more typical of generalized agency, while instrumental relations are more typical of restricted agency.

Ordinarily our lives are a mix of the two forms of agency and relations. In closely-knit communities, such as families, we experience generalized agency and personal relations. There is an identity of individual and common interest: we are there for each other and we all benefit from the mutually supportive relations. In the workplace, on the other hand, we are more likely to encounter restricted agency and instrumental relations. We cannot achieve fulfilment of our needs, and then only partially, unless we submit to the demands of our employer. In dealing with customers or clients, we are again governed not by their needs but by the employer's needs. We find ourselves in the contradictory position of being able to help the customer or client only within the constraints set by the employer. If the employer's interests are primarily those of the clients, then there will be a closer approximation between individual and common interests. But employers live in a world in which they can only function by competing with other employers for profit, market share, etc. These are powerful 'needs' that are definitely not shared by the employee except indirectly (he/she might not have a job if the firm is unprofitable), and they are certainly not those of the clients/customers.

Owing to the conflict of interests in such a situation, justice necessarily becomes an issue. The structure of the relational situation itself demands that someone gains and someone loses. Consequently, we invent forms of 'justice' that conform to the relational structure, such as treats 'equals equally and unequals unequally', thus appearing to justify unequal treatment of, for example, employers, employees, or clients/customers. When the rules are broken, the convention slides into forms of retributive justice that make the same distinctions: for example, the powerful get their wrists slapped while the underlings are sent to jail.

The moral (and, I would argue, religious) imperative is to extend the limits of generalized agency and personal relations in our lives, to enlarge the human community, and to realize our need for justice. The ideal here, which will doubtless never be attained, is to have the community universal. While this may sound unrealistic and utopian, it is approachable. People are more concerned about what is happening to others in distant parts of the globe today and making efforts to improve their lives than ever before in human history. In the last few centuries, we have seen our overt concerns for community (however only partly realized) extend to ethnic affinities, nations, and more recently to universal human rights and poverty in the Third World.

Morality

Like agency, morality is also inherent in intentional action. As noted above, intentional actions are meaningful actions: they are the ways in which we participate as individuals in the cultural meanings that are embodied in societal practices. Now, these meanings can be detached from the actions, which is what happens in language and thought. We are thus able to distinguish between propositions and actions: the former being assertions about meaning that have no necessary effect on the world around us, and the latter being meaningful bodily assertions that necessarily change the world. For example, to claim that the arctic ice pack is melting has absolutely no effect upon the climate in the polar region, but to meet our needs for warmth by burning fossil fuels does have such an effect. Of course thoughts and verbal claims do have their effects, but only when they prompt an action. It is never the thought or claim that has the effect.

My claim about the arctic ice pack is subject to judgment. It may be true or false, but can be verified empirically. Actions, which necessarily embody meanings, however, are not so judged. It is true that I repaired my sailboat's rudder today, but my repairing of the rudder is not true, nor is it false. The act of repairing the rudder is rather judged as right or wrong. In attempting to repair it, in my intention to repair it, did I do the right thing? With the best of intentions, I could have done what will prove to be the wrong thing and I will be unable to steer the boat in tomorrow's race.

Actions, however, can be right or wrong in at least three different ways: pragmatic, aesthetic, and moral. *Pragmatically*, does the repair of the rudder achieve the end of allowing more effective control of the boat? If so, it was technically, pragmatically the right thing to do.

But pragmatics apply not only to our actions with things, but also to our actions with people. If I want to teach you to sail, my main consideration will be to find the right things to do with you in order to achieve that end. In this case the end of my actions will be the same as yours. But to take another example, if we take part in the same activity, we need not share the same end: if you are selling me something, I need to know how to complete the transaction in a way that satisfies my needs, and this includes knowing the right things to do regarding you as the seller. When we apply pragmatics to social relations the result is the instrumental relations that have already been discussed. When people are the objects of purely technical considerations, they become mere instruments - and of course have the unpleasant feeling of being used.

We avoid this by being polite. We know we went into the store to purchase an object and that our relation to the clerk is merely a means to that end. We could treat the clerk like any other part of the retail apparatus, but mostly we do not. We smile, we chat, and we are polite for no other reason than to ameliorate the necessarily instrumental nature of the relationship. If we did not do this, we would be judged as wrong, but in a different sense than the technical. Yes, we got the goods, but we were unnecessarily rude. To be polite, however, is not to embrace the clerk as one of our own family. We are not creating a personal relationship where one did not previously exist. We are merely smoothing over what might otherwise be socially rough edges. The rightness or wrongness here is *aesthetic*.

It is the same when I repair the rudder. The technical aim has to do with steering the boat, but the job can be done roughly or pleasingly – that is, pleasing or unpleasing to me as well as to others. A jury-rig might do the job, but it is not pretty, and most sailors are fussy about the appearance of their boats as well as about their performance. It is the same with the cars we drive, the houses we live in, and the clothing we wear. And the worker who performs his or her task with style is preferred over the one with no style.

The third kind of rightness/wrongness is *moral*. It has to do directly with our relations to one another. It is more than just being polite. Homicidal psychopaths are said to kill gently and with a smile. Morality touches the very conditions of our existence as human beings. Moral action is that which supports and facilitates the actions of others. Moral action intends the good of the community. It feeds back positively into that social context that makes our own development as human beings possible. Curiously enough, the repairs to my rudder can also be morally judged. I am not doing it for its own sake. I am repairing the rudder so that I can compete fairly with other racers and thus I also contribute to the continuance and further development of a community of people who race their boats. If, however, I intend to use the boat to smuggle drugs that will contribute to the destruction of human relations, then I am not doing the right thing morally.

Every action can be judged regarding the three kinds of rightness/wrongness. Since every intentional action has an aim, it can be judged as to whether it achieves its aim. It can be judged as the style with which it does so. And it can be judged as to its effect upon the community of intentional actors. This community includes of course – indeed it constitutes – the 'I' as well as the 'You'. Thus even seemingly private actions can be so judged. There really is nothing that I can do that does not ultimately affect my relation to others.

Recalling that it is the intention that makes action distinct from other behaviours, it is clear that the moral judgment concerns the intention. If I fail in my attempt to save my neighbour's life, my intention would still have been morally right.

The underlying moral intention of all specific acts is, as already noted, the maintenance of the community of agents. This is necessarily the same for all agents because it arises from the very nature of intentional action. Thus it is universal and provides the norm of rightness and wrongness for all actions. It is a corollary of this that the good achieved is itself a universal good. It is, in short, the common good. Moral actions, however prosaic or dramatic, strive for the common good. Those that offend against the common good are immoral and sometimes vicious.

This implies that there is no such thing as an individual good that can conflict with the common good, but rather an identity of the particular and the universal. I may gain an object, indeed even satisfy a need, by stealing from others, but in so doing I violate the universal right to personal property (not private property, which is a different matter) which makes my things mine. In short, stealing from others violates my own rights. Similarly with murder: to take the life of another is to violate the universal right to life that protects me from intrusions by others. It may appear that gaining something for myself at the expense of another is a 'good' for me, but this is a mistake because good must be defined precisely as that which preserves and promotes the community upon which my own life and personal development depend. Apparent 'goods' that are bad for others are illusory and false.

Realizing the common good is realizing oneself as a human being. Such realization is an ongoing process that begins at birth. We become fully realized as human beings, as persons, only through inclusion in social practices as members of the community of agents, through which I am given the power to satisfy my own needs. To be denied that power – or at least as much of such power as the current historical development of society allows – has the effect of stunting my development as a human being. In the ideal society, each member of society would be fully integrated into the collective production for the needs of all. In historical fact, however, this is rarely achieved. Poverty and unemployment are the obvious signs of failure.

The individual's relation to the common good is spoken of in terms of duties and rights. In 1948 the General Assembly of the United Nations proclaimed the *Universal Declaration of Human Rights*, recognizing the inherent rights of all individual human beings to rights of life, liberty, security of person, education, freedom of conscience and religion, property, etc. This was a milestone in human history, articulating an ideal by which history itself may be judged. Most significant from a moral-theoretical point of view was the explicit recognition of rights as *universal* and as *inherent* in our being human.

We have already seen that the moral, the good, rights and the like are nothing if they are not universal. Moreover, we have claimed that they must be inherent in our humanness. But the question may be seen to remain as to that in which they are inherent. Kant and many other important philosophers before and after him in the modern period believed that rights inhered in the individual. But the moral, the good, and rights make no sense outside of the social context of the individual. I have no right if you do not recognize it. The right exists in its recognition. Moreover, I acquire the right by virtue of being a member of society. In short, rights are inherent in society. Only in society can the individual realize his or her rights; only in society can one act morally and for the good; indeed only in society can we, strictly speaking, act at all. As we have seen, it is only in human action that the moral, the good, and our rights are manifest.

As mentioned, the rights of one depend on their recognition by others. Thus there are two sides to rights, the second side being that of duty. We all have the moral duty to observe the rights of others, which is another way of repeating that the 'I' exists only in relation to the 'You'.

JUSTICE

Justice is above all being fair in our dealings with others as well as with ourselves. It is unquestionably a moral idea and thus belongs to that which makes us human. But, as John Macmurray (1961, p. 188) pointed out, justice – or fairness – has a peculiarly ambiguous status in relation to morality. As he says, justice seems so meagre and universal as to be hardly a virtue at all. It expresses the minimum of reciprocity and interest in others. With mercy, generosity, and benevolence it is apparent that I am prepared to sacrifice self-interest for the sake of others. It is not obvious that justice or fairness toward others is quite so demanding or costly. Indeed, one can imagine fairness without self-sacrifice or morality of any kind. I can be as ungenerous to one as to another, making no distinction as to race, colour, or creed. As Macmurray (1961, p.189) warned, 'to be more than just to some and less than just to others is to be unjust to all'.

But if we try to imagine morality without justice, a quite different picture emerges. To be unevenly generous to others puts the morality of the act in question. For a parent to love one child more than another is to love the one at the expense of the other and is thus morally dubious. Without justice, Macmurry reminds us, morality becomes illusory and sentimental, the mere appearance of morality.

Justice is absolutely essential to morality, because justice guarantees the inclusiveness of the moral intention. It ensures that morally intended acts are aimed not just at particular others but at the generalized other. It safeguards the actors' intention of community, and the universality of that intention, which in turn assures the morality of the act.

In short, justice or fairness without morality is thinkable but morality without justice is not. Justice is not morality itself but it is a necessary condition for morality. If it is correct to say that we have a need to be human – and it appears that we do – and it is the case that morality is at the heart of being human, then the necessary condition for morality is the necessary condition for our very humanity. Justice is that condition and is thus a fundamental need, just as the need for food is fundamental for our biological survival.

Conclusion: Justice Is a Fundamental Human Need

Justice is basic to everything that makes us truly human. While we can and do live with injustice, we cannot live without justice altogether. It is in this sense that justice is the absolutely necessary condition for the existence of humanity. We cannot act intentionally without agency; we have no agency without morality; and we have no morality without justice. Justice is thus the first and most basic *human* need. Our need for justice, for ultimate fairness and genuine equality, as envisioned in such documents as the *Universal Declaration of Human Rights* is basic to our being societal human beings as opposed to biological animals. We daily feel that need locally and globally. We intuit, however vaguely, that justice for one is justice for all, that there is finally an identity of individual and common interests, an identity of our good with the common good. What remains is to see what stands in the way of universal justice and to understand what we can do to achieve it.

References

Hegel, G.W.F. (1977). *Phenomenology of Spirit* (Trans. A.V. Miller). Oxford: Oxford University Press. (Original work published 1807).

Holland, J.S. (2004). Tool time, monkey style. *National Geographic*, 202, 1, xxi.

Holzkamp, K. (1983). *Grundlegung der Psychologie.* Frankfurt: Campus Verlag

Macmurray, J. (1961). *Persons in relation.* London: Faber and Faber.

Wittgenstein, L. (1953). *Philosophical investigations.* New York: Macmillan.

Woolfson, C. (1982). *The labour theory of culture.* London: Routledge and Kegan Paul.

Wright, R.V.C. (1972). Imitative learning of a flaked stone technology: The case of an orangutan. *Mankind*, 8, 296-306.

In: Justice as a Basic Human Need
Editor: Anthony Taylor, pp. 25-38
ISBN 1-59454-915-X

Chapter 3

THE MEANING OF JUSTICE: INSIGHTS FROM THE BIBLICAL TRADITION

Christopher D. Marshall

ABSTRACT

The aim of this chapter is to identify some characteristic features of the Bible's teaching on justice. It observes that the Bible has had a lasting impact on the Western cultural and intellectual tradition, and still has insights to offer on the meaning and character of justice. It makes clear that, according to biblical tradition, a commitment to justice should be a central feature in the religious life of individuals and the communities in which they live. It reviews the many complexities surrounding both the concept of justice itself and the interpretation of the biblical materials relating to it. It discusses issues of distribution, equity, power, and rights, and presents a challenge for those impelled to right the wrongs they see around them.

INTRODUCTION

Christians regard the Bible as a uniquely important source of guidance on matters of belief and practice. What the Bible has to say about justice, therefore, ought to be of great significance for shaping Christian thought and action on the subject today. The Bible also has had a profound impact on the development of Western culture in general, so that exploring biblical perspectives on justice can help illuminate some of the convictions and values that have helped shape Western political and judicial thought in general. Admittedly the wellsprings of Christian nurture are drying up in secular society. But the Christian tradition has important and distinctive insights into the meaning of justice that are still worth listening to. Every religious tradition has something valuable to offer to the unending quest for better justice in the world. What Christianity has to contribute is the accumulation of centuries of faith, reflection and experience preserved for us in the ancient biblical text.

Yet coming to grips with biblical teaching on justice is by no means easy. There are many complexities to cope with. For starters, there are hundreds of texts in the Old and New

Testaments that speak explicitly about justice, and hundreds more that refer to it implicitly. Justice is in fact one of the most frequently recurring topics in the Bible. The data is also diverse. Different biblical writers address different historical circumstances, and they sometimes take different positions on what justice entails (this is especially true with respect to criminal justice). In what follows I will concentrate on broad areas of theological agreement among the writers. But we do well to remember that, especially on issues of justice, the difficulty is always in the detail. It is also always important to remember that biblical reflection on justice takes place within a larger cultural and religious worldview that is, in many respects, quite unlike that of contemporary secular society. Understanding the justice dimension of biblical teaching requires us to cross over into a different and foreign world to our own, and that is never an easy thing to do. Then, having crossed over, modern readers need to decide what, if anything, they want to bring back with them that might be relevant and applicable to their world, a task requiring considerable hermeneutical sophistication.

Added to these factors is the complexity that surrounds the concept of justice itself. What actually *is* justice? Does justice have an objective existence, or is it simply the product of social agreement? Is there an unchanging essence to justice – such as fairness or equality or balance – or does it mean different things to different people in different settings? Where does justice come from? How is justice known? How should it be defined? What is the relationship between social, moral, political and legal justice? How are justice and love related? These are all very difficult questions which cannot be addressed in any detail here. But even without traversing the difficult terrain of moral and legal philosophy, it is evident even from everyday discourse that justice is a paradoxical value.

The Justice Paradox

Justice is one of those ideas that combine tremendous emotional potency with a great deal of semantic ambiguity. It is both a self-evident reality and, at the same time, a highly disputed one. On the one hand, we all have a strong intuitive sense of what justice is. We appeal to the criterion of justice all the time. We instinctively recognise when it has been violated. Even very young children have a powerful, innate sense of justice. Think of how often children complain that something is just so unfair! To declare some action or state of affairs to be unfair or unjust is to make one of the strongest moral condemnations available. And when individuals make this complaint, they usually assume that the injustice in question will be patently obvious to anyone who cares to look.

But what appears obvious to one person is not always obvious to others. People may agree that justice is the fundamental principle to consider, but they frequently disagree on how the principle translates into practice. Some, for example, defend capital punishment as a matter of just deserts, a life for a life, the re-balancing of the scales of justice. Others decry it as an affront to human dignity, an awful imitation of the injustice it claims to denounce or correct. Or again, some consider it to be a matter of basic justice that women have the right to choose an abortion, since it is their bodies that are affected. For others however abortion is a deadly injustice to an unborn child, the unjustifiable taking of innocent human life. Similar disputes on justice litter human history, and there have been huge shifts in social consensus from age to age. Aristotle considered slavery to be compatible with, even essential to, a just society. For later British and American abolitionists, slavery was the very the epitome of injustice.

So we have a paradoxical situation. We all know that justice is important, we all feel obligated towards the demands of justice, we all sense the primordial pull of justice. But we cannot say exactly what justice is, or how best to define it, or why standards of justice vary so much down through the centuries and across different cultures.

Key Conceptual Components

Obviously then justice is not a straightforward or singular concept. Like love, justice is a generic term embracing a variety of meanings and applications. This makes it very difficult to reduce justice to a simple, all-encompassing definition. Yet most expositions of justice seem to involve at least four key ingredients:

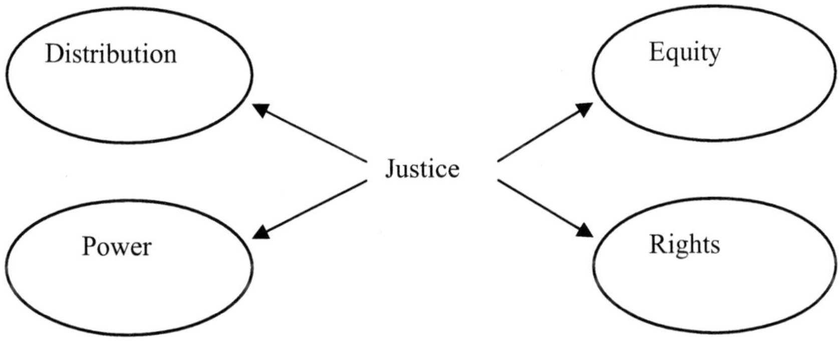

- ***Distribution:*** Justice entails the appropriate distribution of social benefits and penalties among contending parties. Justice dictates that people get their fair share in society's goods and rewards (social justice), and that they are not subjected to punishments or penalties unless they are morally deserved (criminal justice).
- ***Power:*** Justice involves the exercise of legitimate power, whether to arbitrate between conflicting claims, or to implement social benefits, or to enforce legal obligations, or to impose suitable sanctions. Injustice occurs when power is misused to deny or rob people of what they are rightfully due.
- ***Equity:*** Justice requires fairness and balance. Similars should be treated as similars, and dissimilars as dissimilars. Disputes should be adjudicated even-handedly, without regard to irrelevant, secondary considerations that will arbitrarily disadvantage one party.
- ***Rights:*** Justice has to do with honouring the rights or entitlements of people, especially in conflict situations. A right is where someone has a legitimate moral or legal claim on some good, which others have a duty to respect or uphold. Justice gives moral legitimacy to such rights.

At the broadest level, then, justice entails the exercise of legitimate power to ensure that benefits and penalties are distributed fairly and equitably in society, thus meeting the rights and enforcing the obligations of all parties. Where disputes arise is in deciding who should exercise power, what kind of power is appropriate, what benefits or penalties particular parties deserve, what constitutes a fair distribution of resources in view of the different characteristics and contributions of people, and whose rights take precedence when there is a clash between the legitimate rights or claims of various groups.

Making decisions in such disputes is never easy. It requires careful consideration of all the factors bearing on each situation. How these factors are distinguished and measured depends, in turn, on the larger worldview or belief system within which human communities operate. It is here that justice intersects with religious understandings and meanings. For arguably those beliefs, values, stories and symbols that make up a worldview are, by definition, religious in nature inasmuch as they presuppose or give answers to life's ultimate questions (in this sense even secularism has a religious character since it constitutes a particular interpretation of life's meaning and value).

Most philosophers now agree that the content of justice cannot be determined simply through the exercise of objective, disembodied reason. No such faculty exists. Reason does not operate in splendid isolation from the rest of human experience. Human beings can only ever think about justice (or anything else for that matter) within the context of particular historical and cultural traditions. In other words, our reasoning, and thus our understanding of justice, is unavoidably contextual or historical in character. This need not mean, as is often assumed today, that justice itself is merely the product of human reflection, that it has no objective transcendent existence; it simply means that our knowledge of actual justice is always going to be limited and partial. Indeed from a Christian theological perspective, justice must have a real objective existence, because justice derives from God, and God exists apart from human speculation. Justice is real because God is real. But our capacity to know God's universal justice is unavoidably conditioned by the way of looking at life and the world given to us by the particular historical and religious traditions we belong to. This is where the Bible comes in.

The Bible's Contribution

Christianity insists not only that justice exists because God exists, but that it is possible to know something substantial about the nature of justice, just as it is possible to know something substantial about the nature of God. And the place where Christians can learn about justice, first and foremost, is the biblical narrative of God's creative, sustaining and redeeming activity in the world. For the biblical writers, the meaning of justice is not discovered through abstract philosophical speculation. It is known primarily through God's revelation in history, with the biblical writings comprising the record of that revelation. It is from the biblical story of God's self-disclosure, in both word and deed, then that Christians can come to understand more of what justice entails.

In the biblical narrative, two events stand out as uniquely important in understanding God's justice. The first is the liberation of the Hebrew slaves from Egypt and their formation into a covenant community living under God's law. Over and over again, the prophets and poets of Israel declare that God's justice has been made visible in this momentous intervention. The second great event is the coming of Jesus Christ, who also brings deliverance from servitude and inaugurates a new covenant. For the New Testament writers the Christ-event, even more than the exodus from Egypt, is *the* decisive 'revelation of God's justice' (Romans 1:16-17: 3:21-26). In between and around these two great events, the biblical writers speak eloquently and repeatedly of justice, both divine justice and human justice. Before trying to summarise what they say, a little more needs to be said about the theological worldview within which they talk of justice.

Biblical reflection on justice gives expression to a range of worldview assumptions or core values. Many could be mentioned, but there is room for comment here on just three – Shalom, Covenant and Torah. S*halom* is the Hebrew word for peace. But peace in the Bible is more than the negative absence of armed conflict or violence. Shalom denotes the positive presence of harmony and wholeness, of health and prosperity, of integration and balance. It is the state of soundness or flourishing in all dimensions of existence – in our relationship to God, our relationships to each another, our relationship with nature, and our relationship with ourselves. Shalom is where everything is as it ought to be. In this sense, shalom encapsulates God's basic intention for humanity – that people live in a condition of 'all rightness' in every department of life. Shalom thus combines in one concept the meaning of *both* justice and peace. They are inseparable ingredients of the same reality. There can be no peace without justice, as we all know. But nor can true justice ultimately be established by belligerence, for there is no justice in war.

Covenant is the Bible's word for committed relationship, or, more accurately, for the formal commitment which brings the relationship into existence and specifies the rights and responsibilities of both parties. At the heart of the biblical story is the covenant made between God and Israel. In an act of undeserved grace, God chooses to enter into a unique relationship with Israel, a relationship which is ultimately intended for the benefit of all other nations as well.

The conditions of this covenant relationship are spelled out in the *Torah*, the law said to be given to Moses on Mount Sinai and gradually unfolded and developed through succeeding generations. This law reveals what is needed for Israel to live in shalom, to experience what the creator God always intended for the human community. The law derives its authority, not from the coercive power of the state, but from the will and purpose of God for human blessing and fulfilment. Peace and justice will result if Israel remains loyal to her relationship with God by living according to God's law. Among other things, this law requires all covenant members to act with justice and mercy towards each other. Biblical justice is therefore covenant justice. It is the practical outworking of Israel's special relationship with God. Justice flows from a life of obedience to the law of God, a law that derives its character from a larger vision of shalom, of God's intentions for human life. Law, justice and covenant are thus overlapping or interpenetrating concepts in the Bible.

We should note in passing that biblical law is not legislation in the modern sense. Modern law codes are impersonal, technically precise, comprehensive, and self-consistent. Language is used literally in order to eliminate or minimise ambiguity. The primary audience of modern legislation is the professional legal establishment that must interpret and enforce its provisions. Biblical law, by comparison, has a more pronounced pedagogical or educational function. It is addressed not just to legal specialists but to the entire community, spelling out in simple terms what life in covenant relationship with God entails. Torah really means 'instruction'; it is God's means of instruction in righteousness and justice. The array of diverse stipulations that make up the Mosaic Torah are not hard and fast rules; they are better understood as representative samples of legal reasoning, built up steadily over time and in widely different circumstances, from which guidance could be drawn for other situations. In drawing such guidance, judges had considerable discretion. They were guided by the written Torah but 'do justice and only justice' (Deuteronomy 16:18-20), not simply to enforce positive legislation.

The Contours of Biblical Justice

We are now in a position to identify some of the emphases and insights that give biblical teaching on justice its distinctive character. Space does not permit a thorough analysis of each feature, nor extensive citations from the biblical text to substantiate each (for which see Marshall, 2005). It is possible here only to highlight the most prominent contours of the landscape of biblical justice and to try to view them from within the biblical worldview. The place to begin is where, for the biblical writers, justice itself begins – in the nature of God.

An Attribute of God

The biblical writers consider justice to be, before all else, a personal quality or virtue of God. This explains the enormous concern they have for the subject. Justice belongs to the very being of God. Justice is not something God aspires to; it is the heart of who God is and what God does. As an attribute of the Creator God, justice also furnishes the ground plan of creation. It is, according to the psalmists, the 'foundation' of God's throne, the fundamental principle of the cosmos (Psalms 89:14; 97:2). Justice designates the 'right ordering' of the universe, i.e. the way God intends reality to operate. It is not merely the product of cultural consensus. It is this conviction that drives the biblical writers to condemn injustice wherever they find it, not just in Israel. All nations are answerable to God, for God 'will judge the world with righteousness, and the peoples with equity' (Psalm 98:9).

It is such unwavering belief in the inherent justice of God that gives rise to the painful problem of theodicy (literally the justification of God). How can the goodness and justice of God be vindicated in light of empirical evil? How can the all-powerful Creator, the Deity who 'loves justice' (Isaiah 61:8), tolerate such brutal injustices in the world? The biblical writers are as keenly aware of this dilemma as are modern thinkers. Yet despite the apparent triumph of evil in everyday affairs, the biblical authors never dispute the reality of God's own justice and integrity. Whatever the contradictions of present experience, they never toy with the possibility that God's personal justice might somehow be flawed or God's power limited. For them, there can be no doubting that Yahweh is perfect in justice. Why? Because Israel herself had witnessed the triumph of God's justice in her own history. She had seen God intervene to liberate her from the oppression of slavery, to lead her safely through the wilderness and constitute her as a free, independent people. Israel's own concrete experience had proved forever that 'Yahweh is a God of justice' (Isaiah 30:18).

Yahweh's justice was also confirmed in the gift of the Torah to Israel. In this law, God requires the covenant people to act towards one another in the same way God has acted towards them – with justice, mercy and equity. 'You shall not deprive a resident alien or an orphan of justice; you shall not take a widow's garment in pledge. *Remember* that you were a slave in Egypt and the LORD your God redeemed you from there; *therefore* I command you to do this' (Deuteronomy 24:17-18).

So, for the biblical authors justice is rooted in God's very being and determines all God's interactions with the world. When the great American civil rights leader Martin Luther King declared 'the universe is on the side of justice', he was echoing a fundamental presupposition of the biblical tradition. Justice is the objective foundation of all reality. This justice is known, not primarily through philosophical speculation, but through observing God's *actions* to liberate the oppressed, and through heeding God's *word* in the Law and the Prophets to protect and care for the weak. Knowledge of justice thus springs ultimately from the knowledge of God, and that there can be no true knowledge of God without an appreciation of God's own unfailing dedication to justice.

An Emulation of God

In the biblical creation narratives, it is only human beings who are made in the image and likeness of God. Humans are created to be icons of God in the world. They are the means by which God's loving rule is to be made visible on earth. Since God is a God of justice, those who bear God's image must also be agents of justice. They are to learn from God what justice means and to reproduce what they learn in all their activities in the world. Tragically the entry of sin distorts humanity's capacity to know the truth about God and to live justly. But God's redemptive activity, beginning with the call of Abraham and the election of Israel, is aimed at reinstalling humankind to its intended role in creation. In God's saving activity toward Israel, the nature of divine justice is disclosed afresh, and its beneficiaries are again instructed to replicate what they have seen. 'He has told you, O mortal, what is good; and what does the LORD require of you but to do justice, and to love kindness, and to walk humbly with your God' (Micah 6:8).

According to the Hebrew prophets, emulating God's justice is the real evidence of what it means to know God. True knowledge of God entails both an appreciation of God's own unswerving devotion to justice and a commitment to live one's personal life in conformity to God's justice. Knowing God, as the prophet Jeremiah affirms, is much more important than possessing of wealth or education or power. But there is more to knowing God than confessing dogmas or having religious experiences. It involves discovering God's personal passion for justice and responding in like manner. 'Let those who boast in this, that they understand and know me, that I am the LORD; I act with steadfast love, justice, and righteousness in the earth, for in these things I delight, says the LORD' (Jeremiah 9:23-24)

An Object of Hope

Biblical hope – that confident expectation of a better future – is rooted in the knowledge of God's justice and faithfulness. Because God is the source and champion of justice, and because God is utterly reliable, there is always hope for positive change. The present may be blighted by evil and injustice, but the 'God of hope' (Romans 15:13), forever on the side of the downtrodden, is moving history mysteriously in the direction of final deliverance. 'Happy are those whose help is in the God of Jacob', the psalmist declares, 'whose *hope* is in the Lord their God...who *executes justice* for the oppressed' (Psalm 146:5-7). So while justice can be known in the present, its full realisation on earth always remains an object of hope. It is something yet to be witnessed.

A belief in eschatological justice has important implications for understanding the present. It means, for example, that no existing political system or economic order can ever be regarded as the full, or even as an adequate, realisation of justice. All human social structures and centres of power are denied ultimate significance. Every human attempt to create justice, when measured against the perfect justice of God's coming kingdom, is inescapably partial and limited. There is therefore always room for criticism, there is never ground for complacency, there is always need for improvement. Never are Christian believers to resign themselves to the evils of the world, while waiting passively for God's coming rule to sweep them away. Instead they are called to work tirelessly with God for the greater attainment of justice here and now, knowing that God shall ultimately bring their efforts to fruition in the renewal of creation. God's coming justice is the culmination of, not a substitute for, human striving for greater justice here and now.

A Primary Obligation

Justice is always an effort. It doesn't spontaneously spring into existence. Nor is it the automatic or accidental by-product of something else, such as the operation of market forces or the spread of Western democracy. Justice requires commitment and struggle. It must be pursued with dedication, for there are powerful forces at work in every society with vested interest in maintaining structures of exploitation and oppression.

The pursuit of justice is therefore the primary obligation of the people of God in the Bible. It is so critical, say the biblical prophets, that without a commitment to justice all other means of worshipping God, even those commanded in God's own law, are bankrupt. In the absence of justice religious performances, such as feasts and festivals, fasting and sacrifices, merely nauseate God. They have no leverage on God where workers are oppressed, violence is perpetrated, and the poor go hungry (e.g., Amos 5:21-25; Micah 6:6-8; Isaiah 1:12-17; 58:1-14).

For the biblical prophets, the holiness to which God's people are called is not primarily a matter of observing prescribed religious rituals, nor is it simply a case of maintaining ethnic distinction, though both these things are required by covenant law. The essential mark of holiness is a lifestyle of justice. Just as 'the LORD of hosts is exalted by justice, and the Holy God shows himself holy by righteousness' (Isaiah 5:16), so too God's people are to be known by their passion for justice. For holiness in the Bible means wholeness as well as separation from sin and impurity; it describes a life of completeness and unity and goodness, a life that reflects God's own integrity and self-consistency, a life that is animated by justice.

A COMMITMENT TO ACTION

Justice in the Bible is not an abstract philosophical idea or a mathematical principle of evaluation. It is a description of what God is like and of how God relates to the world. It is shown most clearly in the way God has acted towards oppressed Israel, and to the oppressed within Israel. Justice is not the maintenance of some precarious balance in society. It is not simply the preservation of law and order, for laws can be unjust and order may depend on violence. The accent in biblical justice falls on positive action, the exercising of power to resist the oppressor and set the oppressed free. Justice requires an activist response to systemic evil, a radical intervention to 'loose the bonds of injustice, to undo the thongs of the yoke, to let the oppressed go free, and to break every yoke' (Isaiah 58:16). This is why the prophet Amos pictures justice not as a neatly balanced set of scales, as in the Western tradition, but as a thundering river sweeping oppression away (Amos 5:21-24).

Understandably it is those who possess authority in society who are most responsible for the pursuit of justice. What is almost universally accepted in political theory is true of the Bible as well – securing justice is the first and foremost task of government. The primary responsibility of the Hebrew king was to ensure that justice prevailed in the land by restraining the strong and defending the weak. Similarly the task of the future Messiah – the coming ideal king – was to bring the fullness of God's justice and peace to earth.

A RELATIONAL REALITY

If justice is a personal attribute of God, and if human beings as God's image bearers are called to emulate God's justice in the way they live with one another in community, it follows that justice is all about relationships. It has to do with God's relationship with humanity and the world, and with the relationship of human beings to each other and to the larger created order.

This, in fact, is one of the most distinctive features of biblical teaching. Biblical justice is comprehensively relational. It is neither a private attribute an individual can have on his or her own, independent of anyone else. Nor is it a set of abstract norms about balance or equity or fairness. Justice means doing all that is necessary to create and sustain healthy, constant and life-giving relationships between persons. Justice is to be measured by the extent to which people honour their obligation to live in relationships that uphold the equal dignity and rights of the other. Both elements are important – relationships that are wholesome, and faithfulness to the demands of such relationships by all parties involved.

The relational character of biblical justice helps to explain why the biblical writers see no tension between justice and mercy. God's mercy in fact is an expression of God's justice. 'He will rise up to show mercy to you', Isaiah, writes, 'for the LORD is a God of justice' (Isaiah 30:18). People today often think of mercy and justice as opposites. To show mercy when wrongdoing has occurred means suspending or disregarding what justice strictly requires. Mercy thus represents a kind of injustice. But this is only the case if we think of justice in strictly arithmetical or legalistic terms. If instead we understand justice in terms of restoring healthy relationships, then mercy is often the best way to get there. Compassionate acceptance of human fallibility is essential to the functioning of healthy relationships. Where failure occurs, as always it will, justice must be seasoned with mercy - else it is not true justice.

A Partiality for the Disadvantaged

We come now to one of the most important insights of biblical teaching on justice – it requires different priorities in different settings. In some circumstances justice requires a disinterested impartiality, a repudiation of all favouritism, but in other circumstances it demands an unequivocal partiality – a definite bias towards the interests of certain parties over those of others. Therefore, depending on the issues at stake, justice can be both impartial and partial, biased and unbiased, equal and unequal.

Biblical law considers impartiality to be critically important when dealing with criminal wrongdoing or in arbitrating disputes between litigants. Unlike other ancient societies, where different laws and different penalties applied to different classes, Israelite criminal and procedural law was radically egalitarian. All members of the community were subject to the same standards, and judges were explicitly required to disregard social and economic status in hearing cases and to refrain from selling justice to the highest bidder (e.g., Deuteronomy 1:16-17). Such procedural fairness was mandated, once again, by an appeal to the equity of God's justice, 'for there is no perversion of justice with the LORD our God, or partiality, or taking of bribes' (2 Chronicles 19:7)

But a quite different emphasis emerges in the Bible with respect to social justice (which deals with the way wealth, social resources and political power are distributed in society). Here a definite partiality is to be exhibited. A special concern is to be shown for the welfare of four groups in particular – widows, orphans, resident aliens, and the poor (e.g., Exodus 22:21-24). Partiality for such groups (sometimes other parties are also included, such as prisoners, the sick and the broken hearted) is commended, yet again, by the nature of God's own justice, for 'the LORD maintains the cause of the needy, and executes justice for the poor' (Psalm 140:12). At first sight, the idea of a presumed bias in favour of certain groups in society seems antithetical to justice. Should not a just society aspire to treat all people exactly the same, irrespective of wealth, nationality or family status? Does not justice require a level playing field? Not necessarily, suggests the biblical tradition.

There are two main reasons why, according to biblical perspective, the struggle for social justice must be biased in favour of certain parties. The first is because some groups in the community are more frequently the victims of injustice than are others. God has created all people equal in worth and given to all equal rights of access to the abundance of creation. But individuals are also created different in gender, race, personality, capacity and gifting. Injustice occurs when these differences are exploited in such a way that some are denied their God-given rights so that others can accumulate unneeded excess. What widows, orphans, migrants and the poor have in common, especially in a patriarchal society, is their vulnerability to exploitation. The widow has no husband to watch over her rights, the orphan has no parents, the poor have no money, the stranger has no friends. Their rights are more easily trampled than are those of the rich and powerful – who still possess legitimate rights but usually have the means to protect these rights by themselves.

The other reason is because the condition of the impoverished and the oppressed violates the Creator's intentions for the world. It is not God's will that some should live in splendour and opulence, while others starve and die. It is not God's will that some should horde food and surplus land, while others languish in debt and servitude. This is why meeting the needs of the poor is not viewed in the Bible as a matter of charity but as an act of justice, for it helps move society in the direction God intends. In biblical understanding, the litmus test for measuring the extent of justice in society is how its most vulnerable members are faring. The most salient indicator of injustice is where people are deprived of access to the essential resources they need to survive and flourish as free and productive human beings.

God's bias or 'preferential option' for the poor is, ultimately, in the interests of equity. In the perennial struggle for social justice, in which the scales seem always to be tipped on the side of the wealthy and powerful, God evens the balance by taking the side of the poor and defenceless. God is not a disinterested observer of the struggle; instead God 'executes justice for the oppressed...gives food to the hungry...sets the prisoners free...opens the eyes of the blind... lifts up those who are bowed down... loves the righteous... watches over the strangers...upholds the orphan and the widow, but the way of the wicked he brings to ruin' (Psalm 146:5-9).

But precisely *how* does God defend the cause of the poor? How does God feed the hungry and show solidarity with the oppressed? How, for the biblical authors, is the bias of God's justice visible in practice? There are several ways. One is through historical precedent. God's intervention to rescue powerless, impoverished Israel from servitude in Egypt proved forever God's active bias to the poor. Another way is through the inclusion in God's law of specific welfare provisions and protections for the poor and vulnerable. Numerous laws guarantee access to food, clothing, shelter and rest even to the most destitute. Sabbath and Jubilee regulations required the periodic remittance of debts, the release of slaves and restoration of land to its original owners. Scholars doubt that these revolutionary provisions were ever fully honoured in practice. But they betokened the recognition of the need for regular political action to counteract the inherent tendency in all economic systems to concentrate wealth and power in the hands of the few at the expense of the many. They also served as a constant and uncomfortable reminder to the community of God's partiality towards the plight of the dispossessed.

Yet another way that God's bias for the poor was visible in practice was through the raising up of prophets to confront the rich and powerful, including the king himself, with God's demand for justice and with dire warnings of judgment should they fail in their duty to care for the weak. The prophets also spoke of a new day coming in which the hungry will be fed, the sick will be healed, captives will be released, and suffering will be ended, a day when 'the meek will inherit the earth' (Matthew 5:5).

A Restorative Activity

God's partiality for the poor in biblical teaching, we have suggested, is because of their greater vulnerability to unjust victimisation. But the poor are not automatically virtuous. They are not always innocent of wrongdoing themselves. Where accusations are brought against them in court, biblical law requires the judicial system to treat all parties impartially, regardless of social status (Leviticus 19:15; Exodus 23:2-3). But impartiality is only essential to establishing guilt or culpability. Once that issue is decided, the fundamental goal of the judicial system was with the restoration of what had been damaged by the offending, with restitution and compensation playing a significant role in biblical legislation. Biblical justice is, predominantly, a restorative justice, with restoration being sought at several levels – the restoration of the victim to wholeness, the restoration of the offender to a right standing in the community, and the restoration of wider society to shalom, to peace and freedom.

It is true, of course, that punishment also plays an important role in biblical legislation. But, as I have argued in detail elsewhere (Marshall 2001a), punishment was mainly seen a means to an end, not as an end in itself. Punishment served an educative more than a retributive function. It helped the covenant community to recognise those kinds of behaviours that constituted the most serious threats to its moral and spiritual wellbeing. The attaching of punitive sanctions to certain offences was intended to mark them out as especially damaging to the community's welfare and distinctiveness. Tellingly, unlike other ancient societies and all European societies up to the 18th century, biblical legislation never prescribed the death penalty for crimes against property, only for crimes against people and for violations of those central obligations of Israel's unique relationship with God, and only rarely was it mandatory to carry out the penalty. This manifests an underlying scale of values in which the protection of human dignity and the preservation of Israel's redemptive vocation in the world was considered to be more important that the protection of property rights or the promotion of individual autonomy.

EMBODIED IN JESUS CHRIST

The liberation of Israel from captivity in Egypt and her establishment as an independent people revealed God's justice to be a liberating, community-creating power that intervenes in oppressive situations to restore shalom. Israel was summoned to emulate God's justice in her own manner of living in the world. Sometimes she did so, but often she failed, experiencing a series of historical catastrophes in consequence. Consequently the hope grew up that one day in the future God's liberating justice would manifest itself on earth in a new way, restoring Israel's fortunes and renewing all creation.

For the New Testament authors, Jesus represents the fulfilment of this biblical hope. Jesus incarnates the justice of God. In him, justice moves from heaven to earth in a new and dramatic way. Jesus is 'the Just One' whose life, death and resurrection constitute the definitive revelation of God's justice on earth. For Christians, therefore, most can be learned about justice from examining the life, teaching and activity of Jesus. There is no room to do that here, sadly. But even a superficial reading of the gospel records shows that every feature of justice outlined above is exemplified in the Jesus story.

At the outset of his ministry Jesus defined his messianic mission as one of bringing justice to the oppressed (Luke 4:16-20). Subsequently he went about proclaiming that the kingdom of God – the long-awaited reign of divine justice on earth – was now getting underway. He summoned his hearers to put the claims of God's royal justice ahead of all lesser concerns (Matthew 6:33). He healed the sick, fed the hungry, delivered the demonised and challenged dominant systems of exclusion and oppression. He repudiated war and violence as having any role in 'bringing justice to victory' (Matthew 12:21). On the contrary, justice can only be realised by confounding the tit-for-tat logic of evil, which is what, for Christians, the story of the death and resurrection of Jesus is all about. But that is another story for another time.

CONCLUSION

In the biblical tradition, justice is a complex, multi-faceted reality. It relates to every dimension of human experience, and has many different applications. The Bible does not contain anything like a carefully worked-out *theory* of justice; this is not the contribution it makes to the ongoing quest for a more just world. Instead it offers a series of vignettes on justice, a range of insights, examples, convictions, values, perspectives and priorities that can inform, modify or enlarge conventional accounts of justice. Biblical justice is theological more than theoretical in character; it describes what God is believed to be like, and what this means for those caught up in the drama of divine redemption.

Arguably the term that best captures the spirit and direction of biblical reflection on justice is the word *restoration.* Justice flows from God's own being and designates the way God intends the world to be. But things have fallen into disorder; the shalom of creation has been ruptured. God responds by seeking to restore the world to the way it ought to be. God acts to reconstruct shalom by overthrowing oppressive powers and setting victims free, and by healing the destructive legacy of sin and death. To know this God is to learn about the meaning of justice. To love this God is to join in God's great campaign to restore justice to the world.

SELECTED REFERENCES

Barnes Lampman, L., and M.D. Shattuck, (Eds.). (1999). *God and the victim: Theological reflections on evil, victimization, justice and forgiveness*. Grand Rapids Mich.: Eerdmans.

Epsztein, L. (1986). *Social justice in the Ancient Near East and the people of the Bible.* London: SCM.

Forrester, D.B. (1997). *Christian justice and public policy*. Cambridge: Cambridge University Press.

Haugen, *G.A.* (1999*). Good news about injustice: A witness of courage in a hurting world.* Leicester/Downers Grove, Ill.: InterVarsity Press.

Haughey, J.C. (Ed.). (1977). *The faith that does justice: examining the Christian sources for social change.* New York: Paulist Press.

Herzog II, W.R. (2000). *Jesus. Justice and the reign of God: A ministry of liberation.* Louisville KY: Westminster John Knox.

Heschel, A.J. (1962). *The prophets.* New York: Jewish Publication Society of America.

Kaylor, R.D. (1994*). Jesus the prophet: His vision of the kingdom on earth.* Louisville Ky: Westminster John Knox.

Knierim, R.P. (1995). *The task of Old Testament theology: Substance, method and cause.* Grand Rapids, Mich:Eerdmans.

Leclerc, T.L. (2001). *Yahweh is exalted in Justice: Solidarity and conflict in Isaiah.* Minneapolis: Fortress Press.

Leech, K. (1985). *True God: An exploration in spiritual theology*. London: Sheldon Press.

Malchow, B.V. (1996). *Social justice in the Hebrew Bible.* Collegeville, MINN: Glazier.

Marshall, C.D. (1993). *Kingdom come: the kingdom of God in the teaching of Jesus.* Auckland: Impetus.

Marshall, C.D. (2001a). *Beyond retribution: A New Testament vision for justice, crime and punishment.* Grand Rapids, Mich.: Eerdmans.

Marshall, C.D. (2001b). *Crowned with glory and honor: Human rights in the biblical tradition.* Telford, Penn: Pandora Press.

Marshall, C.D. (2005). *The little book on biblical justice.* Intercourse, PA: Good Books.

Mott, S.C. (1993a). *A Christian perspective on political thought.* New York/Oxford: Oxford University Press.

Mott, S.C. (1993b). The partiality of Biblical justice. *Transformation*, 10, 1, 23-29.

Weinfeld, M. (1995). *Social justice in ancient Israel and in the ancient near east.* Minneapolis: Fortress Press.

Wright, C.J.H. (1983). *.An eye for an eye: The place of Old Testament ethics* Today. Downers Grove Ill: InterVarsity Press.

Wright, C.J.H. (1995). *Walking in the ways of the Lord: The ethical authority of the Old Testament.* Leicester: Apollos.

Yoder, P.B. (1987). *Shalom: The Bible's word for salvation, justice and peace.* Newton KA: Faith and Life Press.

Zehr, H. (1990). *Changing lenses: A new focus for crime and justice.* Scottsdale PA: Herald Press.

In: Justice as a Basic Human Need
Editor: Anthony Taylor, pp. 39-47
ISBN 1-59454-915-X

Chapter 4

From Darwin to Piaget: The Development and Acquisition of Moral Beliefs

Paul Jose

'He's got more than me' (said by all children at one time or another concerning the distribution of resources within the family)

Abstract

If justice is a basic moral need, as Taylor (2003) has argued, then one should be able to find evidence for it early in a person's developmental history. Indeed, all parents are able to offer numerous accounts of expressed concerns by children concerning fair distribution of food, attention, and other family resources. Parents' immediate response may be of annoyance, but a broader perspective allows them to appreciate the necessity for children to gain experience in such matters. The central thesis of this chapter is that it is critical for children to express themselves and to gain skills in these interactions because their welfare and the continuation of the species is dependent upon their ability to obtain sufficient resources for survival.

Introduction

The majority of research and theory in developmental psychology germane to the question of moral development attempts to answer the questions of "how?" and "when?" but rarely "why?" (Gaulin and McBurney, 2001). In this chapter, I will briefly summarize the four chief theorists of moral development (i.e. Freud, Skinner, Piaget, and Kohlberg), and then move to compare and contrast their views with those of evolutionary psychologists. The evolutionary perspective will be proposed as a compelling position for those who would like to argue that justice is a basic need of humans, in essence, providing an answer to the question of why humans develop a sense of morality.

HISTORICAL VIEWS OF THE DEVELOPMENT OF MORALITY

In his approach to understand the human psyche, Sigmund Freud posited three functional concepts: the id (source of innate drives); the ego (the rational problem solver and decision maker); and the superego (moral rules and the conscience) (Badcock, 1992; Freud, 1927; 1986). He deemed the superego responsible for moral behaviour, and considered that it was derived chiefly through identification with the same-sex parent during the phallic period (early childhood). Freud believed that no individual was able to satisfy the id's desires all (or even most) of the time, so the ego and the superego must serve to police the individual's actions to a great extent. The ego and superego reflect societal restraints on behaviour and constrain the person to behave according to accepted local norms and mores (Freud, 1930). The chief area of restraint that Freud explored concerned sexual desires and behaviour, although, as we will see later, there is no compelling reason to disallow the consideration of other important resources such as food, social respect, and other valuable commodities of human life. Freud was keenly interested in understanding the aetiology of psychological dysfunction, such as psychosis and neurosis, and felt that healthy resolution of the inherent tension among his three given intrapsychic components would allow an individual to live a well-adjusted life. Although his theory was not specifically focused on the matter of moral development per se, his psychodynamic theory opened up new territory in this regard.

B. F. Skinner (1938), also, was not particularly interested in moral development per se, but his general theory of behaviour analysis and modification is sometimes used to explain the acquisition of moral behaviour. He approached the issue of moral behavior by arguing that the operant conditioning of behaviour increased or decreased the incidence of particular behaviours, moral or otherwise. If a parent wishes to increase honesty in her child, she could make praise contingent on truth-telling behaviour and punishment contingent on lying behaviour, and providing she can discriminate between lying and truth-telling and systematically and reliably administer reinforcers over time, then the child's behaviour will evolve toward more honesty. The theory has been labeled as highly contextual insofar as there is no external frame for determining what behaviours might be considered moral or immoral, i.e. it does not accord special status to moral behaviour. In addition, the theory is not developmental in the sense that change is caused by experience with particular reinforcement schedules rather than any growing awareness of ethical principles, and it is not explicitly dependent upon the age (i.e. the biological maturity) of the individual.

The theoretical and empirical work of Jean Piaget and Lawrence Kohlberg is profoundly developmental, because they believed that the age of the child (which roughly reflects the child's cognitive level) strongly constrains the developmental course of moral acquisition. They were united in the belief that the child's acquisition of moral thought, judgment, and behaviour was dependent upon his or her level of cognitive functioning. Piaget articulated a theory of cognitive development that served as the basis for his conclusions about the developmental trajectory of moral development, and Kohlberg (1976) took the matter further in his subsequent theory and research.

The Piaget/Kohlberg approach has attracted considerable attention within psychology and related fields because it describes convincingly the course of moral judgments that children and adolescents experience. To a great extent, it persuasively describes the 'when' and 'how' of moral development, and it has been evaluated as contributing significantly to our knowledge of moral development. However, I would like to point out that Piaget's theory also includes some suggestions about the 'why' of moral development that have been often overlooked. Let us now consider his theory in some detail to identify these explanatory factors. Jean Piaget's (1932) major work on moral development described the results of his interviews, observations, and studies with Swiss children over a period of several years, and he derived a developmental model from interpreting these data in light of his general cognitive developmental theory. The book is replete with creative and insightful methodologies for assessing moral thought and behaviour in children, and it provided a significant basis for social and developmental psychological research for the following 50 years. In particular, two key areas evolved from this work: i.e. 1) distributive justice and 2) retributive justice. The former concerns how an individual allocates finite resources among a number of parties, and the latter is the issue of how one evaluates and treats the moral nature of human behaviour.

In essence, Piaget observed that children pass through discrete stages of reasoning concerning moral judgments. Those in the sensorimotor period of functioning, 2 years and younger, were said to be 'amoral', or premoral. Once they achieve language and symbolic thought, roughly at about 2 years of age, children become 'preoperational' insofar as they have not yet acquired logical operations that permit more complex cognitive functioning. During this period, until about age 10, children are said to be heteronomous, i.e., reflecting distinctive ways of thinking about moral issues (e.g., children consider rules to be external and stemming from parental authority and teachers). A qualitative shift occurs at about age 10 years, after which children become more autonomous, increasingly believing that moral rules are not external to the self and increasingly questioning authority. In essence, their acquisition of more sophisticated cognitive skills (i.e. logical operations) encourages them to think more flexibly and accurately about the foundations of ethical and moral rules.

The development of children's judgments concerning distributive justice generally follows stages of cognitive development described by Piaget. He considered young children before the age of 6 to be egocentric, in that they are likely to have great difficulty in taking the perspectives of others, and in the matter of seeking toys, food, attention, etc., children of this age are chiefly motivated by self-interest. In Freudian terms, the id dominates and promotes behaviour that others often consider to be selfish. A toddler who grabs a toy from another child because she wants it is acting in an egocentric fashion: her desire to have the toy is more important or relevant than the other child's desire for the toy. In Piagetian terms, children possess a scheme (i.e., 'take what you want') that is enacted when they wish to obtain a desired object. As they mature, children receive considerable feedback and instruction from their parents, older siblings, and other children concerning their behaviour around resources. If 4-year-old children persist in taking whatever they want, they will receive strong signals from their environment that their behaviour is undesirable. The state of the child realizing that use of their present schemes does not always result in effective social interactions was termed 'disequilibration' by Piaget. He argued that it motivated cognitive development, and led children to understand that resource allocation was a more complicated process than they had previously envisioned. Disequilibration leads to accommodation, wherein the child modifies his or her cognitive structures in order to interact more smoothly with people and objects in the environment.

The second stage of distributive justice occurs at about 5 or 6 years of age when children begin to take the other's perspective into account to work out when they can play with particular toys, how they can ask for it, etc. Gradually the process refines children's cognitive structures to the point that they adopt a position of equality with regard to resource allocation (i.e., distributive justice) (Damon and Hart, 1988; Thorkildsen, 1989). By then they have reached a new level of equilibration which allows them to share and divide resources in a more socially acceptable fashion. The third level achieved in distributive justice is the equity position (Damon, 1980). It is reached when children who have acquired logical operations are able to apply several criteria simultaneously to determine fair or equitable distribution of resources. For example, a child may recognize that, of several children who worked to complete a joint school assignment, the one who worked the hardest should receive the largest share of the resource. Equity is confirmed when the child of 10 or 11 years begins to show signs of benevolence in their distributive decisions, allowing more resources to be given to those who are needy (Damon. 1980).

At this juncture, I would like to focus on Piaget's concept of adaptation that he considered to be one of the bedrock assumptions of his theory (Ginsburg and Opper, 1988; Pulaski, 1980). He believed that members of the human species are genetically predisposed to become cognitively more sophisticated with age, and that the unfolding of the genetic blueprint over time in conjunction with feedback from the environment pushes individuals to become cognitively more complex as they grow older. He did not believe that age alone determined cognitive or moral development, but instead he emphasized the process of equilibration (the continual to and fro of assimilation and accommodation creating ever increasing sophistication and complexity) that occurs between the child and his environment. The result of continual equilibration produced an organism more suitably adapted to the environment.

Lawrence Kohlberg (1976; 1981) extended Piaget's developmental theory of moral judgments to the period of formal operations (i.e., late adolescence and adulthood). Kohlberg's theory encompassed the age-span from young childhood to adulthood by positing three periods of preconventional, conventional, and postconventional development, each period of which has two lower-level stages. Although a number of critics (e.g., Gilligan, 1982; Shweder, Mahapatra, and Miller, 1990) questioned his methodology, theory, and results, Kohlberg's theory has been hugely influential in stimulating educators and researchers of many disciplines. Like Piaget, Kohlberg felt that higher levels of moral judgment were achieved through social interactions effecting the refinement of cognitive structures underlying moral belief systems. For example, children who are involved in discussions with their parents concerning real world experiences of justice, ethics, and morality are more likely to evidence increases in moral reasoning (Kurtines and Gewirtz, 1987; Walker and Taylor, 1991).

In a prominent review of the literature on moral development, Turiel (1998, p. 868) argued that Kohlberg's legacy in the area of moral development was to stress that the acquisition of highly developed moral rules was 'not solely or even primarily an external or unwanted imposition on (children)'. Rather with a position similar to Piaget's conception of adaptation, he saw children and adolescents as having a strong natural inclination to become more sophisticated and function more effectively in a real world moral sense with age.

Both Piaget and Kohlberg died before the fields of evolutionary psychology, and in particular, evolutionary ethics, developed and became established. Consequently they did not have a chance to consider how their perspectives might fruitfully interleave with these new views. In the remainder of this chapter, I will briefly highlight a number of relevant arguments from an evolutionary perspective, and I will attempt to marry it with previous work in moral development.

EVOLUTIONARY PSYCHOLOGY

The essential position of evolutionary psychology is that over millennia Homo sapiens has been shaped by evolutionary forces, and that present behaviours evident in our species reflect the consequences of these forces. Evolutionary psychology, and the related sub-field of evolutionary ethics, has developed recently in an attempt to answer the question of how these evolutionary pressures have formed our species' moral beliefs, judgments, emotions, and behaviours. A number of theorists from this perspective (e.g., Chisholm, 1999; Farber, 1994; Maienschein and Ruse, 1999; Thompson, 1995; Wright, 1994) have put forward provocative models to explain how evolutionary pressures have created a particular moral sense in humans. Among them Wright's views (1994) will be considered here, not because his are the most authoritative or extensive, but because they are typical of the field and they are very accessible. Other useful accounts of evolutionary psychology (e.g., Buss, 1999; MacDonald, 1998) and evolutionary ethics exist (e.g., Richards, 1995), and these can be read to acquire a broader and deeper sense of this perspective.

Wright argues principally from the writings of Darwin (1859; 1871; 1872), but also from Alexander (1987), Dawkins (1986), Hamilton (1963), Trivers (1971), Williams (1975), and E. O. Wilson (1978). His thesis is that humans come into this world embodying the two opposing tendencies of altruism and self-interest. The organism is self-interested (i.e., wishes to act to continue living) because continued existence conveys an evolutionary advantage upon the ability to pass genetic material on to the next generation. One's genes are more likely to be perpetuated if one can survive to reproductive age, succeed in reproducing, and then live long enough to assist one's offspring to get a good start in life themselves.

However, opposing this self-interest is a tendency toward altruism. Organisms are predisposed to assist others of their species, particularly if providing help does not significantly hinder one's own survival. As Wright (1994) says, "Organisms are things that act as if their welfare were more important than the welfare of all other organisms (except when other organisms can help spread their genes)" (pp. 336-337). Giving assistance to genetically related individuals can help to proliferate one's genes, and it is therefore a general tendency that has been selected for survival. The calculus of genetic relatedness is said to govern altruistic behaviour to a great extent. Thus a parent is highly motivated to ensure the safe-keeping and well-being of his or her children because he or she is highly genetically related to a son or daughter ($r = .50$). A child is more likely to help a sibling ($r = .50$) than a cousin (.25), and so forth.

Nevertheless, a human being cannot be entirely motivated or governed by one of these two countervailing forces, or else the person would quickly feel the force of evolutionary pressures to change his or her stance. In particular, someone cannot be exclusively self-interested or else others will cease to cooperate with him. Similarly, an organism cannot be entirely altruistic or else she will quickly deplete necessary resources and threaten her own survival. The implication that Wright draws out of these two evolutionary gradients coming into contact with each other in the human species is that the competent human learns to balance these two motives and eventually adopts an approach where resources are shared equally (Piaget's equalitarianism) or according to contribution or need (equity).

RAPPROCHEMENT?

The main argument of this chapter is that the literature on developmental psychology and children's moral judgments and behaviour can be usefully interpreted within the context of evolutionary psychology. The central theory of moral development that we have considered here is Piaget's cognitive developmental theory. The question to be considered is whether Jean Piaget, if he were alive today, would find an integration of his perspectives with evolutionary psychology to be sensible and helpful. I believe that he might. In an effort to persuade the reader, let me quote from both Darwin (1871) and Piaget (1932) sequentially. The first quote comes from Darwin's book, *The descent of man and selection in relation to sex*:

> At the moment of action, man will no doubt be apt to follow the stronger impulse; and though this may occasionally prompt him to the noblest deeds, it will more commonly lead him to gratify his own desires at the expense of other men. But after their gratification when past and weaker impressions are judged by the ever-enduring social instinct, and by his deep regard for the good opinion of his fellows, retribution will surely come. He will then feel remorse, repentance, regret, or shame; this latter feeling, however, relates almost exclusively to the judgment of others. He will consequently resolve more or less firmly to act differently for the future; and this is conscience; for conscience looks backwards, and serves as a guide for the future' (reprinted in Thompson, 1995; pp. 57-58).

The passage identifies the two forces discussed above (i.e. self-interest and altruism), and it is notable that Darwin seems to believe that self-interest is generally a more powerful motive than altruism. Further, he notes that the 'social instinct'--the desire to be included in social relations with others--is the force that drives a person to rein in his selfish desires. In expressing this point, he gives emotions a prime function in impelling an individual to consider the moral nature of his actions. And last, Darwin emphasizes the self-regulating nature of this process, with the person attempting to achieve a balance between these two motives.

We now turn to a quote from Piaget's book, *The moral judgment of the child* (p. 318), as a way of drawing parallels between these two theorists:

> . . . it cannot be denied that the idea of equality or of distributive justice possesses individual or biological roots which are necessary but not sufficient conditions for its development. One can observe in the child at a very early stage two reactions which will play a very important part in this particular elaboration. Jealousy, to begin with, appears extremely early in babies: infants of 8 to 12 months often give signs of violent rage when they see another child seated on their mother's knees, or when a toy is taken from them and given to another child. On the other hand, one can observe in conjunction with imitation and the ensuing sympathy, altruistic reactions and a tendency to share, which are of equally early date. But it goes without saying that equalitarianism can never be regarded as a sort of instinct or spontaneous product of the individual mind. The reactions we have just alluded to lead to a capricious alternation of

egoism and sympathy. It is true, of course, that jealousy prevents other people from taking advantage of us, and the need to communicate prevents the self from taking advantage of others. But for true equality and a genuine desire for reciprocity there must be a collective rule which is the *sui generis* product of life lived in common. There must be born of the actions and reactions of individuals upon each other the consciousness of a necessary equilibrium binding upon and limiting both "alter" and "ego". And this ideal equilibrium, dimly felt on the occasion of every quarrel and every peace-making, naturally presupposes a long reciprocal education of the children by each other'.

This section is quoted at length because it encompasses several critical ideas that Piaget held that overlap very neatly with the evolutionary thesis. First, in his opening sentence he mentioned the possibility that distributive justice motives may have biological roots, and although he denies later in the passage that equalitarianism is an instinct, I think it clear that he is suggesting that moral judgment and behaviour have genetic origins. Second, in a very perceptive fashion he noticed and commented upon the twin countervailing motives of self-interest and altruism that Darwin described. Although he names the former jealousy, I believe that a generous interpretation would allow it to be identified as self-interest. Third, he noticed that these contradictory impulses are present from a very young age (i.e., during the sensorimotor period), and that the child vacillates between them. In other words, they seem to exist as relatively intact modules of motivation and action, and, further, they are not typically combined or integrated in the very young child. A significant notion of Piaget's here, is that these two motives stand in contradistinction, and further, both serve a functional purpose. Self-interest prevents others from taking advantage of us, and at the same time, the fact that we must live with others in relative harmony precludes us from taking advantage of others. And fourth, the last portion of the passage is a succinct synopsis of how Piaget thinks that the child engages in equilibration around these issues. Thus Piaget and Darwin seem to agree that individuals tend to be torn by these two particular warring emotions or motives, and that eventually children learn to effect a compromise that allows them to live effectively with others.

In sum, I would argue that the foundation of Piaget's theory of moral development bears a remarkable resemblance to the core ideas of Darwin's views on moral thought.

Piaget referred to himself as a genetic epistemologist (Pulaski, 1980). His theory of cognitive development was firmly rooted in biological and evolutionary ideas, and late in his life he published two books which laid out his views that psychological development occurs on top of the foundation of biological development: Biology and knowledge (1971) and Behavior and evolution (1978). Also his use of the term adaptation to describe cognitive development over time resonates with its use in genetics and biology. Given that his early training was in zoology and biology (his doctorate was in malacology, the study of mollusks), it is not a difficult leap in induction to think that Piaget would have found himself to be quite sympathetic to many of the concepts espoused in evolutionary psychology.

Is Justice a Basic Human Need?

Notwithstanding the difficulty inherent in deciding what a *basic* human need might be (see Maslow, 1970 and Taylor, 2003), the clear implication of the juxtaposition of the cognitive developmental and evolutionary ethics positions described here is that striving for justice would seem to be an essential part of human life. Piaget's view that cognitive development is driven by adaptation, is congruent with the Darwinian perspective that organisms well adapted to their environment are more likely to survive and procreate. Piaget did not explicitly contextualize his moral development theory in an evolutionary sense, but he was certainly aware, and I believe sympathetic, with the hugely influential writings of Darwin that were published 60-70 years before he published his own book on morality. Certainly we can recognize the vastly functional purposes of being able to judge the fairness of resource distribution and the fairness of human actions. A human being who can do neither well, will soon be shortchanged in resource allocation, and will be mistreated by untrustworthy acquaintances. To be able to make an accurate judgment of whether one has been treated fairly by others confers an evolutionary advantage. Thus, I believe it fair to argue that a motivation to achieve a sense of justice is basic for the human species.

REFERENCES

Alexander, R. D. (1987). *The biology of moral systems.* Hawthorne, NJ: Aldine de Gruyter.

Badcock, C. (1992). *Essential Freud.* (2nd edn.). Oxford: Blackwell Publishers.

Buss, D. (1999). *Evolutionary psychology: The new science of the mind.* Boston: Allyn and Bacon.

Chisholm, J. S. (1999). *Death, hope, and sex: Steps to an evolutionary ecology of mind and morality.* Cambridge: Cambridge University Press.

Damon, W. (1980). Patterns of change in children's social reasoning: A two-year longitudinal study. *Child Development,* 51,1010-1017.

Damon, W. and Hart, D. (1988). *Self-understanding in childhood and adolescence* Cambridge: Cambridge University Press.

Darwin, C. (1859). *The origin of species.* New York: Penguin Books (1968).

Darwin, C. (1871). *The descent of man, and selection in relation to sex.* Princeton, NJ: Princeton University Press (1981).

Darwin, C. (1872). *The expression of emotions in man and animals.* Chicago: University of Chicago Press (1965).

Dawkins, R. (1986). *The blind watchmaker.* New York: Norton and Co.

Farber, P. (1994). *The temptations of evolutionary ethics.* Berkeley, CA: University of California Press.

Freud, S. (1927). *The ego and the id.* London: Hogarth Press

Freud, S. (1930/1963). *Civilisation and its discontents.* London: Hogarth Press and the Institute of Psycho-analysis.

Freud, S. (1986). *The essentials of psycho-analysis.* London : Hogarth Press and the Institute of Psycho-Analysis.

Gaulin, S. J. C., and McBurney, D. H. (2001). *Psychology: An evolutionary approach.* Upper Saddle River, NJ: Prentice-Hall.

Gilligan, C. (1982). *In a different voice : Psychological theory and women's development.* Cambridge, MA: Harvard University Press.

Ginsburg, H. P., and Opper, S. (1988). *Piaget's theory of intellectual development.* (3rd edn.). Englewood Cliffs, NJ: Prentice Hall.

Hamilton, W. D. (1963). The evolution of altruistic behavior. *American Naturalist, 97*, 354-356.

Kohlberg, L. (1976). Moral stages and moralization. In T. Lickona. (Ed.). *Moral development and behavior.*(pp. 31-53) New York: Holt, Rinehart, and Winston.

Kohlberg, L. (1981). *Essays on moral development.* San Francisco: Harper and Row.

Kurtines, W. M., and Gewirtz, J. L. (Eds.). (1987). *Moral development through social interaction.* New York: John Wiley and Sons.

MacDonald, K. (1998). Evolution and development. In A. Campbell and S. Muncer (Eds.), *The social child* (pp. 21-49). Hove, England: Psychology Press.

Maienschein, J., and Ruse, M. (Eds.). (1999). *Biology and the foundation of ethics.* Cambridge: Cambridge University Press.

Maslow, A.H. (1970). *Motivation and personality.* (2nd ed.). New York: Harper and Row.

Piaget, J. (1932). *The moral judgment of the child.* New York: The Free Press. (1965).

Piaget, J. (1971). *Biology and knowledge.* Chicago: University of Chicago Press.

Piaget, J. (1978). *Behavior and evolution.* New York: Random House.

Pulaski, M. A. S. (1980). *Understanding Piaget: An introduction to children's cognitive development.* New York: Harper and Row.

Richards, R. J. (1995). A defense of evolutionary ethics. In P. Thompson (Ed.), *Issues in evolutionary ethics* (pp. 249-291). Albany, NY: SUNY Press.

Shweder, R. A., Mahapatra, M., and Miller, J. G. (1990). Culture and moral development. In J. Stigler, R. A. Shweder, and G. Herdt. (Eds.). *Cultural psychology: Essays on comparative human development* (pp. 130-204) New York: Cambridge University Press.

Skinner, B. F. (1938). *The behavior of organisms: An experimental analysis.* New York: Appleton-Century-Crofts.

Taylor, A. J. W. (2003). Justice as a basic human need. *New Ideas in Psychology, 21*, 209-219.

Thompson, P. (1995). (Ed.). *Issues in evolutionary ethics.* Albany, NY: SUNY Press.

Thorkildsen, T.A. (1989). Pluralism in the children's reasoning about social justice. *Child Development, 60*, 965-972.

Trivers, R. (1971). The evolution of reciprocal altruism. *Quarterly Review of Biology, 46*, 35-56.

Turiel, E. (1998). The development of morality. In W. Damon and N. Eisenberg (Eds.), *Handbook of child psychology.* (5th edn.). *Volume 3: Social, emotional, and personality development* (pp. 863-932). New York: John Wiley and Sons.

Walker, L. J. and Taylor, J. H. (1991). Family interactions and the development of moral reasoning. *Child Development,* 62, 264-283.

Williams, G. C. (1975). *Sex and evolution.* Princeton, NJ: Princeton University Press.

Wilson, E. O. (1978). *On human nature.* Cambridge, MA: Harvard University Press.

Wright, R. (1994). *The moral animal: Evolutionary psychology and everyday life.* New York: Pantheon Books.

In: Justice as a Basic Human Need
Editor: Anthony Taylor, pp. 49-60
ISBN 1-59454-915-X

Chapter 5

CRIMINAL JUSTICE AND GOOD LIVES

Lynne Eccleston and Tony Ward

ABSTRACT

Crime and bad lives are the measure of a State's failure, all crime in the end is the crime of the community - *A Modern Utopia, 1905, ch. 5, reprinted in The Works of H. G. Wells. vol. 9, 1925.*

'A society should be judged not by how it treats its outstanding citizens but how it treats its criminals' - *Fydor Dostoevsky.*

Concern for rehabilitating offenders leads to a consideration of the ethics and morality of punishment and of the various models of sentencing that have emerged to put them into effect. This chapter covers the range from therapeutic jurisprudence and restorative justice to risk needs assessment, strengths-based rehabilitation, and good lives. It underscores the necessity for engaging offenders more keenly in the process of reappraising themselves and their lives, if justice is to serve one of its major purposes – i.e. the protection of the community and the recovery of offenders as worthwhile citizens.

INTRODUCTION

Philosophers have debated theories of justice for centuries. Plato and Aristotle commented that individuals within a rigid hierarchy of social classes were naturally unequal. In essence, they argued that it was unjust to treat individuals with varying levels of ability equally. Moreover, they posited that governments evolved purely because mankind has a social instinct to gather under powerful councils in their demands for justice (Solomon, 1993). Hobbes contended to the contrary that equality was a natural fact and that it was the role of the government to enforce peace and security for all citizens. He argued that justice only came into existence through a social contract in which everyone in a given society agreed to abide by defined rules and to cooperate towards their mutual benefit rather than compete with each other. Philosophers, psychologists, and theologians today continue to ponder on the ethical, moral, and social issues underlying justice as a means to attain human rights and the conditions necessary to attain and maintain the good life (Solomon, 1993, Thompson, 1992; and the chapters by Marshall and Tolman in the present book).

Among psychologists Maslow (1970) was the first to map out a hierarchy of human needs that individuals should fulfil if they were to reach their full potential and lead healthy and fulfilled lives. Although he did not include justice specifically as in his list of basic needs, he placed it together with fairness, honesty and orderliness as 'almost' a prerequisite, and he cautioned that injustice could be viewed as an impediment to human development. In the light of the wide-ranging evidence that has since accumulated about the fundamental importance of justice in human affairs, Taylor (2003) argued that Maslow would doubtless have included justice were he still alive. For that reason Taylor (this volume) proposes that justice should in fact be regarded as a basic 'safety need', because individuals need to be treated fairly to ensure that they 'thrive cognitively, emotionally and socially', acquire society's morals and values, and make adjustments to laws to better the lot of mankind. Further, he contends that although justice is fundamental to moral philosophy and to jurisprudence, forensic psychology has typically focused on justice in relation to the causes of crime and has neglected the underlying moral issues.

As psychologists working with criminals we agree that morality and social justice are central to offender rehabilitation, and that they warrant greater consideration and debate. Another reason we say this, is because at present the focus of correctional departments across Australia and New Zealand, and elsewhere, is on the rehabilitation of offenders. Previously retributive programmes were in place, but they brought widespread disillusionment stemming from Martinson's (1974, p.25) despairing conclusion from review of 231 controlled outcome studies conducted between 1945 and 1967, that 'nothing works...with few and isolated exceptions, the rehabilitative efforts that have been reported so far have had no appreciable effect on recidivism'. Subsequently the Australian Law Reform Commission (ALRC 15, 1980) released a report entitled *Sentencing of Federal Offenders* that made several recommendations for offenders, including the desirability of finding new alternatives to imprisonment. The Commission recognised that existing prison conditions fostered deep resentment in offenders and contributed to continuing criminality rather than to a reduction in re-offending, and it commented that although the economic cost of building and maintaining prisons was enormous, the cost in human terms was perhaps even larger to offenders and their victims.

Widespread dissatisfaction with the legal system *per se*, the growing realization that punishment was an ineffective method of reducing recidivism, and the need for victims to have a voice in the proceedings, also led to the emergence of 'therapeutic jurisprudence' in some countries, notably North America (see Wexler, ch.6 in this volume) and to 'restorative justice' programmes in New Zealand and Australia (see Maxwell and Morris, ch.7 in this volume). Both involved a variety of alternative methods to imprisonment to reduce the risk that re-offending would occur (Braithwaite 1989), each with a slightly different emphasis on humanizing court procedures, sharing decision-making power between key players, and offering different settings in which the proceedings might take place. Since then empirical studies have shown that recidivism can be reduced more through these new methods for the rehabilitation of offenders than through punishment and imprisonment alone (Andrews, Bonta and Hoge, 1990; Andrews and Bonta, 1998; Hollin, 2002).

Thus for the past two decades a paradigm shift has occurred in criminal jurisprudence towards a 'what works' philosophy. However, we raise questions from our clinical practice because some high-risk offenders continue to commit offences despite participating in programs that specifically target their criminogenic needs (i.e. the dynamic risk factors behind each individual's offences). Therefore in our view, the next phase of offender rehabilitation should capitalise on the strengths of risk management theory by embedding it in 'the good lives model' (GLM) of offender rehabilitation (Ward, 2002a; 2002b). Thus in the treatment of offenders, the risk factors – i.e. the missing or incomplete internal and external conditions necessary to achieve community valued outcomes - would command attention rather than continue to be ignored.

In the remainder of this chapter we touch on the ethics of punishment, say more about the punitive versus restorative models of justice, and focus on the key elements of risk management in treatment. Our proposition is that the needs of offenders, both criminogenic and non-criminogenic, should be integrated into a more holistic rehabilitation framework based on the 'good lives' model – the difference being that criminogenic needs are the dynamic attributes of offenders and their circumstances that, when changed reduce recidivism (Andrews and Bonta, 1998). In our conclusion we accept that social justice goes some way to providing the necessary context for the attainment of primary human goods, but we consider that the propensity to attain justice is fundamentally biological and is expressed through the mediation of cultural and social structures and processes (Ward and Stewart, 2003a).

ETHICS OF PUNISHMENT

The courts and the legal system under which they operate have the dual purpose of allocating blame and administering punishment on offenders who have broken society's rules (Price, 1997). While the processes involved in the allocation of blame have tended not to be so much within the province of psychologists – except for the insights that Wexler, both a psychologist and a practicing lawyer, brings to bear in his system of therapeutic jurisprudence – the administration of punishment has been a concern because of the implications of learning theory from classical conditioning to operant conditioning and incidental learning (Bandura, 1976).

To open the debate, punishment can broadly be defined as the deliberate infliction of harm by duly authorized agents of the state. It involves the imposition of sanctions that would be considered morally wrong were they not within the law, such as the deprivation of the right of offenders to freedom (Glaser, 2003). Even when punishment is legally ratified, it still involves ethical obligations concerning the humanitarian management and care of prisoners (cf. *UN Standard minimum rules for the treatment of prisoners*, 1955-1977).

The legal system thus metes out justice by inflicting statutory penalties when the voluntary admission of the crime can be accepted, when intent can be proven; when the punishment is matched in severity to the wickedness of the crime; and, when punishment for an evil act is morally right within the law (Ho, ForsterLee, ForsterLee, and Crofts, 2002). But the same researchers comment that when no other sanction can achieve the objectives contemplated by law, the imposition of severe punishment is not 'justified'. By implication they raise the issue of whether punishment should ever be a means to an end, or whether it should be an end in itself that requires no evaluation of its effectiveness: i.e. an offence has been committed and the punishment simply expresses society's condemnation.

However, the issue of whether punishment should represent either the social condemnation of deviant behaviour or the prevention of future offending is not easily resolved (cf. Oswald, Hupfeld, Klug and Gabriel, 2002). No matter what the purpose of punishment might be, unless the offence has been quite horrific and beyond the pale, calling for absolute life detention, society expects it to change an offender's behaviour.

Then questions arise about how far punishment should be proportional to the offences committed - because individuals perceive justice as the process of establishing an equitable balance between action and reaction (cf. Lerner, and Lerner, 1981). Within that 'just world' perspective, punishment is also assumed to recompense the victims of crime – although there the obligation to research its effectiveness does arise.

The general failure of the sentencing policies has led courts and jurisdictions to become more punitive and to focus on principles of 'just deserts' and proportionality in sentencing (McGuire, 2000). Yet the evidence shows that punitive sanctions rarely improve the behaviour of persistent offenders, and that sometimes it makes it worse (Walker, 1991; McGuire, 2002). It is thought that retributive punishment disempowers offenders and discourages their involvement in behaviour change. And even attempts within an alternative utilitarian framework to introduce other forms of punishment, such as home detention and electronic monitoring, and sending juvenile offenders to military induction 'boot camps' to learn teamwork and leadership skills to divert them away from the criminal justice system, have had little success (Fass and Pi, 2002). Similarly unsupervised community restrictions, intensive supervision, extensive surveillance, and restrictions on liberty, have not reduced recidivism rates (McGuire, 2002). Finally, punishing offenders only partially satisfied the feelings of revenge their victims might have (Orth, 2004). To reiterate Martinson's (1974) finding of despair, we know that punishment in and of itself still 'does not work'.

RESTORATIVE JUSTICE

In response to the demonstrated inefficacy of conventional and modified conventional forms of punishment, a renewed interest in restorative justice has arisen in Australia, Canada, England, Wales and New Zealand (Van Ness, Morris and Maxwell, 2001). Its primary aim is to widen the focus of the justice system beyond the state and the offender to include the victim and community as active participants. Such participation is to ensure that for justice to be served the important concepts of 'empowerment', 'dialogue', 'negotiation', and 'agreement' are addressed (Ashworth, 2002; Maxwell and Morris, 2001). Under its umbrella a variety of diverse practices such as family group conferencing, victim-offender mediation, sentencing circles, community reparation boards, and restitution programs have been developed (Morris, 2002).

In general, follow-up research studies suggest that victims find the restorative justice process more beneficial than the previous punitive approaches to offending. They report less fear, and have a better understanding of the reasons why they were targeted. Offenders comment that they feel more involved with the process, appreciate the opportunity to express their opinions, understand the strategies employed to help them redress their offending behaviour, are satisfied with the restorative justice processes, and view them as fair. Empirical studies also show the outcome to be somewhat more successful than residential or custodial sentences in reducing the number of reconvictions (Morris, 2002; Orth, 2004).

STRENGTHS-BASED RESTORATIVE JUSTICE

The benefits gained from the restorative ethos of punishment during the 1990s led to the emergence of the 'strengths-based' paradigm of justice (Maruna, 2001: Van Wormer, 2001; Maruna and LeBel, 2002) – the difference being that, whereas the earlier restorative models functioned in general with professionals, victims, offenders and the community at the macro level to achieve equity and justice, the strengths-based approach operates at the micro level by focusing on developing the capabilities of the offenders themselves. It asserts that individuals can learn to help themselves by focusing on the good rather than the bad in themselves, and that, with the thoughts that they are able to change, they are able to look towards the future positively rather than to continue to dwell on the negativity of the past. It is claimed that the focus on strengths rather than deficits or weakness, helps offenders to realize a capacity for making useful contributions to society rather than to remain focused on their liabilities. As an example Maruna (2001) reported that when offenders redefined the way they perceived themselves in relation to substance abuse as 'not like that anymore', they were more likely to desist from offending and they had a strong desire to help others who were struggling with the same issue.

This 'strengths-based' perspective is consistent with the 'helper principle' of the *New Careers Movement* whereby individuals derive benefit from helping others (Maruna, and Lebel, 2002). Such helping has been found to increase the self-respect and levels of competence of the helpers – elements of recovery that are most pertinent to offenders who normally continue to re-offend, not because of some internal deficits, but because they are stigmatized and labelled as 'offenders'. It provides opportunities for them to realize that they have positive contributions to make to others, and that they have potential for good. It gives them courage to make amends for their crimes, goes some way indirectly towards repairing any damage they have caused to victims and the community, and so enables them to begin to redeem themselves by learning how to lead the 'good life' (Braithwaite, 2001; Maruna and LeBel, 2002).

THERAPEUTIC JURISPRUDENCE

As we have said, David Wexler (in press) himself has a chapter in the present volume outlining the application of therapeutic jurisprudence (TJ), but we thought it appropriate to mention it here in sequence with restorative justice and strengths-based justice. Essentially TJ focuses on the relationship between the law and its legal agents, and the behaviour of individuals who come into contact with the legal system (Wexler, 1990; McGuire, 2000). It developed from Wexler's (1996) pioneering study of mental health law and has since been extended to other specialist areas within the law. His position is that the law has a 'healing' role in offender rehabilitation that goes beyond the imposition of punishment (Glaser, 2003).

With a focus on offenders, according to Birgden (2002), first the process of implementing the law directly impacts on their wellbeing, either to their benefit or detriment. Second, it follows that the law should harness the optimal time that offenders are in the system to trigger pro-social behaviours and lifestyle. Third, all representatives, therapeutic and legal, from different professions within the legal context, should work together within a scientist-practitioner model to enhance offender wellbeing. Fourth, legal considerations including individual autonomy and community protection take precedence over therapeutic objectives. Fifth, TJ is theoretically normative and adheres to implicit value judgments whilst maximising the overarching arms of the law.

Treatment refers to any form of interventions with offenders, individual or group, that have the capacity to help reduce the rate of recidivism. TJ in this context can encompass psycho-educational and employment programs, general counselling or rehabilitative services, or therapeutic programs designed to target criminogenic needs by changing pro-criminal attitudes and deviant self-concept (McGuire, 2000). TJ can thus be used to work constructively with offenders within a conceptual framework of 'tertiary prevention' (Gendreau and Andrews, 1990), and it can easily be integrated into legal systems and practices. McGuire (2000), however, stresses that more research into TJ is required, and in particular he suggests that measures could be taken to determine the therapeutic or anti-therapeutic impact of the law in attempting to restructure cognitive distortions of specific groups of offenders, for example, sexual offenders. In fact the evidence suggests that TJ has taken a punitive stance with regard to that particular group, with a primary position of risk management that gives them longer sentences than other offenders (Birgden, in press: Winick, 2003).

A further point is that although advocates of TJ argued that the term 'therapeutic' refers to the promotion of psychological wellbeing in offenders, critics say that in some circumstances it might sacrifice individual rights and justice to adhere to a misguided agenda of quasi-treatment or punishment (Schopp, 1999, and also the combination of therapy with the primary aim of protecting the community blurs the boundaries between therapy and punishment (Glaser, 2003). In other words, the treatment of sexual offenders once more could become subordinate to punishment and prevention.

The Risk Needs Approach to Offender Rehabilitation

Continuing the focus on offenders, according to Howells, Day, Byrne, and Byrne (1999a), prison and community programs for changing their attributes, reducing recidivism, and ultimately causing less community harm follow the principles of *risk*, *need*, *responsivity*, *program integrity*, and *professional discretion*. The *risk principle* matches an offender's risk level with the amount of treatment warranted, thus those at high-risk should receive most treatment of at least 100 hours of cognitive behavioural interventions over a three to four month period (Hollin, 1999). The *need principle* suggests programs should target criminogenic needs, or the offender characteristics directly related to recidivism for particular types of crime (e.g., sexual, violent or drug-related) rather than simply for crimes in general. For example, among the criminogenic needs that should be targeted in sexual offending programs, Hanson and Harris (2000) identified deviant sexual arousal, intimacy deficits and loneliness, and difficulties with emotional regulation. The *responsivity principle* ensures that a given program content makes sense to the offenders for whom it was designed, and it eliminates factors of gender, learning styles, ethnicity, and treatment motivation that might impede learning (Andrews and Bonta, 1998). *Program integrity* insists that the implementers are competent to deliver a program and adhere to specific treatment protocols. Finally, *professional discretion* allows clinicians to use their judgment to override the *risk, needs* and *responsivity* principles under certain circumstances, allowing for a documented degree of treatment flexibility and the use of innovative interventions (Andrews and Bonta, 1998).

LIMITATIONS OF THE RISK NEED MODEL

Although the risk-need model provides a theoretically sound and empirically defensible framework to guide offender rehabilitation, the theory does have weaknesses associated with each of its key principles that we believe impact on how we can effectively conceptualise treatment. Firstly, within Andrews and Bonta's (1998) theory, *risk* and *need* are inter-related concepts - since criminogenic needs are perceived as dynamic risk factors. In essence, the theory proposes that low-risk offenders compared to high-risk offenders have few, if any, criminogenic needs. Although Ward and Brown (2003) acknowledge that marrying risk and need simplifies offender rehabilitation, they argue that estimates of risk should not always determine the type and extent of criminogenic needs to be assessed in treatment, because offenders assessed as low risk might have high needs or clinical problems such as depression, anxiety, relationship problems that although not criminogenic, could still require therapeutic attention and have an impact on rehabilitation. More importantly, without appropriate coping skills or supports in place such non-criminogenic needs could elevate an offender's risk level from low to high if not adequately addressed.

Further, for the allocation of offenders correctly into treatment programs, it is essential that the range and severity of an individual offender's clinical problems are known, in combination with a clear understanding of the complex relationship between risk, needs and criminal acts. This is because some offenders could have distinct and well-defined problems that place them at risk of recidivism, but they do not display a *wide range* of problems. A high-risk low-need sexual offender, for example, might have deviant sexual preferences but possess good social skills and demonstrate no obvious interpersonal or self-regulatory deficits (Ward and Siegert, 2002). Therefore, in effect, the relationship between risk and need is more complex than that proposed in the risk-need model.

Secondly, another problem is the assumption that, because high-risk offenders have a greater number of needs, they do better if they are treated more intensively, medium risk offenders do better with moderate amounts of treatment, and so on. But some offenders might have a small number of intense or severe needs (low need), such as psychotic symptoms, or sexual abuse trauma, that require *prolonged* treatment to shift.

Thirdly, the notion of always basing treatment on risk management is problematic, because it implies that the major task of rehabilitation is to reduce the chances of harm to the community by focusing on eliminating or modifying pro-criminal factors (criminogenic needs). However, basing a treatment model on risk factors alone is too reductionist, too negative, and not sufficiently attuned to the psychological reality of everyday life.

In summary, the risk-need model fails to allow for the complexities, such as individual strengths and non-criminogenic needs, that also place offenders at higher or lower risk of recidivism. Offender rehabilitation should therefore encompass holistic measures that can offer offenders concrete possibilities for living worthwhile lives, based on their individual abilities, circumstances, interests, and opportunities, and culminating ultimately in lasting lifestyle changes and reduced recidivism rates (Ward, 2002a, 2002b).

The Good Lives Model of Offender Rehabilitation

To go beyond the risk need model for offender rehabilitation, Ward and Stewart (2003a, 2003b) offer the enhancement or *good lives* model (GLM) that builds on those actions, states of affairs, characteristics, experiences, and states of mind that are intrinsically beneficial (i.e, primary human goods) to human beings that are therefore sought for their own sake rather than as means to ends (Deci and Ryan, 2000; Emmons, 1996; Emmons, 1999; Schmuck and Sheldon, 2001). It requires the construction of well-designed individual treatment plans that will equip offenders with the necessary conditions (non-criminogenic factors) to meet basic needs in different, more prosocial ways, and ultimately live more balanced and fulfilling lives (e.g., close relationships, rewarding employment, leisure time, self-respect, a sense of meaning and purpose, creativity, etc).

The fulfilment of these needs requires internal and external conditions and results in human wellbeing. The internal conditions refer to psychological characteristics of individual offenders, such as skills, competencies, beliefs, attitudes and values. The external conditions refer to the social, cultural and interpersonal factors that facilitate the development of those internal psychological characteristics - they include education, effective parenting, vocational training, social support, and opportunities to pursue important goals. The presence of internal and external obstacles results in impaired social and psychological functioning, and hence, a less fulfilling life.

Although the enhancement model might seem radical, support for it can be found in contemporary research. Firstly, there is ample evidence from motivational psychology (goal theory and research), personality psychology, social psychology, evolutionary theory, moral philosophy, and philosophical anthropology that human beings seek primary human goods (Ward, 2002a, 2002b). In particular, as Deci and Ryan (2000) have expressed in their Self-Determination Theory of Needs, human beings are inherently active, self-directed organisms that are naturally predisposed to seek the needs of *autonomy, relatedness,* and *competence. Autonomy* refers to the propensity to self-regulate and organise their experiences: *relatedness* to the propensity to establish a sense of emotional connectedness to other human beings: and *competency* to the propensity to establish a sense of mastery over one's environment, to seek challenges, and to master them: They argue that these needs outline the conditions essential for psychological wellbeing and fulfilment, and individuals can only flourish if they are met, and the failure to meet them inevitably result in psychological distress and maladaptive behaviour.

Since human beings are contextually dependent organisms, rehabilitation should always consider the match between an offender's characteristics and the environment in which offenders function. Here the experience of justice becomes of particularly relevance, because the striving for autonomy, relatedness, and competence involves (a) the realization of a particular GLM requires that conditions of fairness exist and effectively regulate the resources and opportunities open to individuals, and (b) the natural inclination of human beings by virtue of their evolutionary history to seek fair treatment in the evolutionary race (Tooby, and Cosmides, 1992).

Maruna's (2001) recent research gives further support for the enhancement model of offender treatment, because he found no differences in the personality traits of desisting and persisting offenders, except for the construction of their lives. His persistent offenders appeared to live their lives according to a *condemnation script*: they saw themselves as victim, and believed that the structure and tone of their lives was set in stone. Thus, they exhibited a poor sense of self-efficacy and felt powerless to change the fate that was set out for them. Their antisocial behaviour enabled them partially to restore a sense of personal control over their lives. Conversely, his desisting offenders lived their lives according to a *redemption script*: they saw themselves as good people who had become corrupt or overwhelmed by external influences, with a criminal lifestyle giving them power over their bleak circumstances. But by discovering their true selves (i.e. becoming aware of their more positive skills, abilities, roles, traits, etc); establishing a sense of empowerment and control over their lives; and learning to give something back to the community, their family and other offenders, the desisters were able to create new identities quite different to the criminal. In a sense, forming the new identity involved offenders to make sense of their earlier crimes and experiences, and to create a bridge between their former undesirable lives and the new way of living they intended to adopt (Ward, 2002b).

CONCLUSION

The most effective way to rehabilitate offenders is to ensure that they possess the competencies, values, opportunities, and resources to live good lives' in the particular contexts in which they are to function in society. The shift from antisocial to prosocial lifestyles should encompass a holistic approach – i.e. one that involves addressing the factors that relate to offending behaviour (i.e. criminogenic needs), *as well as* addressing offenders' psychological distress (i.e. non-criminogenic needs) - in order to instil in them the skills, knowledge and resources to live different kinds of lives. Further, although all human beings have the same basic needs, they are influenced dramatically by the cultural and social structures and processes they encounter in the particular environments in which they strive to satisfy them. By this we, mean that their lives are characterized by the realization of primary human goods in a way that makes sense in the light of offenders' values and interests. Good lives are also meaningful lives.

REFERENCES

Andrews, D. A. and Bonta, J. (1998). *The psychology of criminal conduct.* (2nd.edn.). Cincinnati, OH: Anderson.

Andrews, D.A., Bonta, J., and Hoge, R.D. (1990). Classification for effective *rehabilitation: Rediscovering psychology. Criminal Justice and Behavior*, 17, 19-52.

Ashworth, A. (2002). Responsibilities, rights and restorative justice. *British Journal of Criminology*, 42, 578-595.

Australian Law Reform Commission, ALRC. (1980). Sentencing of Federal Offenders Interim Report 15 – accessed from www.austlii.edu.au/au/other/alrc/publications/reports/15/.

Bandura, A. (1976). *Social learning theory.* New York: Pearson.

Birgden, A., (2002). Therapeutic jurisprudence and 'good lives': A rehabilitation framework for corrections. *Australian Psychologist*, 37, 180-186.

Birgden, A., (in press). Therapeutic jurisprudence and sex offenders: A psycholegal approach to protection. *Journal of Sexual Abuse*: *Research and Treatment.*

Braithwaite, J. (1989). *Crime, shame and reintegration.* Cambridge: Cambridge University Press.

Braithwaite, J. (2001). Restorative justice and a new criminal law of substance abuse. *Youth and Society,* 33, 227-248.

Deci, E.L, and Ryan, R.M. (2000). The 'what' and 'why' of goal pursuits: Human needs and the self-determination of behaviour. *Psychological Inquiry*, 11, 227-268.

Emmons, R. A. (1996). Striving and feeling: Personal goals and subjective well-being. In P.M. Gollwitzer and J. A. Bargh (Eds.). *The psychology of action: Linking cognition and motivation to behavior.* (pp. 313-337). New York: Guilford.

Emmons, R. A. (1999). *The psychology of ultimate concerns*. New York: Guilford.

Fass, S.M., and Pi, Chung-Ron. (2003). Getting touch on juvenile crime: An analysis of costs and benefits. *Journal of Research in Crime and Delinquency,* 39, 363-399.

Gendreau, P., and Andrews, D.A. (1990). Tertiary prevention: what the meta-analyses of the offender treatment literature tells us about 'what works'. *Canadian Journal of Criminology*, 32, 173-184.

Glaser, B., (2003). Therapeutic jurisprudence: An ethical paradigm for therapists in sex offender treatment programs. *Western Criminology Review*, 4, 143-154.

Hanson, R.K., and Harris, A.J.R. (2000). Where should we intervene? Dynamic predictors of sexual offense recidivism. *Criminal Justice and Behavior*, 27, 6-35.

Ho, R., ForsterLee, L., ForsterLee, R., and Crofts, N. (2002). Justice versus vengeance: Motives underlying punitive judgements. *Personality and Individual Differences*, 33, 35-377.

Hollin, C. R. (1999). Treatment programs for offenders: Meta-analysis, "what works " and beyond. *International Journal of Law and Psychiatry*, 22, 361-372.

Hollin, C. R. (2002). An overview of offender rehabilitation: Something old, something borrowed, something new. *Australian Psychologist,* 37, 159-164.

Howells, K., Day, A., Byrne, S., and Byrne, M. (1999). *Risk, needs and responsivity in violence rehabilitation Implications for programs for indigenous offenders.* Paper presented at the Best Practice Interventions in Corrections for Indigenous People Conference, Adelaide. 13-15 October.

Lerner, M.J., and Lerner, S.C. (1981). *The justice motive in social behaviour: Adapting to times of scarcity and change.* New York: Plenum.

Martinson, R. (1974). What works? Questions and answers about prison reform. *The Public Interest*, 35, 22-54.

Maruna, S. (2001). *Making good: How ex-convicts reform and rebuild their lives.* Washington, DC: American Psychological Association.

Maruna, S., and LeBel, T.P., (2002). Revisiting ex-prisoner re-entry: a buzzword in search of a narrative. In S. Rex, and M. Tonry. (Eds.). *Reform and punishment: The future of sentencing*. (pp.3-26). Cambridge MAS: Willan.

Maslow, A.H. (1970). *Motivation and personality.* (2nd Ed.). New York: Harper and Row.

Maxwell, G., and Morris, A. (2001). Family group conferences and reoffendng. In A. Morris and G. Maxwell. (Eds.). *Restorative justice for juveniles: Conferencing, mediation and circles.* (pp. 243-263). Oxford: Hart.

McGuire, J. (2000). Can the criminal law ever be therapeutic? *Behavioral Sciences and the Law*, 18, 413-426.

McGuire, J. (2002). Criminal sanctions versus psychologically-based interventions with offenders: *A comparative empirical analysis. Psychology, Crime and Law*, 8, 183-208.

Morris, A., (2002). Critiquing the critics: A brief response to critics of restorative justice. *British Journal of Criminology*, 42, 596-615.

Orth, U. (2004). Does perpetrator punishment satisfy victims' feelings of revenge? *Aggressive Behavior*, 30, 62-70.

Oswald, M.E., Hupfeld, J., Klug, S.C., and Gabriel, U. (2002). Lay-persepctives on criminal deviance, goals of punishment, and punitivity. *Social Justice Research*, 15, 85-98.

Price, M. (1997). Can mediation produce justice: A restorative discussion for mediators. *Signal, 1*, 1-6.

Schopp, R.F. (1999). Therapeutic jurisprudence: Integrated inquiry and instrumental prescriptions. *Behavioral Sciences and the Law*, 17, 589-605.

Schmuck, P. and Sheldon, K. M. (2001). (Eds.). *Life goals and well-being.* Toronto, Ontario: Hogrefe and Huber.

Solomon, R. (1993). *Introducing philosophy*. San Diego CA: Harcourt Brace Jovanovich.

Taylor, A.J.W. (2003). Justice as a basic human need. *New Ideas in Psychology*, 21, 209-219.

Thompson, J. (1992). *Justice and world order: A philosophical inquiry*. London: Routledge.

Tooby, J. and Cosmides, L. (1992). The psychological foundations of culture. In J. H. Barkow, L. Cosmides, and J. Tooby. (Eds.). *The adapted mind: Evolutionary psychology and the generation of culture.* (pp. 19-136). New York: Oxford University Press.

United Nations Standard Minimum Rules for the Treatment of Prisoners. Adopted August 30, 1955, by the First United Nations Congress on the Prevention of Crime and the Treatment of Offenders, U.N. Doc. A/CONF/611, annex I, E.S.C. res. 663C, 24 U.N. ESCOR Supp. (No. 1) at 11, U.N. Doc. E/3048 (1957), amended E.S.C. res. 2076, 62 U.N. ESCOR Supp. (No. 1) at 35, U.N. Doc. E/5988 (1977).

Van Ness, D., Morris, A., and Maxwell, G., (2001). Introducing restorative justice. In A. Morris and G. Maxwell (Eds.). *Restorative justice for juveniles: Conferencing, mediation and circles.* (pp. 3-16). Oxford: Hart.

Van Wormer, (2001). *Counseling female offenders and victims: A strengths-restorative approach.* New York: Springer.

Walker, N. (1991). *Why punish? Theories of punishment reassessed.* Oxford University Press.

Ward, T. (2002a). Good lives and the rehabilitation of offenders: Promises and problems. *Aggression and Violent Behavior, 7*, 513-538.

Ward, T., (2002b). The management of risk and the design of good lives. *Australian Psychologist,* 37, 172-179.

Ward, T., and Brown, M., (2003). The Risk-Need Model of Offender Rehabilitation: A Critical Analysis. In T. Ward, D. R. Laws, and S. M., Hudson. (Eds.). *Sexual Deviance: Issues and Controversies.* (pp.338-353). Thousand Oaks, CA: Sage.

Ward, T., and Siegert, R. (2002). Toward a comprehensive explanation of child sexual abuse: A Theory Knitting Perspective. *Psychology, Crime, and Law, 9,* 319-351.

Ward, T., and Stewart, C. A. (2003a). Criminogenic needs and human needs: A theoretical critique. *Psychological, Crime, and Law,* 10, 125-143.

Ward, T., and Stewart, C. A. (2003b). The management of risk and the design of good lives. In T. Ward, D.R. Laws, and S. M. Hudson. (Eds.). *Sexual deviance: Issues and controversies.* (pp.21-44). Thousand Oaks, CA: Sage.

Wexler, D.B. (1990). *Therapeutic Jurisprudence: The law as a therapeutic agent.* Durham, NC: Carolina Academic.

Wexler, D.B. (1996). Therapeutic jurisprudence and the criminal courts. In D.N. Wexler and B.J. Winick (Eds.). *Law in a therapeutic key: Developments in therapeutic jurisprudence.* (pp.157-170). Durham, NC: Caroline Academic.

Winick, B. J. (2003). A therapeutic jurisprudence analysis of sex offender registration and community notification laws. *Protecting society from sexually dangerous offenders: Law, justice and therapy.* (pp. 213 - 229). Washington, DC: American Psychological Association.

In: Justice as a Basic Human Need
Editor: Anthony Taylor, pp. 61-69
ISBN 1-59454-915-X

Chapter 6

THERAPEUTIC JURISPRUDENCE[1]

David B Wexler

ABSTRACT

The emergence of therapeutic jurisprudence from the conventional practice of law is catching on in many jurisdictions, because it restructures the judicial process in such a way as to encourage more satisfactory participation from the major participants – the judge, the offender, and the victim. It sprang from the need to make the proceedings more relevant for the purpose of justice - i.e. the reparation of harm done to the victim, and the reformation of the offender. This chapter describes the process and underlines the key concepts that are already in operation in some jurisdictions. The outcome so far is sufficiently positive to encourage its adoption elsewhere.

INTRODUCTION

In 2000 *Court Review* (the official journal of the American Judges' Association) devoted a special issue to the topic of therapeutic jurisprudence (often called, simply, TJ) in which Judge William Schma, a leading judicial voice in therapeutic jurisprudence, noted that 'it is important for judges to practice TJ because - like it or not - the law does have therapeutic and anti-therapeutic consequences'. In fact, in August 2000, a joint resolution of the Conference of US Chief Justices and the Conference of State Court Administrators endorsed the notion of problem-solving courts and calendars that utilize the principles of therapeutic jurisprudence, and noted that well-functioning drug treatment courts represent the best practice of these principles (cf. Hora, Schma, and Rosenthal, 1999). Specifically, the resolution stated:

> 'There are principles and methods founded in therapeutic jurisprudence, including integration of treatment services with judicial case processing, ongoing judicial intervention, close monitoring of and immediate response to behavior, multi-disciplinary involvement, and

[1] 'This chapter is adapted from Wexler, D.B. (2001). Robes and Rehabilitation: How Judges Can Help Offenders "Make Good," *Court Review,* 38, 18-23.

collaboration with community based and government organizations. These principles and methods are now being employed in these newly arising courts and calendars, and they advance the application of (*other policy initiatives, such as*) the trial court performance standards and the public trust and confidence initiative'.

According to Lurigio, Watson, Luchins, and Hanrahan (2001), problem-solving courts, such as those involved with drug treatments, mental health (Kondo, 2000) and domestic violence (Fritzler and Simon, 2000), might be the most obvious examples of 'therapeutic jurisprudence in action'. But it is crucial to recognize the potential application of therapeutic jurisprudence *generally* (Abrahamson, 2000: Wexler, 2000a; District Court for Clark County, Washington, 2003), as well as in civil cases (Leben, 2000), appellate cases (VandeWalle, 2000), family law cases (Babb, 1998) and, of course, in criminal and juvenile cases (Wexler, 1993; 2000b).

Criminal Law Context

In the context of criminal law, the challenge for therapeutic jurisprudence includes a concern not only for defendants, but also for others drawn into the process, such as victims (Wiebe, 1996) and jurors (Shuman, Hamilton and Daley 1994). The remainder of this chapter, however, will focus on offenders and on the opportunity for courts to contribute to their rehabilitation and reform. Of course, judicial opportunity will be enhanced by the presence of a group of lawyers practicing therapeutic jurisprudence (Stolle, Wexler, and Winick, 2000). Such a bar is indeed emerging (Daicoff, 2000). Dallas lawyer John McShane (Wexler, 2002), for example, has a substantial criminal law practice that focuses solely on rehabilitation and mitigation of punishment. Although McShane is free in his private practice to pick and choose clients, he takes only those who agree to use the crisis occasioned by the criminal case as an opportunity to turn their lives around. Always he seeks to defer disposition so as to allow the client an opportunity for rehabilitation. His hope, of course, is that the court will be impressed by, and take into account, such post-offence rehabilitation efforts and gains (United States v. Flowers, 1997: Winick, 1999). His procedure is to assemble a package of mitigating information each offender might gather for submission to the prosecutor in an effort at plea bargaining, or, failing that, to the court at sentencing. The information might consist of items such as a log of attendance Alcoholics Anonymous (AA) meetings, a sequence of urine-analysis lab reports, reports from evaluating and treating mental health professionals, and letters of support from various people in the community, such as AA sponsors, employers, co-workers, clergy, family, and friends.

The excellent role model provided byTJ defense attorney raises questions about the comparable role of the judge. What guidance does therapeutic jurisprudence give to judges interested in furthering offender rehabilitation, apart from the important legal niceties such as the possibility of deferred sentencing and the possibility of mitigating the sentence for acceptance of responsibility (United States v. Jeter, 2001) and for post-offense rehabilitation? The answer is that some of the most exciting therapeutic jurisprudence work offers an excellent opportunity for partnership between academia and the judiciary, crafting creative proposals for importing promising behavioral science developments (such as important research on rehabilitation) into the legal system and into the day-to-day work of lawyers and judges (Wexler, 1991; 2000b). In those reports I explored how judges might use some of such basic principles to increase offender compliance with conditions of release and to consider how courts could encourage defendants to engage in relapse prevention planning.

Compliance

My compliance project was inspired by Meichenbaum and Turk's (1987) book that had nothing to do with law: the book dealt with improving patient adherence to medical advice. Some of the principles the authors enunciated are completely commonsensical, such as speaking in simple terms to help patients to get the message, but others are not so obvious. For instance, when patients make some sort of public commitment to persons above and beyond the immediate health care provider, it has been found that their compliance is likely to increase. Similarly, if family members are aware of a patient's promise, the patient is again more likely to adhere to the agreement.

Consider how these compliance principles might operate in a legal context. If a judge were considering a petition for the conditional release of an insanity-acquitted offender, or if at a sentencing hearing a judge were deciding whether to grant probation, the court could conceptualize the conditional release not simply as a judicial order, but as a type of behavioral contract that could have a bearing on relapse prevention planning. In addition, the hearing could serve as a forum in which criminal defendants could make a public commitment to comply – as also could some offenders found not guilty on the grounds of insanity at the time they committed offences but who since have recovered - and their compliance would be enhanced were family members present at the hearing.

Relapse Prevention

As with the compliance project, my interest in importing relapse prevention planning into the legal arena was triggered by a particular book, this time by James McGuire (1995), geared to teaching certain rehabilitation techniques. The gist of McGuire's book is that because offenders often act impulsively they need to be taught certain problem-solving skills, and those of the cognitive behavioral variety seem to be particularly promising for the purpose. His aim is to help offenders firstly to understand the chain of events that often lead to high-risk situations, and then either to learn to stop, to think, and plan avoidance strategies, or to cope adequately with such situations should they arise. He argues that once offenders develop such an understanding, they prepare their own relapse prevention plans.

The application of this cognitive/behavioral rehabilitation program to the legal process could begin with the court (with the assistance of counsel and others) making defendants responsible for thinking through their situations and vulnerabilities. Thus, a judge about to consider a defendant for probation might say, 'I'm going to consider your penalty, but I want you to come up with a type of preliminary plan that we will use as a basis of discussion. I want you to figure out why I should grant you probation and why I should feel comfortable that you're going to succeed. In order for me to feel comfortable, I need to know what you regard to be high-risk situations and how you're going to avoid them or cope with them without messing up. And, speaking of messing up, I want you to tell me what happened that led you to mess up last time, and why you think the situation is different this time around.'

Through such an approach, a court would be promoting cognitive self-change as part and parcel of the sentencing process itself. The process might lead an offender simply to respond by saying: 'I realize I mess upon Friday nights, and from now on I will stay home on Friday'. Note that the condition would not be the product of judicial fiat. Instead, the defendant would have thought through a serious high-risk situation and in essence have come up with his or her own condition of probation. The offender is thus likely to regard the condition as fair and, linking back to our earlier discussion, more likely to comply with the arrangement than if it had simply been imposed by the court.

According to the 'what works' research, cognitive self-change programs seem promising, but, of course, they do not work for everyone. If offenders were committed to continue offending, for example, even a substantial exposure to a program of problem-solving skills would not lead to desistance. On the other hand, if they had self-concepts of being basically good people who often found themselves in difficulty, or in the wrong place at the wrong time, or mixing with the wrong crowd, they might well decide to straighten out and take control of their lives. For them, a cognitive skills development program geared to helping them understand the chain of events leading to high-risk situations and teaching certain problem-solving skills, might induce them to prepare their own relapse prevention strategies – such as stopping to think, avoiding high risk situations, and managing such situations should they arise.

DESISTANCE

Who decides to change course, and *how* and *why*, seem to be questions locked away in what Shadd Maruna (2001) calls the 'blackbox of the what works' literature. To explore the matter further, he conducted the 'Liverpool Desistance Study' in which he interviewed both persistent offenders and those who, after a steady life of crime, eventually became 'desisters'. He used a narrative approach, i.e. consistent with the notion of narrative therapy, to see how the two different types of offender described and made sense of their lives. Generally, he found that in their narratives the desisters established themselves as basically good; that they became victims of society by adverse circumstances who turned to crime and drugs to cope with a bleak environment, and then became trapped in a vicious cycle of repeated criminal activity and imprisonment until someone in conventional society believed in them and recognized their potential for good and helped them to make good. He concluded that compared to persistent offenders, the ex-convict desisters began to develop a 'coherent prosocial identity' when they understood how their checkered past lives could lead to reformation – although there was much drifting and zigzagging in and out of criminal activity until finally they stopped offending. As a result he saw desistance as a maintenance process, rather than as a specific event, and he regarded the explanatory narratives of offenders not merely a *result* of desistance behavior, but factors that helped them to *sustain* their desistance.

In Maruna's study (2001, p.156), the desisters seemed almost obsessed with establishing the authenticity of their reform. During the interviews, many provided letters of support from college teachers and parole officers, and gave copies of offence records showing the date of their last convictions. Others urged the investigator to seek confirmation independently by speaking with family members, girlfriends, or to the staff of a drug treatment clinic. In his final chapter, Maruna proposed the introduction of redemption rituals like graduation ceremonies upon successful completion of correctional programs. In other words he would have courts empowered not only to re-imprison each felon after the commission of further offences, but also to recognize officially their efforts toward reform and to 'rebiograph' the records of reformed offenders through formal expungement procedures.

HOW COURTS CAN HELP

Following Maruna, the suggestion is that the courts should place some real responsibility on defendants and get them to think through their personal situations and vulnerabilities. The proposal would be interactional in nature, because desisting persons must in some way accept conventional society and conventional society must in turn accept them. In particular, two judicially related proposals mentioned by Maruna – the graduation ceremonies and reentry courts – attract considerable attention. In drug treatment courts, for example, applause is commonly heard when offenders have completed their programs satisfactorily, and, in some courts, even judicial hugs are by no means a rare occurrence (Lasker, 2001). In Judge Judy Mitchell-Davis's Chicago courtroom, offenders often invite their friends and family to attend their graduation ceremonies in the courthouse. Some of the graduates make speeches, and all receive a 'diploma' from the court. In some such courts, participants have asked that their arresting officer be present at their graduation.

These lessons from drug treatment courts can be extended, of course, to other specialized treatment courts and to ordinary juvenile and criminal cases. Judicial praise, family and friend attendance, and graduation ceremonies can all occur, for example, at the successful completion or early termination of a period of probation imposed in routine criminal cases. The ceremonies would acknowledge the progress of former offenders and, taking a page from Maruna, might at the same time *contribute* to the maintenance of desisting behavior. The strong suggestion that these ceremonies are themselves therapeutic and not merely ceremonial, might readily justify their widespread use and easily justify their time-consuming nature.

The apparent success of drug treatment courts, based on a team approach and ongoing judge-defendant interaction, led Maruna to propose its extension to a judicial process to acknowledge prisoner re-entry to the community (Office of Justice Programs, 1999; Maruna, and LeBel, 2003). Re-entry courts established for the purpose could tap many principles of therapeutic jurisprudence, and serve an important function in the rehabilitation program. The problem, however, is that, at least in most jurisdictions in the United States except in the courts for juveniles, the authority for reentry issues is not within the judicial branch. But Americans might profit from interacting with legal structures overseas that provide for the judicial monitoring of offender progress. For example, in Italy therapeutic jurisprudence has typically been exercised in a very traditional, legalistic manner - and the system there might profit from the American experience with specialized treatment courts, and the like (cf. Ciappi, Wexler, Agrait, and Traverso, 2001).

The main point is that the function of the Courts need not be confined to hearing violations of probation and conditional sentences. Already the courts in many legal settings have the discretion to set review hearings at intervals shorter than those mandated by law, and Judges should consider taking action even when they are not especially worried about an offender's compliance, for such hearings could indeed recognize and applaud an offender's efforts and so contribute to the maintenance of desistance. Recall that desistance is best thought of as a 'maintenance process', and desisters, especially at the early stages of desistance, desperately need outside validation to convince *themselves* of their conversion.

Judges are of course the appropriate prestigious persons to confer public and official validation on offenders and the efforts they are making for reform. Ideally, either at a deferred sentencing hearing or at an "all is going well" review hearing, judges also can comment favorably upon the sorts of matters that Maruna found to be so important to desisting offenders. When all goes well, of course, it is relatively easy for the judiciary to constitute the respected members of conventional society willing to 'believe in' the defendant and to see the defendant's real persona - the diamond in the rough. But all does not always go well. Review hearings will often be rather mixed, sometimes court orders will require revocation, the sentencing hearings will not invariably lead to probationary dispositions, and often judicial discretion regarding disposition will be severely circumscribed.

Even in these far from favorable situations, the court can play a highly important and longer range function than usual in potential offender reform. Consider the Vision Statement of the District Court of the State of Washington for Clark County (2003) that specifically embraces the use of principles of therapeutic jurisprudence to 'make a positive change in the lives of people who come before the court'. Some of its guiding values relate remarkably well to Maruna's findings regarding desister narratives. One such is that individuals are not condemned to a life of crime or despair by mental condition or substance abuse, and that everyone can achieve a fulfilling and responsible life. Another is the belief that everyone, no matter whom, has something positive within their make up on which they can build.

A judge committed to this vision is unlikely to tell a woman that she is simply no good as a mother, and even when imposing a severe sentence, such a judge is not going to say 'You are a menace and a danger to society. Society should be protected from the likes of you'. Instead, especially in light of Maruna's findings, a judge committed to the vision statement would search for and comment on whatever favorable features might eventually be woven together by the offender to constitute the 'real me'. Sometimes, such a favorable feature might mitigate the sentence. But even if not, and the judge took pains to emphasize a positive attribute as a real quality and not simply a routine mitigating factor, the words might eventually constitute a meaningful component of the offender's self-identify. Such a judge might say something like this:

> 'You and your friends were involved in some pretty serious business here, and I am going to impose a sentence that reflects just how serious it is. I want to add one thing, however. There's been some testimony here about how you showed some real concern for the victim. I'm going to take that into consideration in your case. You know, according to some of the letters that were submitted, it looks like that sensitive nature is something you displayed way back in grade school Nowadays, it seems to peek out only now and then. But if I could peel away a few layers, I'll bet I could get a glimpse of a pretty caring person way down there. In

> any case, under the law in this state, I'm able to reduce your sentence by a year for what you did when that caring quality came peeking out last March'.

Sometimes, a search for and discovery of a favorable feature or quality might not influence the disposition at all, but none-the-less plant a helpful seed, like this:

> 'I don't really know what went wrong here. I do know you committed a robbery and someone was hurt. And I know that it is only right that I impose a sentence of such-and-such. What I don't understand is why this all happened. You are obviously very intelligent and were always a good student. Your former wife says that, until a few years ago, you were a very good, caring, and responsible father. You obviously have a real talent for woodworking, but it's been years since you spent time on a real woodworking project. Beneath all this, I see a good person who has gotten on the wrong path. I hope you'll think about this and change that path. With your intelligence, personality, and talent, I think you can do it if you decide you really want to'.

CONCLUSION

Even in instances where desistance seems not to have occurred, judges can use principles of therapeutic jurisprudence in the hope that their judicial behavior might constitute the building blocks of eventual reform and rehabilitation. This sort of judging can therefore have both short-term and long-term benefits. Ultimately the benefits may be for offenders, and, in turn, for society as a whole. And let's not forget the benefits to the judges, whose sense of professional satisfaction may soar. Who would not feel immense satisfaction receiving letters, as Chicago drug treatment court Judge Judy Mitchell-Davis (dubbed "Judge Judy" by defendants) often does, like this:

> 'Judge Judy, I just want to thank you for being the loving and caring woman that you are. You've really helped make a positive change in my life. I believe I'm going to make it. It feels so amazing to control my own thoughts and feelings. I feel so good about myself for the first time'.

REFERENCES

Abrahamson, S.S. (2000). The appeal of therapeutic jurisprudence. *Seattle University Law Review,* 24, 223-230.

Babb, B.A. (1998). Fashioning an interdisciplinary framework for court reform in family law: A blueprint to construct a unified family court. *Southern California Law Review*, 71, 469-531.

Conference of Chief Justices Resolution 22 and Conference of State Court Administrators Resolution 4, adopted August 3, 2000 - accessed from www.problem-solvingcourts.org.

Chase, D.J., and Hora, P.F. (2000). The implications of therapeutic jurisprudence for judicial satisfaction. *Court Review*, 37, 12-31.

Ciappi, S., Wexler, D., Agrait, F., and Traverso, G.B. (2001). Therapeutic Jurisprudence: Alcune considerazioni su di una concezione postliberale del dirotto e della pena. *Rassegna Italiana di Criminologia*, 6, 355-373.

Court Review. (2000). Special Issue on Therapeutic Jurisprudence. 37, 1-68.

Daicoff, S. (2000). The role of therapeutic jurisprudence within the comprehensive law movement. In D.P. Stolle, D.B. Wexler, and. B.J. Winick. (Eds.). *Practicing therapeutic jurisprudence: law as a helping profession.* (pp. 465-492). Durham: Carolina Academic Press.

District Court of the State of Washington for Clark County. Vision Statement. In Winick, B.J. and Wexler, D.B. (Eds). (2003). *Judging in a therapeutic key: Therapeutic jurisprudence and the courts*. (p. 124). Durham: Carolina Academic Press.

Fritzler, R.B. and Simon, L. (2000). The development of a specialized domestic violence court in Vancouver, Washington: Utilizing innovative judicial paradigms. *University of Missouri at Kansas City Law Review*, 69, 139-177.

Hora, P.F., Schma, W.G., and Rosenthal, J. T.A. (1999). Therapeutic jurisprudence and the drug treatment court movement: Revolutionizing the criminal justice system's response to drug abuse and crime in America. *Notre Dame Law Review,* 74, 439-530 - available online under the heading "publications" in Judge Hora's website (www.judgehora.com).

The International Network on Therapeutic Jurisprudence at http://www.therapeuticjurisprudence.org

Lasker, A.W. (2001). Her stock in trade is 'therapeutic jurisprudence'. *Chicago Daily Law Bulletin*, June 13, p.3.

Leben, S. (2000). Thoughts on some potential appellate and trial court applications of therapeutic jurisprudence, *Seattle University Law Review*, 24, 467-476.

Kondo, L.L. (2000). Advocacy of the establishment of mental health specialty courts in the provision of therapeutic justice for mentally ill offenders, *Seattle University Law Review*, 24, 373-481.

Lurigio, A.J., Watson, A., Luchins, D.J., and Hanrahan, P. (2001). Therapeutic jurisprudence in action: Specialized courts for the mentally ill. *Judicature*, 84, 184-187.

Maruna, S. (2001). *Making good: How ex-convicts reform and rebuild their lives.* Washington DC: American Psychological Association.

Maruna, S., and LeBel, T.P. (2003). Welcome Home? Examining the "Reentry Court" Concept from a Strengths-based Perspective. *Western Criminology Review*, 4, 91-107.

McGuire, J. (1995). *What works: Reducing reoffending: guidelines from research and practice*. Chichester; New York

Meichenbaum, D., and Turk, DC. (1987). *Facilitating treatment adherence: A practitioner's guidebook.* New York: Plenum.

Monk, G., Winslade, J., Crocket, K. and Epstein, D. (Eds.). (1997). *Narrative therapy in practice: the archaeology of hope.* New York: Jossey-Bass.

Office of Justice Programs. (1999). *Re-entry Courts: managing the transition from prison to community: A call for concept papers*. Washington D.C.: U.S. Department of Justice, Office of Justice Programs.

Schma, W. (2000). Special issue overview: Judging for the new millennium, *Court Review*, 37, 4-9.

Shuman, D.W., Hamilton, J.A., and Daley, C.E. (1994). The health effects of jury service, *Law and Psychology Review*, 18, 267-307.

Stolle, D.P. Wexler, D.B. and. Winick, B.J. (Eds.). (2000). *Practicing therapeutic jurisprudence: Law as a helping profession*. Durham: Carolina Academic Press.

United States v. Flowers. (1997). *Federal Supplement - United States District Court for the Eastern District of New York*. 983, 159-183.

United States v. Jeter. (2001). *Federal Reporter*. (3rd ed.). 263, 1032-1045.

VandeWalle, G.W. (2000). A sea of change in the appellate process? *Seattle University Law Review*, 24, 567-570.

Wexler, D.B. (1991). Health care compliance principles and the insanity acquittee conditional release process. *Criminal Law Bulletin*, 27, 18-41.

Wexler, D.B. (1993). Therapeutic jurisprudence and the criminal courts. *William and Mary Law Review*, 35, 279-297.

Wexler, D.B. (2000a). Therapeutic jurisprudence in the appellate arena. *Seattle University Law Review*, 24, 217-225.

Wexler, D.B. (2000b). Just some juvenile thinking about delinquent behavior: a therapeutic jurisprudence approach to relapse prevention planning and youth advisory juries. *University of Missouri at Kansas City Law Review*, 69, 93-107.

Wexler, D.B. (2001). Robes and Rehabilitation: How Judges Can Help Offenders 'Make Good'. *Court Review*, 38, 18-23.

Wexler, D.B. (2002). Some reflections on therapeutic jurisprudence and the practice of criminal law. *Western Criminology Review*, 38, 205-215.

Wexler, D.B. (in press). Spain's JVP ('Juez de Vigilancia Penitenciaria) Legal Structure as a Potential Model for a Re-Entry Court. *Contemporary Issues in Law*.

Wiebe, R.P. (1996). The mental health implications of crime victims' rights. In Wexler, D.B., and Winick, B.J. (Eds.). (1996) *Law in a therapeutic key: Developments in therapeutic jurisprudence*. (pp. 213-241). Durham: Carolina Academic Press.

Winick, B.J. (1999). Therapeutic jurisprudence and preventive law's transformative potential for particular areas of legal practice: Criminal Law: Redefining the role of the criminal defense lawyer at plea bargaining and sentencing: A therapeutic jurisprudence/preventive law model. *Psychology, Public Policy and Law*, 5, 1034-1086.

Winick, B.J. and Wexler, D.B. (Eds). (2003). *Judging in a therapeutic key: Therapeutic jurisprudence and the courts*. Durham: Carolina Academic Press.

In: Justice as a Basic Human Need
Editor: Anthony Taylor, pp. 71-84
ISBN 1-59454-915-X

Chapter 7

MEETING HUMAN NEEDS: THE POTENTIAL OF RESTORATIVE JUSTICE

Gabrielle Maxwell and Allison Morris

ABSTRACT

The conventional criminal justice system can be criticized for its failure to respond to offending in ways that meet human needs for identity and self-esteem, forgiveness, healing, repair, and reintegration. Further, the existing system leads to high levels of reoffending, adds considerably to costs in keeping offenders for longer periods in prison, fails to protect the community adequately from offending, and leads to dissatisfaction among victims. In contrast, the processes of restorative justice provide options that go some way towards reversing these trends and, at the same time, towards better meeting basic human needs. In this chapter, we describe the values that underlie restorative justice and the processes that have been developed in New Zealand that exemplify them. We assess the evidence on empowering victims and offenders, increasing their involvement in the processes, on repairing harm, and on reintegrating into society those who have been alienated from it.

INTRODUCTION

In the first chapter of this book, Taylor pointed to the human need for security and safety, fairness and equity, and forgiveness as components of a basic need for justice. Others (for example, Ericson 1950) have argued for the recognition of self-esteem and identity needs that often have their foundation within the culture to which the individual belongs. To this list we would add the need to heal the harm and if possible repair the damage done to victims, and the need to get offenders to take responsibility for their actions. At a societal level, there is also a need to restore the balance in the relationships among those affected and to reconnect both victims and offenders with society as a whole. The conventional criminal justice system (CCJS) has failed to meet these needs, but not only that, being based on responses that emphasise deterrence and retribution, has resulted in high rates of reoffending and high costs associated with imprisoning increasing numbers of offenders for longer periods[1]. At the same time, it has often overlooked the specific human needs of victims and offenders, and, as a consequence, some victims remain bitter, angry and vengeful while some offenders are left shamed and alienated (Retzinger, and Scheff 1996; Tangney, and Dearing, 2002).

Restorative justice (RJ) represents a challenge to the CCJS, and it places a value on human needs. The idea of RJ is not new: traces of it can be found embedded in the judicial systems of many pre-modern societies (Zehr, 1989). Small communities often developed ways of meeting to resolve conflicts and restore harmony. They put the emphasis not wholly on punishment but rather on healing and restoration. As nations developed, the State came to play a larger hand in determining responses to transgressions and, to a considerable extent, the ownership of the conflict passed from those most immediately affected to a supposedly more impartial criminal justice system designed to give better protection for the rights of offenders and more consistent responses to their offending. At the same time, victims were often overlooked, the harm caused by the offending was not repaired, and the criminal justice system failed to reintegrate offenders. Over the last twenty years, there has been growing advocacy for a return to the values and processes underpinning these earlier models and a de-emphasis on retribution and deterrence (for example: Zehr, 1990; Van Ness and Strong 1997).

In the first part of this chapter, we contrast CCJS and RJ by comparing the characteristics and underlying values of the two systems and the implications for both the principal participants and for society in general. In the second part, we describe how restorative values have been translated into practical reality in New Zealand. In the third part we summarise the findings of research on the outcomes that are relevant to the debate on the effectiveness of restorative justice in meeting human needs.

Part 1. Contrasting Conventional Restorative Justice Values

Contrasting Values

The conventional criminal justice system emphasizes the centrality of State authority, and gives primacy to the interests of the State through a process of detached and impersonal decision-making by professionals. It is based on an ethic of individualism and individual culpability at both the trial and the sentencing stages of legal procedures. It gives priority to legal rights that ensure equality before the law and consistency of practice, and focuses primarily on the symbolic and expressive functions of punishment. It also signifies that the State has a role in the care of its citizens, softened only to a limited degree by the establishment of rehabilitative programmes. And in all respects, it is distinctly mono-cultural, and restricted in its ability to meet the needs of both victims and offenders.

[1] Rehabilitation is sometimes seen as a secondary goal of conventional criminal justice systems. While there is some evidence that the introduction of rehabilitative programmes does make some difference to reoffending rates, they are very difficult to implement within the confines of the conventional justice system, and, at best, they have limited impact (Andrews, 1994; Andrews and Bonta, 1998).

By contrast, restorative justice gives primacy to the interests of those most affected – the victims, offenders and their communities of care. It endorses a collective ethos and collective responsibility in which the State no longer has a monopoly over decision-making, but rather the principal decision makers are the parties themselves. It emphasizes human rights and the need to recognize the social impact of substantive injustice, rather than simply to provide offenders with legal or formal justice and the victims with no justice all. It recognizes shared values that can be used to address offending and its consequences, and to reintegrate victims and offenders in their local communities. It is premised on the belief that the reasons behind the offending, and hence the solutions to it, lie with the community. And finally, it encourages cultural relativity and sensitivity rather than cultural dominance, because it allows the parties themselves to shape the processes and outcomes. In essence, the social values underlying restorative justice rely on connections between offenders, victims and communities, rather than on exclusion and separation.

Contrasting Processes

The conventional system takes the form of a public ritual, with formal and complex language, rules and procedures, that Wexler in his chapter sets out to 'humanise' but which RJ seeks to change. Professionals representing the State - judges, lawyers, police officers and court staff - are the principal players in that ritual. Lawyers are responsible for most, if not all, of the dialogue; and judges make the decisions. All of this ritual, of course, does have purpose and meaning. It signifies how society regards crime and criminals, but it also expresses and signifies the authority of the State. Even the structural and spatial arrangements of the courtroom, and the positioning of the parties involved in the proceedings, indicate who has the real power and who the real participants are. For victims and offenders, the consequences of this are profound. We will return to this later.

In contrast, restorative justice is a relatively flexible, informal, and private process. The parties themselves often choose the venue and the procedures to be followed, thus allowing for considerable flexibility. It brings together all parties with a stake in a particular offence - victims, offenders and 'communities of care' – who, with the aid of a facilitator, resolve how the offence should be dealt with to the satisfaction of the parties concerned.

Contrasting Outcomes

Within the conventional criminal justice system, the outcomes tend to be punitive. Their aim is to reassert the particular values underpinning the criminal law and thus to perform a wider educative function; they are supposed to deter others; and they are intended, through the choice of sanction, to denounce the offence and the offender. Any outcomes that might be intended to have a rehabilitative or reparative focus tend to be additional to the punishment process rather than an integral part of it.

The aims of restorative justice processes, on the other hand, are primarily to hold offenders accountable for their offending in meaningful ways and to try to get them to make amends to victims certainly in a symbolic sense and, where possible, in a real sense. Thus RJ outcomes focus on producing apologies, reparation or community work, as ways of restoring the property stolen or compensating for the injuries endured. But it does not exclude the protection of society and the gravity of the offending from consideration; rather these are secondary objectives. In fact, any outcome - including a prison sentence - can be restorative if the outcome is agreed and considered appropriate by the key parties.

One of the principal hopes of RJ is that reconciliation between the offender and victim will occur. But although this is not always possible - the victims may remain angry or bitter and offenders may remain unmoved and untouched - there is no doubt that reconciliation often does take place between victims and offenders. Overall, the principal objective of restorative outcomes is to reintegrate victims and offenders into their respective communities.

Contrasting Victims' Experiences

In the conventional criminal justice system, where there is a 'guilty' plea, the effects of offences on victims are mainly communicated to the court, if at all, through a victim impact statement presented by the prosecutor in written form. Under that system, even when victims do attend court, they are merely witnesses for the prosecution or observers. They are not able to participate meaningfully in the process. Consequently, the victims, particularly of serious offences, frequently feel alienated by the process; they receive little to aid their healing, and they end up with an understandable sense of grievance.

At restorative justice meetings, the attendance of victims is, of course, voluntary. But many victims want to meet the person who has offended against them, and their presence (or the presence of a representative or spokesperson) is central to the success of the process. It gives them the chance of telling offenders how they feel about their actions and what the consequences were for them. Typically these are emotionally powerful occasions far removed from the conventional courtroom scene. For victims, being present at restorative meetings can offer further potential benefits, such as providing opportunities for healing, and for understanding why the offences occurred. In short, successful restorative justice processes put victims at the heart of what happen, and opens the path for closure.

Contrasting Offenders' Experiences

By and large, offenders have much the same experience of conventional criminal justice processes as victims. Pre-trial and trial procedures do not engage them. As a result, they rarely participate. They are only able to communicate with the court through the police or lawyers, they feel alienated from the justice process, and afterwards they often have only a vague idea of what has happened to them. They are discouraged from direct dialogue with their victims, and they are not effectively held accountable in meaningful way. Overall, they remain fundamentally untouched by both judicial processes and outcomes.

In contrast, restorative justice processes require not just the presence of the offender, but their inclusion in the proceedings. They are expected to directly participate in the process, to speak about their offending and matters associated with it, to interact with the victim, to express their remorse about what has occurred, to apologize for what they have done, and to contribute to decisions about eventual outcomes. From all this, offenders are expected to have a better understanding of their offending and its consequences, to become accountable for the offending in ways which they understand and to contribute to repairing the harm. The presence of victims also means that their justifications for offending - the 'she could afford it', 'he is insured', and other such superficial explanations - can be challenged. Overall, the intention of the restorative justice process is to touch, and perhaps to change, the hearts and minds of offenders and victims.

Summarising the Arguments So Far:

The present policies of conventional criminal justice demand reconsideration. Penal populations are growing at considerable cost to the community, with little likelihood of reducing rates of re-offending. There is little in either psychological theory or criminological research to support the belief that punishment, denunciation, shaming, and incarceration are likely to have a positive impact on offenders or reduce the probability of others committing crime. Furthermore, the policies largely ignore the needs of both victims and offenders, while fears about personal safety and the sense of injustice grow among them and in society at large.

In the meantime, restorative justice has begun to command community support, and it is growing in piecemeal fashion. Through it, we might be able to reverse the criminal justice trends mentioned above and, in particular, to find ways to respond more effectively to individual and social needs in ways that benefit all concerned. In the next sections we provide detailed information on the potential of restorative justice first, by describing experience with the processes that have been adopted in New Zealand, and second, by presenting data from research on the extent to which these processes can meet their objectives and respond to the needs of all those affected by their offending.

PART 2. EXAMPLES OF RESTORATIVE JUSTICE IN PRACTICE

New Zealand Models

Three main examples of restorative justice in practice in New Zealand demonstrate how restorative justice values can be translated into everyday penal practice: family group conferences for young offenders, community panel, and court-referred restorative justice conferences for adult offenders[2]. The different projects described here all provide offenders, victims, and their communities of care with a voice in a meeting with a facilitator that focuses on offender accountability and responsibility and takes victims' interests into account. But they differ in the types of offences they deal with, where they are located within the structure of the criminal justice system, who decides how to deal with the offending, and the role of victims in the procedures. At the same time, the use of these processes does not involve the abandonment of courts and prisons, because the determination of guilt or innocence remains

[2] In addition, there are a number - it is difficult to be precise about how many - of restorative justice programmes operating without state funding at a local community or marae level to which judges can refer offenders, at their discretion. Some prisons in New Zealand also offer a restorative justice programme through the Prison Fellowship of New Zealand i.e. the Sycamore Tree Programme –see Prison Fellowship International (2004) and Te Ara Whakatika (2002)

the tasks of judges and jurors, custodial sentences can still be imposed, and the processes can be optional.

Family Group Conferences

Family group conferences in New Zealand are used for all medium-serious and serious offending by young people - except murder and manslaughter. They operate as an alternative to courts for young people who have not been arrested or charged in the Youth Court, and they also provide a mechanism for making pre-sentence recommendations to the judge when young people have been charged in the Youth Court (see flow-chart Figure 1). The meetings involve the victims, young people and their families to enable the offending and its impact to be discussed, to provide an opportunity for the offenders to repair the harm they have caused and for the meetings as a whole to make recommendations to prevent further offending. One important feature is that at some point in the meetings, families and their youngsters are given the opportunity to discuss privately how they think the offending should be dealt with. When the conferences reconvene with all the participants present, the family plans are then discussed among all those present, and agreement is sought or amendments made.

The intended focus of the discussion and the resulting outcomes are on the young person's offending and matters related directly to the circumstances of that offending. However, the *Children, Young Persons and Their Families Act 1989* s206(g) also states that, in determining outcomes, due regard should be paid to the interests of the victim(s). This requirement invites the consideration of apologies, reparation and community work. Other outcomes are limited only by the imagination of the parties. These might include donations to a charity, involvement in some kind of training programme, supervision by a social worker or community organization, a residential placement (for a short time) and, occasionally, a period in custody.

Each party to the conference, at least in theory, has a veto and can register their disagreement with the plans that might be proposed. If they cannot reach agreement the matters can be referred back to the police or the Youth Court. But if they all agree, and, where relevant, once they are accepted by the Youth Court judge, the plans and decisions are binding.

Community Panels

In 1995 a number of community panel pilot schemes were funded in New Zealand to divert adult offenders from having to reappear before the criminal courts. They began operating in 1996, and two of these *Project Turnaround* and *Te Whanau Awhina* are still in operation. The offences dealt with by the projects range from the more ‘routine’ offences of willful damage, theft and burglary to cases of aggravated robbery, threatening to kill, driving causing death, driving with excess alcohol. And although there are important differences between them, both schemes have elements of restorative justice in the way they operate.

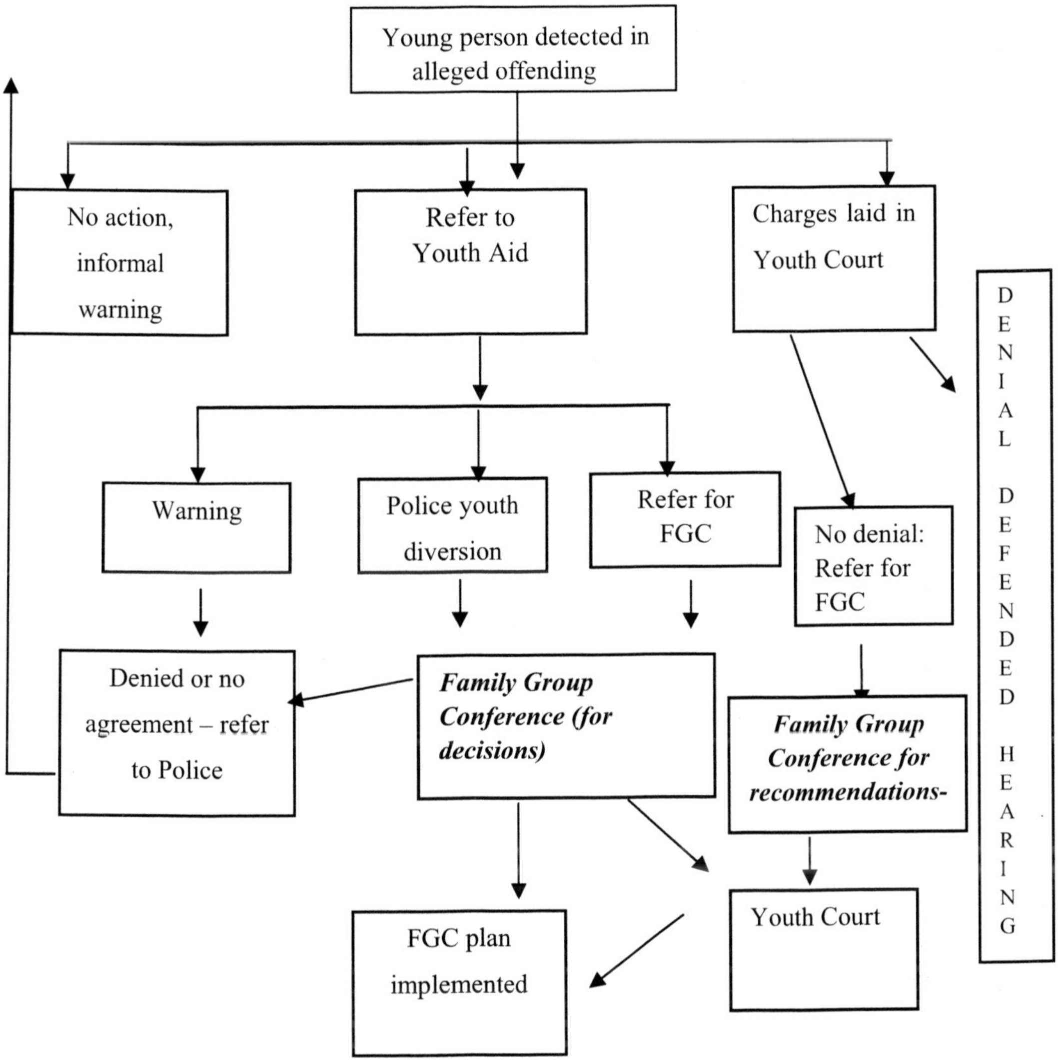

Figure 1. Pathways through the New Zealand youth justice system – Line on left side needs to connect with bottom left box (Denied or no agreement – refer to police)

Project Turnaround (PT) is situated in Timaru, a provincial South Island city, and it shares its offices with the Safer Community Council and the Community Police. Most of the offenders referred to it are New Zealanders of European origin. Judges divert selected offenders to the scheme on the first appearance at court, and, if the subsequent conditions are met, the offender makes no further court appearance and the police withdraw their evidence. The panel members are volunteers who are selected to represent the community. Normally they have a police officer present, and frequently also the victims. The procedure can be contrasted with a fully restorative process where decisions are made by those who are most directly affected by the offending rather than by appointed representatives of the community. However, the plans decided at the meetings involve making amends to the victim and the community, and making arrangements for the offender of both a reintegrative and a rehabilitative nature. This focus on recompensing the victim and the community is consistent with a restorative justice approach.

Te Whanau Awhina (TWA) is situated on a marae (a communal centre including a meeting house and other buildings for customary activities as well as educational and training facilities) in Auckland, the largest city in New Zealand, and the community panel meetings are held in the wharenui (a traditional meeting house). Almost all the offenders referred are Maori (the indigenous people of New Zealand). As in *Project Turnaround*, they are referred to the scheme by the judge at a court hearing. However, offenders who appear before a panel at *Te Whanau Awhina* are not necessarily diverted from further court appearances and sanctions. Typically the panel consists of three or four Maori elders, one of whom chairs the meeting, and the programme coordinator whose role includes that of providing support for the offender. Family and friends of the offender may also attend, but usually neither the police nor direct victims of the offending are present. Those managing the conference speak on behalf of victims and characteristically identify both the offender's family and the Maori community as victims. The outcome of these meetings involves the offender in accepting plans relating to obtaining employment, job training, participation in marae-based programmes, as well as deciding on ways of making amends to the direct victims.

Despite the irregular attendance of direct victims at Te Whanau Awhina meetings, the focus on repairing the harm to victims and to the community, and reintegration of the offender with family and the wider community are consistent with aspects of a restorative justice.[3]

Court-Referred Restorative Justice Conferences

A pilot scheme of court referred restorative justice conferences began operation in 2001 in the District Courts in four areas of New Zealand. After offenders plead guilty, Judges refer selected cases for a conference. These cases can include those involving property offences with maximum penalties of two years imprisonment or more and other offences with maximum penalties of one to seven years, but not cases involving domestic violence and sexual offences.

A coordinator employed by the Department in each of the courts then meets the offender is determine if the offender is willing and able to participate in the restorative justice process. At that stage, in some cases, the coordinator might also have contact with the victim. If the preliminary indications are satisfactory, the coordinator makes referrals to trained restorative justice facilitators from provider groups contracted by the Department for Courts. Two facilitators[4] then meet with the victim and offender separately, and they convene a joint conference if the offender still appears able to participate safely and both victim and offender are willing (see flow-chart Figure 2).

[3] Since these early beginnings, a number of Community Panel Diversion Schemes have been publicly funded. Mainly, these are modeled on *Project Turnaround* in that they involve the offender and victim meeting with a community panel, but some have incorporated additional developments. By mid 2004, in total there were 18 programmes in operation, and it is estimated that by the end of the year these programmes will deliver about 900 conferences.

[4] Ideally, the facilitators are matched to the offender and victim in some ways - for example, with respect to gender and ethnicity.

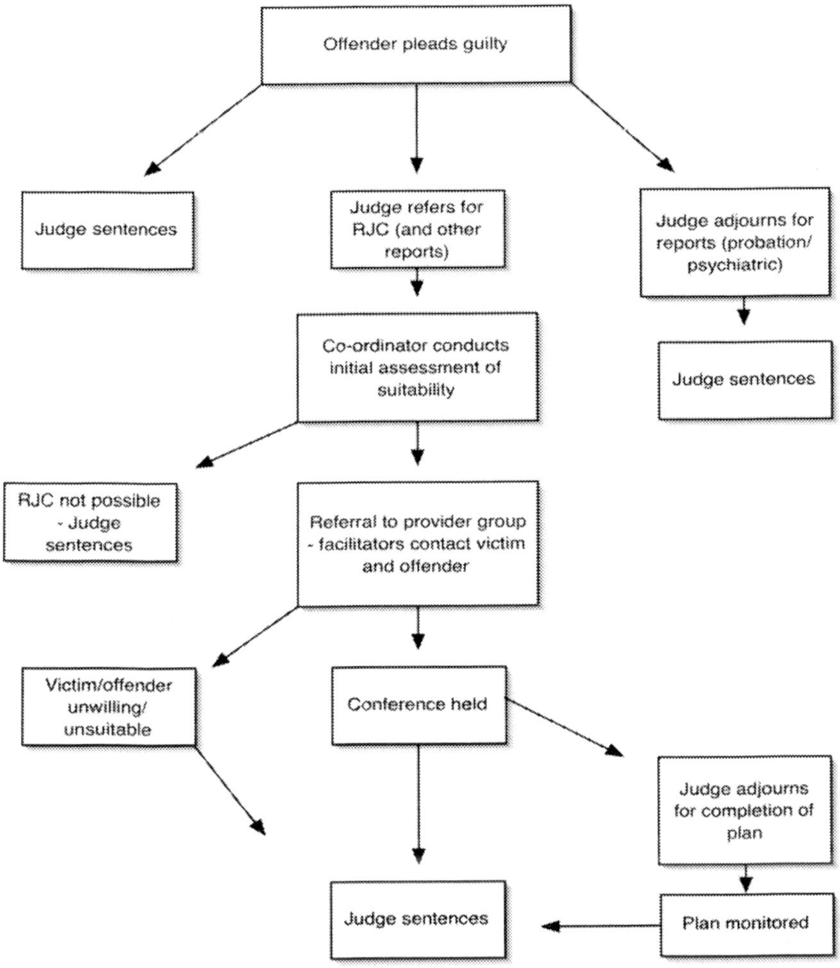

Figure 2. Court-referred restorative justice process

The subsequent restorative justice conferences are relatively informal. Victims and offenders must be present and their respective support people are usually present too. The police, probation officers and the youth advocate are invited to attend, but in practice they do not always do so. The intention is for the conference to provide an opportunity for victims to have their say, and for offenders to take responsibility for putting things right. In this way, the conferences are more like family group conferences than community panels, in that they rely on the victims and their support people - not panel members - to come up with a plan or agreement. However, they differ from family group conferences in that both the victim and offender must both agree to participate. The outcome is a report that can include specific steps that the offender agrees to take to put things right (for example, payment of money to victims or offenders carrying out specific work), and it might also contain rehabilitative features (for example, the attendance by offenders at anger management or job-training courses).

In a given case the judge, the prosecutor, and the probation officer, are each provided with a report of the interactions of the restorative justice conference with any agreements reached. Then, as obliged by law, the judge takes the report into account along with any other pre-sentence reports in deciding on the appropriate sentence[5]. Judges, however, retain the discretion whether or not to incorporate into the sentence all or part of any agreement reached. In some cases, instead of imposing a sentence at this stage, the judge might choose to adjourn the case in order for the offender to carry out the agreements reached at the restorative justice conference – in which case a report is later provided to the judge as to whether or not the required tasks have been completed, and the offender will either be discharged or sentenced. The explicit aim of the pilot projects is to offer better outcomes for offenders, victims, and the community, to increase their satisfaction with the criminal justice system, and to reduce re-offending.

PART 3. EVALUATING RESTORATIVE JUSTICE

Three New Zealand Studies

In this final section, we draw from our research and experience in New Zealand to assess the potential of restorative justice processes in meeting human needs. Detailed findings from our research are reported in Maxwell and Morris, 1993, 1999; Maxwell, Kingi, Robertson, Morris, and Cunningham, 2004, and Maxwell, Kingi, Robertson, and Morris, 2004. In selecting what to present in this chapter, we focus on a) the impact on both victim and offenders of: participation and involvement in decisions; b) offenders accepting responsibility for their offending and attempting to repair the harm that was done; and c) the steps being taken to reintegrate offenders into the community. We also examine critical aspects of the family group conference experience for offenders in leading to positive life outcomes and reducing the probability of their re-offending.

The critical outcomes that we have identified include many of the same critical correlates of a sense of justice identified by Harlow and Newcomb (1990) that Taylor described in the first chapter of this book. They comprise the quality of relationships with peers, intimates and family; a sense of purpose in life and a perception of opportunities; satisfaction with work and health; and an absence of meaninglessness and powerlessness. The prediction of these characteristics, along with whether or not reoffending occurred, was the main target of the 1999 and 2004 research.

We derived data for the 1999 study by examining files and interviewing 108 of the 161 offenders whose conferences we had observed, interviewed and reported on previously in 1993. In 2004 we were able to go further by drawing data and from interviews with 520 young offenders who had a family group conference in 1998 (the retrospective sample), plus another 105 young offenders who had a conference in 2000-2001 (the prospective sample). We also interviewed 100 victims whose offenders had conferences in 2000-2001, observed the 100 conferences in which these victims and offenders were involved and we interviewed the co-ordinators and youth aid police officers who had been involved in a large number of the family group conferences in 1998 and 2000-2001.

For research data on the two community panels described earlier – i.e. *Project Turnaround* and *Te Whanau Awhina* – we examined the files of 200 offenders who had been

[5] Recently this obligation was strengthened by legislative changes (i.e. the *Sentencing Act 2002* and the *Victims' Rights Act* 2002).

dealt with by the panels during 1995, interviewed a sample of them (Maxwell, Morris and Anderson, 1999), and contrasted their offending with 200 matched offenders who were dealt with solely in the criminal courts. We also collected information on the reconvictions of 200 participants in the two pilot schemes, and on the sample of 200 matched offenders who had been dealt with through the court. The two samples were randomly matched for age, sex, ethnicity, previous offending, and number of charges, with a control subjects who were convicted of the same offence (or the same most serious offence where the participants were charged with committing more than one offence) and dealt with by conventional court processes during the year 1995. We used records of further convictions as the measure for assessing recidivism, and, because the participants and controls were not all exposed to the risk of committing offences for the same length of time A 'survival analysis'was carried out to take account of the different length of the follow-up period available for each offender.

The latest publication evaluating the pilot project of court referred restorative justice conferences (Ministry of Justice, 2005). It drew information from a wide range of sources: i.e. from files and documents, observations of conferences, postal surveys to all participants and facilitators, interviews with the offenders and victims referred to these conferences (after the conference, after the offender's sentence, and 12 months after the conference), questionnaires to key informants (such as judges, co-ordinators, police and facilitators during the first year of the evaluation and 12 months later), and interviews with a sample of offenders and victims whose cases were dealt with only in the courts (soon after their cases were dealt with, and again 12 months later).

Research Findings

Victims' views: The research showed that victims did not always take advantage of the opportunity to attend restorative processes. Only about a half attended family group conferences (that occur regardless of whether or not a victim attends), and at least half the referrals for adult restorative conferences in the presence of victims did not occur because the victims did not wish to take part. Their reasons for not participating included: not wanting to meet the offender, that the cost of involvement seemed disproportionate to their loss, or that they had already put the matter behind them. On the other hand, those victims who attended the conferences usually found it a positive experience - they felt it was a good way to resolve the situation, they wanted to give offenders another chance, they wanted to confront offenders and inform them of the impact that their offending had had, and they wanted to have a say in the outcome. Those who attended usually said that it had been a positive experience and that they agreed with the outcomes.

Offenders' views: Most offenders who attended family group conferences or restorative conferences said that they gained a better understanding of what had happened. They appreciated the chance to have their say, they understood the victim's point of view, and agreed with the outcomes. However, young offenders did not always report being fully involved, perhaps, because adults were often not willing to hear and value young people's views, especially when they have offended.

Critical elements of the process: The research on family group conferences used multi-variate analyses to identify critical factors in the process that contributed to a lower probability of reoffending and to positive life outcomes. The critical factors included being fully involved in the decisions, not being shamed by the process (Maxwell and Morris, 2002), feeling remorse, being able to make amends for what they had done, feeling supported and that they had been forgiven, and experiencing outcomes that contributed to their reintegration into society. Particularly important were the opportunities offenders were given to gain further educational qualifications or skills, to find employment, and to have positive relations with family, friends and partners.

Critical outcomes for society: Two other key features of interest to the justice system and to society as a whole, are the impact of restorative processes on reoffending and the financial costs of the process. Research on the outcome of community panels was able to demonstrate that, compared to control groups, those involved in the restorative process were less likely to reoffend, and also the costs to the system were considerably reduced compared to those incurred when more traditional processes were used to make decisions and more traditional penalties were put in place. The savings were greatest when the offences were more serious, because in these cases that might otherwise have resulted in custodial sentences, alternative community solutions were often found.

Conclusion

The effectiveness of restorative and conventional justice systems cannot readily be contrasted, since the primary objectives of both are so different. But even in terms of the objectives to which the conventional system gives priority (but which restorative justice makes secondary) it seems that restorative justice does no worse and on some dimensions may even do better. For example, there is little evidence that the ritualistic nature of conventional justice and the abstract nature of most of the sanctions it imposes are any more likely to express society's abhorrence of offending or to operate as a deterrent to other potential offenders than restorative approaches, provided they incorporate meaningful accountability and are viewed as 'right' by the parties, including their 'communities of care'. Being confronted by one's victim, for example, is not the 'soft option' often portrayed with respect to restorative justice.

Also, although the rhetoric of the conventional criminal justice system places emphasis on the protection of the public, and in particular on the use of imprisonment for that purpose, it in fact pursues that objective in a haphazard and often completely misconceived way. The conventional criminal justice system does, of course, provide some protection of the public, but there is no reason to believe that restorative justice, which of course can retain the option of imprisonment, is incapable of doing so at least as well.

Although reducing re-offending is not the primary objective of the conventional criminal justice system, in this respect it also seems to do fairly poorly, The reconviction rates from those imprisoned are high and the reconviction rates for those sentenced to community-based sanctions are not much better. Also, while there is some evidence that rehabilitative programmes under the conventional criminal justice system can make some difference to re-offending rates, they are very difficult to implement within the confines of the conventional system, and at best have a limited impact. Further, psychological theory does not suggest that a reliance on punishment and denunciation will be effective in changing behaviour. On the other hand, there are some encouraging data on reconviction with respect to restorative justice, and importantly, the research indicates that the probability of reconviction is *reduced* when certain of the potentially restorative justice aspects are achieved. However, when the two systems of justice are contrasted in their ability to respond to human needs of offenders and victims, it is clear that the restorative system is more likely to be effective. The development of RJ in New Zealand supports the key elements of the theory: i.e. the need for those involved to be empowered and to have control over what happens, to be supported by others and to have positive relationships with those closest to them, and to be reintegrated into the social fabric. The research[6] points to the importance for healing of offenders making amends and being forgiven, and of victims having a voice. The data also point out that the less punitive and costly solutions can reduce reoffending, and hence the mounting costs of imprisonment. Moreover, the probability of successful reintegration into civil society is greater for offenders who have experienced an effective restorative process.

Many countries across the world have expressed interest in the development of restorative justice approaches to dealing with offending – especially in relation to young people. Enabling legislation in relation to young people has already been passed in most of the Australia States, England and Wales, Canada, Ireland and Singapore. Legislation is currently being developed or being introduced in Belgium, Macao and Brazil. Pilot schemes for young offenders are operating or being set up in many other countries including South Africa, Sweden, Netherlands, Hong Kong and Brazil. Restorative approaches to adult offending through victim offender mediation are also developing in other jurisdictions, for example in some of the states in the USA.

In addition, the international research literature is developing rapidly with results now available from most of the countries mentioned above. In all cases, the findings are consistent with ours in reporting increased satisfaction with restorative processes and the outcomes for victims. Although studies of reoffending are relatively few almost all indicate that effective processes result in reductions in reoffending, especially when the offences are not trivial.

We would like to make an important caveat. Although restorative justice has a long history, the processes described here have been developed relatively recently. Therefore more time is needed to ensure that the critical values of restorative justice are translated into good modern day practices. So far New Zealand is the only country that has legislated for a nation-wide mandatory system of restorative justice for young people, and even there, its implementation is not without problems. In addition, there are many schemes in a variety of different countries that claim to be examples of restorative justice but fail to meet its key values. Therefore the label 'restorative justice' must be treasured; otherwise poor practices will provide ammunition for critics to undermine it.

There is much that is exciting here for the student of human behaviour. The developments we describe, demonstrate that it is possible to create a humane system of justice that is more responsive to the needs of the people most affected by offending. Furthermore, what works is consistent in many respects with the theory and understanding of human needs for fairness, for feeling safe, for being given a voice and having control over our own lives, for not being shamed or stigmatised, for being forgiven, and for achieving meaningful and purposeful life outcomes.

---

[6] Not all the evaluations we have carried out provided information on all these factors. However, the most comprehensive of the published studies (Maxwell et al, 2004) identifies the important characteristics of family

REFERENCES

Andrews, D.A. (1994). *An overview of treatment effectiveness: Research and clinical principles.* Ottawa: Department of Psychology, Carleton University.

Andrews, D.A., and Bonta, J, (1998). *The psychology of criminal conduct.* (2nd edn.). Cincinnati: Anderson Publishing.

Ericson, E.H. (1950). *Childhood and Society.* New York: Norton.

Harlow, L.L.and Newcomb, M.D. (1990). Towards a general hierarchical model of meaning and satisfaction in life. *Multivariate Behavioural Research*, 25, 3, 384-405.

Maxwell, G.M., and Morris, A. (1993). *Families victims and culture: Youth justice in New Zealand.* Wellington: Social Policy Agency and Institute of Criminology, Victoria University of Wellington.

Maxwell, G.M., and Morris, A. (1999). *Understanding reoffending.* Wellington, Institute of Criminology, Victoria University of Wellington.

Maxwell G.M., and Morris, A. (2002). Shame, guilt and remorse. In E. Weitekamp and H-J. Kerner. (Eds). *Restorative justice: Theoretical foundations.* (Ch, 13). Cullompton, Devon: Willan.

Maxwell, G.M., Morris, A. and Anderson, T. (1999). *Community adult pre-trial diversion: Supplementary evaluation.* Wellington: Crime Prevention Unit, Department of Prime Minister and Cabinet and Institute of Criminology, Victoria University of Wellington.

Maxwell, G. Kingi, V., Robertson, J., Morris, A. (2004). *Achieving effective outcomes in youth justice: Final report to the Ministry of Social Development.* Wellington: Ministry of Social Development.

Maxwell, G.M., Kingi, V., Robertson, J., Morris, A. and Cunningham, C. (2004). *Achieving effective outcomes in youth justice in New Zealand.* Wellington: Ministry of Social Development.

Ministry of Justice (2005). *Court-referred Restorative Justice Pilot evaluation.* Wellington, Ministry of Justice.

Prison Fellowship International website (2004). *The Sycamore Tree Project* http://www.pficjr.org/programs/stp/

Te Ara Whakatika (2002) Newsletter. Issue 7, page 4 .Wellington: Ministry of Justice.

Tangney, J.P. and Dearing, R.L. (2002). *Shame and guilt.* New York: Guilford Press.

Retzinger, S.M. and Scheff, T. J. (1996). Strategy for community conferences: Emotions and social bonds. In J. Hudson and B Galaway. (Eds). *Restorative justice: International perspectives.* Monsey: Criminal Justice Press.

Van Ness, D. and Strong, K. (1997). *Restoring justice.* Cincinnati: Anderson Publishing.

Zehr, H. (1990). *Changing lenses: A new focus for crime and justice.* Scottsdale. PA: Herald Press.

---

group conferences, while the Community Panel evaluation provides a control group sample for the purposes of determining the impact of restorative process on recidivism and financial costs.

In: Justice as a Basic Human Need
Editor: Anthony Taylor, pp. 85-93
ISBN 1-59454-915-X

Chapter 8

JUSTICE: SOCIAL-PSYCHOLOGICAL PERSPECTIVES

Ronald Fischer and Linda J. Skitka

ABSTRACT

The aim of the current chapter is to share eight fundamental insights that have been gleaned from over fifty years of social psychological theorizing and research relating to justice. These insights are that:

1. Justice is an important subjective phenomenon
2. People have a need to believe in a just world
3. Outcomes, procedures, and treatment impact perceptions of justice
4. Perceptions of justice are important for both individuals and groups
5. People care about justice for a number of different reasons
6. Feelings of injustice are tied to notions of accountability and blame
7. Justice judgments are formed through social comparisons
8. Justice judgments are shaped by cultural values

INTRODUCTION

Social psychology is the study of the ways that people collectively shape their thoughts, feelings, and behavior. For example, imagine a person growing up alone on a desert island. What need would he or she have for a conception of fairness or justice? Then imagine that one day a second party arrives at the island. As soon as there are two people, questions of fairness dominate many of their social interactions: Who is entitled to the available food supply, and how much should each be able to harvest? If one works to gather the firewood, is the other entitled to share the fire? Thus fairness and justice are fundamentally social concepts that require an examination of the social interactions between two or more people.

Justice Is a Subjective Perception

The first major lesson social psychological research offers about justice is that the notion of justice is a subjective construction that is formulated by individuals according to their expectations and feelings of righteousness and 'deservingness'. For this reason social psychological researchers and theorists do not lay down what is just and unjust, and how justice can be achieved. Rather, they study *how* people decide what is just and unjust under given circumstances, and they examine the consequences of these perceptions, while recognising that such perceptions are not necessarily in agreement with philosophical imperatives or objective realities. Take for example the normative criteria outlined by the philosopher John Rawls (1971), one of which was that rules for the allocation of scarce resources should not injure the least well off within a society and should provide for a minimum level of existence for all members. Although Rawls may have identified a normative justice, it is not an empirically validated one. Empirical research has demonstrated that variability exists between individuals and groups about fair allocation (e.g. Lissowski, Tyszka, and Okrasa, 1993).

Therefore social psychologists working on this topic follow Folger and Cropanzano (1998, pp. xiv-xv) in theorizing that:

> 'an act is 'just' because someone thinks it is just and responds accordingly. This definition is subjective and socially constructed. As one might imagine, two or more people can disagree. Justice, then, is a perceptual cognition. People perceive a certain event. They then make judgments regarding that event and store them in memory. Justice is a means by which individuals make sense out of their social worlds'.

Early research in occupational settings relating to pay confirmed the notion that justice is often in the eye of the beholder and depends on comparisons with others. For example, in their study of African American soldiers stationed in the southern United States, Stouffer, Suchman, DeVinney, Star, and Williams (1949) found that the soldiers were more satisfied with their pay, than were their counterparts stationed in the northern United States. The southern soldiers compared their pay and treatment to that of other Blacks in the south, and felt comparatively fairly treated. When northern soldiers compared their situations to that of other Blacks in the north, in contrast they felt disadvantaged. Similarly, Crosby (1982) reported that women felt they were fairly paid when they compared their pay and treatment with that of other women, but when asked explicitly to compare their treatment to men, they thought otherwise.

The Need to Believe in a Just World

There is also evidence to suggest that people have an inherent need to believe in a just world – i.e. to believe that good things happen to good people and bad things happen only to bad people. When this belief is threatened by contrary evidence, such as when innocents are victimized, people often engage in a variety of behaviors that range from helping or compensating the victim to making psychological rationalizations for the victim's fate; e.g., perceiving the fate as deserved (and, therefore, less unfair) due to an unworthy character. For example, Lerner and Simmons (1966) found that people reacted by compensating an innocent victim of harm when they believed they could effectively do so. Under these conditions, people appeared to recognise the unfairness of a situation, and it motivated them to respond with compassion. However, when they had the expectation that the victim might continue to suffer, people denigrated the victim and blamed her for her plight.

It seems that the need to believe in a just world - developed in early childhood as a necessary step toward learning to defer gratification - has a motivational quality. People need to believe in a just world, in part because the belief provides a sense of predictability and meaning in life as well as giving some assurance that behaviour and characteristics will be appropriately rewarded or punished in the long run (Dalbert, 2001; Lerner, 1980). Should the belief in a just world be threatened by contrary evidence, like the victimization of innocents, people engage in a variety of behaviors that help them to maintain their original belief. Such behaviours might range from helping or compensating the victim, to the rationalization of the victim's fate; e.g., perceiving the fate as deserved (and, therefore, less unfair) because of some an unworthy character trait. In short, the need to believe in a just world can sometimes have ironic consequences, such as blaming innocent victims for their plight.

Outcomes, Procedures and Interpersonal Treatment Impact on the Perception of Justice

The most basic distinction between factors that shape people's perception that something is fair or unfair is procedures versus outcomes (Greenberg, 1990). Distributive justice refers to perceptions of outcomes, e.g., whether people think their outcomes are fair. Although people clearly care about whether they get positive or negative outcomes, they often care more about whether positive or negative outcomes are deserved and are therefore fair (Skitka, Winquist, and Hutchinson, 2003).

Fairness judgments are also shaped by *how* decisions are made, i.e, the procedures used to decide outcome distributions. Leventhal (1980) proposed six general criteria for fair procedures - (1) following consistent procedures, (2) lacking self-interest, (3) seeking accurate information, (4) allowing opportunities to correct decisions, (5) having the important interests of all concerned parties represented, and (6) acting consistent with moral and ethical standards. Lind and Tyler (1988) have also found that having an opportunity to have a voice in decision-making processes is also important in shaping people's belief that procedures are fair.

In addition to formal aspects of procedures, more recent research has also found that interpersonal treatment - i.e., the degree that authorities treat people with dignity and respect - may be more important than formal or structural aspects of procedures on people's fairness reasoning (Bies and Moag, 1986).

In sum, social psychological research has found that outcomes, procedures, and interpersonal treatment are each important factors that people used to judge whether something is fair or unfair. Although it is clear that each of these classes of variables affect people's fairness reasoning, social psychologists have not isolated which of these factors are necessary, rather than sufficient, causes of variance in justice reasoning.

Perceptions of Justice Are Important for Individuals and Groups

The judgment that something is fair or unfair can have a number of adverse consequences for individuals and for groups. For individuals, unfairness can evoke feelings of anger, psychological depression, moral outrage, prejudice, self-esteem, affect political attitudes, work output, organizational commitment, induce sabotage, theft, and protest (Tyler, Boeckmann, Smith, and Huo, 1997). At the group level, the widespread perception of economic and material disadvantage or deprivation can lead to riots and collective actions to redress those feelings (Gurr, 1970). A recent review of the literature found that these effects do not reflect anger, disappointment, and so forth simply because people do not get what they want: The degree that people perceive outcomes and procedures as fair or unfair emerges as a stronger predictors of organizational commitment, retaliation, and so forth than does whether outcomes are simply favorable or unfavorable (Skitka, Winquist and Hutchinson, 2003).

People Care about Justice for Various Reasons

So far attention has been paid to the subjective judgments people make about outcomes, procedures, and interpersonal treatment, and to the effect these have on attitudes, feelings and behaviour. But why are people concerned with justice? The answer is that people are concerned with justice because it serves their (a) long-term self-interests, (b) social identity needs, and (c) need to express or defend their sense of themselves as morally authentic. According to the instrumental or self-interest explanation, individuals are concerned with justice because it facilitates the achievement of their economic goals. To survive and thrive they need to be able to engage in socially cooperative behaviour with those who behave fairly (e.g., Thibaut, and Walker, 1975; Walster, Berscheid, and Walster, 1978).

However, the instrumental view has been challenged by those who argue that people are not primarily concerned about maximizing their economic interests, but are concerned more about establishing and maintaining their social identities (Rousseau and Parks, 1992, Tyler, and Blader, 2003). Fair treatment, for example, communicates the degree that one is a valued and respected member of the group. According to this view, justice is rooted in concerns about relational aspects of group membership. Consistent with this idea, Lind, Kanfer and Earley (1990) found that procedures had positive effects on justice judgments even when they had no instrumental or self-interest value. Subsequently, Tyler and Lind (1992) argued that the use of such procedures also communicated group values to individuals, and that treatment of individuals by groups and their leaders reflected the prevailing quality of their relationships. As Lind, Tyler, and Huo (1997, p.767) went on to say, procedures are described as fair when they 'offer reassurance that the person will not be excluded from the group or relegated to second-class status, with accompanying diminution of social identity'. For individuals who have the freedom to join and leave multiple groups, is important for them also to know whether or not they might be exploited by their groups.

A number of theorists have also argued that people care about fairness for moral reasons, and not only because justice serves people's instrumental or social identity concerns (e.g., Folger, 2001; Leung and Tong, 2003, Skitka, 2001; Skitka and Mullen, 2002). According to this view, people have a need to express, defend, and live up to personal values and convictions about right and wrong, morality and immorality.

In a recent experimental demonstration of the power of moral concerns in shaping people's perceptions of fairness, Skitka and Houston (2001) found that people rated vigilantism and due process of law as equally fair procedures for punishing a defendant whom they were confident was guilty. The respondents had a strong moral mandate that the guilty must be punished – it was a concern that shaped their judgment of fairness much more than even an egregious violation of due process.

It is becoming increasingly clear that sometimes justice judgments will be shaped primarily by instrumental concerns, at other times by social identity needs, and yet at others, by concerns about morality. Although still in their infancy, a number of attempts have been to develop contingency theories to explain when each of the different concerns are more likely to shape thoughts, feelings, and behaviour in matters of justice (e.g., Schroeder, Steel, Woodell, and Bembenek, 2003; Skitka, 2003).

Feelings of Injustice Are Tied to Notions of Accountability and Blame

The next two insights deal with the factors that shape reasoning about justice, and more specifically, about the foundations of the perception of injustice. Feelings of injustice arise if individuals can hold someone accountable and assign blame for an action or inaction that threatens another person's material or psychological wellbeing (Folger and Cropanzano, 1998; 2001). In cases where no person can be blamed, no social injustice is perceived to exist, and explanations are sought in other domains of experience. Three elements are of particular importance to judging something unfair: First, individuals need to perceive that someone is negatively affected and at a disadvantage. Second, the harm must be attributable to discretionary conduct. For example, the fact that it is raining on the day you were planning to have an out-door birthday party is unlikely to lead to perceptions of injustice because it is not a consequence of intentional action. Third, the discretionary actions need to violate an applicable moral or ethical standard, because individuals tend not to direct hostile responses toward those who did what they were supposed to do. Hence although a supervisor's actions initially might have seen unfair, employees tend to withhold hostile responses when they perceive that the supervisor acted in full accord with relevant moral precepts.

Justice Judgements Are Formed through Social Comparisons

As mentioned at the beginning of this chapter, justice is fundamentally a social construct - it does not arise in a social vacuum. How do people know whether their outcome is favourable or unfavourable? How can one decide whether one's supervisor has treated you fairly or unfairly? The best way of finding out is to observe reactions of other people (van Prooijen, van den Bos, and Wilke, 2002). What do they get, how are they treated, and how does this compare to one's own outcomes and treatment? Adams' (1965) proposed that individuals compare the ratio between their inputs (contribution to a social exchange) and outcomes (rewards received within that exchange) with the ratio of some referent others. Similarly, people have to determine whether they have been treated fairly by authorities. To arrive at judgments about whether authorities actually followed and applied these criteria, people will observe their social environment and will sample reactions from their fellow group members. Perceptions of procedural fairness, like perceptions of outcome fairness, are therefore affected by social comparisons.

Justice Judgments are Shaped by Culture

So far we have focused on individual differences and argued that perceptions of justice are subjective (e.g., depending on each individual's view), but the culturally shared conceptions of the topic also have to be considered. Culture is a system of shared meaning within a group or population that serves many purposes. It helps people to make sense of their everyday lives, to evaluate individuals, their behaviour and events, and allows individuals to act in meaningful ways within their groups. In short, culture refers to views of the world. Therefore, it is likely that the way we perceive our social world, that is, our culture, will also influence how we deal with issues related to fairness or justice.

Although the tendency to rely on standards to define what is fair appears to be universal, what is considered a relevant standard can be culturally variable. For example, in many parts of the world, people think equal allocations are more fair than those based on merit. This preference for equality is particularly strong in cultures that by definition have no strong differentials between those at the top and at the bottom of the social hierarchy (Fischer and Smith, 2003). For example, Israeli Kibbutzim were very egalitarian, and all of their members received the same rewards regardless of their efforts and contributions.

Standards of procedural justice are also known to vary across cultures. A study by Smith, Misumi, Tayeb, Peterson, and Bond (1989) found that in Japan and Hong Kong local employees thought it fair and acceptable for employers to discuss them behind their back with other employees, but those from Britain and the United States did not. Fischer and Smith (2004a) found that different cultural values obtained. In Britain and the former East Germany more culturally homogeneous groups influenced what criteria were seen as fair. Specifically, employees endorsing self-enhancement values (relating to individual achievement and power) perceived human resource decisions as much fairer if managers considered individual work performance, as compared with those who were more egalitarian and benevolent (relating to self-transcendence).

Individuals from more collectivist and hierarchical cultures also show greater commitment to their groups and engage in more prosocial behaviour at the expense of procedural justice. Similarly people with a secure place within a group do not have pressing social identity needs, and they too will be committed to their group and engage in prosocial behaviour without so much consideration for procedural justice (Farh, Earley and Lin, 1997; Fischer and Smith, 2004b; Lam, Schaubroeck and Aryee, 2002). Polynesian communities with their importance of the family group (whanau) and the larger tribal community (the iwi and the hapu) for individuals are a good example, because in such communities, group approval and considerations are paramount for membership, and individual self-interest is not.

But there are three other reasons why individuals in different cultures might have different perceptions of justice. Firstly, in cultures of scarcity, instrumental concerns are paramount, because the concern of individuals is to survive physically (e.g. having food, shelter, water). This might explain why people from India, a country with great inequalities with many people living below the poverty line, are more likely to focus on need rather than any other distribution norm (see for example, Murphy-Berman, Berman, Singh, Pachauri, and Kumar, 1984). Secondly, in some cultures people care about injustice because something violates their *personal* feeling of moral authenticity (Skitka and Mullen, 2002), whereas people appear to care about injustice because something violates a *group* or *social* convention. Thirdly, people in different cultures have different notions about accountability, and they are likely to choose different individuals or standards for purposes of comparison.

CONCLUSION

In sum, social psychologists have been doing research on the foundations and consequences of justice judgments for several decades. The goal of this chapter was to provide a brief and selective review of some of the insights about the factors that shape perceptions of justice and injustice, as well as about the consequences of these judgments on people's subsequent thoughts, feelings, and behavior. Perhaps the strongest insights we offer are that (a) justice is in the eye of the beholder, and therefore is likely to be culturally variable, (b) justice is fundamentally a social construct, and one that occurs only when two or more parties consider how both the benefits and burdens of social cooperation are to be shared, and (c) judgments of justice and injustice have a number of wide-ranging consequences for people's subsequent thoughts, feelings, and behavior.

REFERENCES

Adams, J.S. (1965). Inequity in social exchange. In L. Berkowitz (Ed.), *Advances in experimental social psychology* .(vol. 2). 267-296. New York: Academia Press.

Bies, R.J. and Moag, J.S. (1986). Interactional Justice: Communication criteria of fairness. In R.J. Lewicki, B.H. Sheppard and B.H. Bazerman (Eds.), *Research on negotiation in organizations.* (vol. 1). (pp. 43-55). Greenwich, CT: JAI Press.

Colquitt, J.A., Conlon, D.E., Wesson, M.J., Porter, C.O.L.H. and Ng, K.Y. (2001). Justice at the millennium: A meta-analytic review of 25 years of organizational justice research. *Journal of Applied Psychology*, 86, 425-445.

Cropanzano, R. and Greenberg, J. (1997). Progress in organizational justice: Tunnelling through the maze. In C.L. Cooper and I.T. Robertson (Eds.), *International review of industrial and organizational psychology.* (vol.12). (pp. 317-372). Chichester: Wiley.

Crosby, F. J. (1982). *Relative deprivation and the working woman.* New York: Oxford University Press.

Dalbert, C. (2001). *The justice motive as a personal resource: Dealing with challenges and critical life events.* New York: Kluwer/Plenum.

Deutsch, M. (1975). Equity, equality, and need: What determines which value will be used as the basis of distributive justice? *Journal of Social Issues*, 31, 137-50.

Farh, J., Earley, P.C., and Lin, S. (1997). A cultural analysis of justice and organisational citizenship behaviour in Chinese society. *Administrative Science Quarterly*, 42, 421-444.

Fischer, R. and Smith, P. B. (2003). Reward allocation and culture: A meta-analysis. *Journal of Cross-Cultural Psychology*, 34, 251-268.

Fischer, R. and Smith, P. B. (2004a). Values and organizational justice: Performance and seniority-based allocation criteria in UK and Germany. *Journal of Cross-Cultural Psychology*,

Fischer, R. and Smith, P. B. (2004b). Who cares about justice? The moderating effect of values on the link between organisational justice and work behaviour. Paper submitted for publication.

Folger, R. (2001). Fairness as deonance. In S. W. Gilliland, D. D. Steiner, and D. P. Skarlicki. (Eds.). *Research in social issues in management.* (vol. 1). (pp. 3 – 33). Greenwich, CT: Information Age Publishers.

Folger, R. and Cropanzano, R. (1998). *Organizational justice and human resource management.* Thousand Oaks: London, Sage.

Folger, R. and Cropanzano, R. (2001). Fairness theory: Justice as accountability. In J. Greenberg and R. Cropanzano (Eds.), *Advances in organizational justice.* (pp.1-55). Stanford, CA: Stanford University Press.

Greenberg, J. (1990). Organizational Justice: Yesterday, today and tomorrow. *Journal of Management,* 16, 399-432.

Gurr, T. T. (1970). *Why men rebel.* Princeton, NJ: Princeton University Press.

Lerner, M. J. (1975). The justice motive in human behaviour: Introduction. *Journal of Social Issues,* 31, 1 -20.

Lerner, M. J. (1980). *The belief in a just world: A fundamental delusion.* New York: Plenum.

Lerner, M. J., and Simmons, C. H. (1966). Observer's reaction to the "innocent victim": Compassion or rejection? *Journal of Personality and Social Psychology,* 4, 203-210.

Lam, S.S.K., Schaubroeck, J., and Aryee, S. (2002). Relationship between organisational justice and employee work outcomes: A cross-national study. *Journal of Organisational Behaviour*, 23, 1-18.

Leung, K. and Tong, K. K. (2003). A normative model of justice. In D. Skarlicki, S. Gilliland, and D. Steiner (Eds.), *Research in Social Issues in Management.* (vol. 3). (pp. 97-120). Greenwich, Connecticut: Information Age Publishing.

Leventhal, G. S. (1976). The distribution of rewards and resources in groups and organizations. In L. Berkowitz and E. Walster. (Eds.). *Advances in experimental social psychology.* (vol. 9) (pp. 91-131). New York: Academia Press.

Leventhal, G. S. (1980). What should be done with equity theory? New approaches to the study of fairness in social relationships. In K.J. Gergen, M.S. Greenberg, and R.H. Willis. (Eds.). *Social exchange: Advances in theory and research.* (pp. 27-54). New York: Plenum.

Lind, E. A. (2001). Fairness heuristic theory: Justice judgments as pivotal cognitions in organizational relations. In J. Greenberg and R. Cropanzano. (Eds.). *Advances in organizational justice.* (pp.56-88). Stanford, CA: Stanford University Press.

Lind, E.A., Kanfer, R. and Earley, P.C. (1990). Voice, control and procedural fairness instrumental and noninstrumental concerns in fairness judgments. *Journal of Personality and Social Psychology, 59*, 952-959.

Lind. E. A., Kulik, C.T., Ambrose, M., and de Vera Park, M.V. (1993). Individual and corporate dispute resolution: Using procedural fairness as a decision heuristic. *Administrative Science Quarterly,* 38: 224-251.

Lind, E. A., and Tyler, T. R. (1988). *The social psychology of procedural justice.* New York: Plenum.

Lind, E.A., Tyler, T.R. and Huo, Y.J. (1997). Procedural context and culture: Variations in the antecedents of procedural justice judgments. *Journal of Personality and Social Psychology,* 73, 767-780.

Lissowski, G., Tyszka, T. and Okrasa, W. (1991). Principles of distributive justice: Experiments in Poland and America. *Journal of Conflict Resolution, 35*, 98-119.

Murphy-Berman, V., Berman, J., Singh, P., Pachauri, A., and Kumar, P. (1984). Factors affecting allocation to needy and meritorious recipients: A cross-cultural comparison. *Journal of Personality and Social Psychology, 46,* 1267-72.

Rousseau, D.M., and Parks, J.M. (1992). The contracts of individuals and organizations. In B. Staw and L. L. Cummings (Eds.), *Research in Organizational Behavior.* (vol.15). (pp. 1-44). Greenwich, CT: JAI Press.

Schroeder, D. A., Steel, J. E., Woodell, A. J. and Bembenek, A. F. (2003). Justice within social dilemmas. *Personality and Social Psychology Review, 7,* 374 – 387.

Skitka, L. J. (2003). Of different minds: An accessible identity model of justice reasoning. *Personality and Social Psychology Review, 7*, 286 – 297.

Skitka, L. J. and Houston, D. (2001). When due process is of no consequence: Moral mandates and presumed defendant guilt or innocence. *Social Justice Research, 14*, 305-326.

Skitka, L. J. and Mullen, E. (2002). Understanding judgments of fairness in a real-world political context: A test of the value protection model of justice reasoning. *Personality and Social Psychology Bulletin*, 28, 1419-1429.

Skitka, L. J., Winquist, J. and Hutchinson, S. (2003). Are outcome fairness and outcome favorability distinguishable psychological constructs? A meta-analytic review. *Social Justice Research*, 16, 309 – 341.

Stouffer, S. A., Suchman, E. A., DeVinney, L. C., Star, S. A., and Williams, R. A. (1949). *The American Soldier: Adjustments during army life.* (vol. 1). Princeton, NJ: Princeton University Press.

Thibaut, J. and Walker, L. (1975). *Procedural Justice: A psychological analysis.* Hillsdale, NJ: Lawrence Erlbaum Associates.

Tyler, T. R., and Lind, E. A. (1992). A relational model of authority in groups. In M. P. Zanna. (Ed.). *Advances in experimental social psychology.* (vol. 25). (pp.115-19). San Diego, CA: Academia Press.

Tyler, T.R., Boeckmann, R. J., Smith, H.J., and Huo, Y.J. (1997). *Social justice in a diverse society.* Boulder, CO: Westview.

Van Prooijen, J.W., van den Bos, K., and Wilke, H.A.M. (2002). Procedural justice and status: Status salience as antecedent of procedural fairness effects. *Journal of Personality and Social Psychology,* 83, 1353-1361.

In: Justice as a Basic Human Need
Editor: Anthony Taylor, pp. 95-111
ISBN 1-59454-915-X

Chapter 9

MENTAL HEALTH CONSUMERS, SOCIAL JUSTICE AND THE HISTORICAL ANTECEDENTS OF OPPRESSION

Palmer Reg Orovwuje and A. J. W. Taylor

ABSTRACT

People suffering from mental disability and mental illness are among the most disadvantaged groups in society. They suffer severe personal and distress, and they are stigmatized, discriminated against, marginalized, and often left vulnerable. They are denied civil, political, and social rights, and are treated less than fairly in legal procedures, clinical practice, and institutional management. Consumers themselves in recovery have likened their plight to those of other oppressed minority groups.

This paper illustrates the theme, and argues that the 'demonisation' of the mentally ill does not have its foundations in the early days of primitive superstition, so much as in the more recent period of European Enlightenment and the Age of Reason. It suggests that the change of intellectual climate brought socio-political measures of exclusion that made social justice virtually unattainable for people with mental illness. But it also points to the emergence of strong family and mental health support groups, together with the relatively recent recognition of human rights for all, and some aspects of consumerism, that collectively have brought a change of response from bureaucrats and health professionals that is beginning to redress the wrongs. It exemplifies the thesis that justice is indeed a basic human need that no person should be denied.

INTRODUCTION

The personalized nature of mental illness obscures from general view the intolerable burden of private and public distress that people with serious mental illness carry. Invariably the mentally ill encounter rejection and humiliation that is in some way tantamount to a 'second illness' (Perlin 2000; Schulze and Angermeyer, 2003). The combination either disrupts or puts beyond reach the usual personal and social life stages of marriage, family life, raising children, sexual relationships, choice of treatment, affordable housing, transportation, education and gainful employment. It severely restricts participation in politics, legal processes, cultural events, recreational activities, and social circles. Lacking financial and social support, if not rejection from society, the mentally ill tend to neglect themselves and their diet, and frequently they delay seeking treatment. When finally they do go for help their reception often is poor, their mental and physical state is difficult to assess, and their response to medication is unpredictable. Too commonly iatrogenic effects arise from their treatment to compromise further their health and life expectations (Cohen, 2002; Drukker, and van Os, 2003)[1].

Accordingly, this chapter will focus on the social, economic, and political circumstances surrounding the mentally ill, and on the underlying historico/philosophical justifications for the psychiatric treatments they received. It will touch on matters of social injustice, refer to the stigma that prevails against the illness, and to the stereotypical attitudes and prejudices held against the patients that militate against their recovery. Then it will make a brief excursion into the history of psychiatry, before relating all these matters to the New Zealand scene.

The Legacy of the European Enlightenment and the Age of Reason

Without attempting to précis Zilboorg and Henry's (1941) authoritative exposition on the ancient and medieval aspects of the topic, the continuing legacy of discrimination against the mentally ill is thought principally to stem from the so-called Age of Reason and Enlightenment. Despite the benefits of using reason to overcome centuries of bigotry, superstition, and religious explanations for mental illness, the epoch inflated the value of reason at the expense of the membership of society. Certainly, coming after the enrichment of creativity in the Renaissance, the period brought freedom to examine the notions of progress and advancement, and the potential use science for the benefit of mankind. But the concern for reason and order led the protagonists to criticize, condemn, and crush whatever they considered to be foolish and unreasonable. Its adoption led society to rid itself of 'unreasonable' elements, and to build huge institutions in the form of mental hospitals (and prisons) for the containment and social exclusion of 'unreasonable' people (Foucault, 1971). The rationale was that persons experiencing mental illness menaced the proper functioning of an orderly, efficient, progressive, rational society, and they should be treated accordingly (Porter 1987). Inevitably, the movement of the mentally ill from the general population to the outskirts of society, literally and metaphorically, deprived them of full citizenship with the right to make their own choices on the pathway through life.

The newly established institutions for the insane gave psychiatrists statutory powers for the compulsory committal and discretionary treatment of patients. No matter how unjustified, the belief was widespread that medical science was the best way of tackling madness (Bracken, and Thomas, 2001). In the words of the medical historian Roy Porter (2002, p.200) 'the medical treatment of the institutionalised saw striking therapeutic innovations, some

[1] The adverse effects of clinical treatment are well known, with a recent report showing that they account for 12.9% of all hospital admissions (Davis, Lay-Yee, Briant, Schug, Scott, Johnson, and Bingley, 2001).

effective, many dubious, a few dangerous'. For example, Julius Wagner von Jauregg won the Nobel Prize in 1927 for developing a technique of taking blood from patients with tertian malaria and injecting it into patients with paresis. Subsequent trials of the same treatment for patients with schizophrenia were less successful, and even more questionable (Valenstein, 1986: Frese, 1997). Other therapeutic long-shots included the over-confident introduction but intellectually indefensible camphor and insulin injections to induce coma, anxiolytic drugs, benzodiazopines and the phenothiazines, prolonged sleep-therapy induced by barbiturates, and electroconvulsive therapy (ECT)[2]. Then Egas Moniz developed prefrontal lobotomy as a conventional psychiatric treatment, and in 1949 he too was awarded the Nobel Prize although the widespread adoption of such neurosurgery was questionable (Donnelly, 1980). As Bracken and Thomas (2004) commented, or perhaps lamented, while few people question the enterprise of general medicine, many do not hesitate to be critical of psychiatry – witness the growth of several strong anti-psychiatry movements over the last 50 years, and the scepticism of psychiatry as a science (Ingleby, 1980; Davis1997).

Aside from such 'treatments' – that should have brought into prominence the dictum that the first obligation of the clinician is to do no harm to patients - isolation in hospitals that society imposed on the mentally ill, deprived them of the capacity to fend for themselves, and it compounded their internal feelings of distress (Kierkgaard, 1941: Arendt, 1958). Hospital routines brought boredom, monotony, and depersonalization that Barton (1959) termed 'institutional neurosis'. To the perceptive it made clear once again the importance for human beings to interact with their regular environments[3], and to receive individual psychological treatment. The perception gave rise to schools of phenomenology and psychoanalysis that, with few exceptions the established health professionals, steeped as they were in the reductionism of biological psychiatry, resisted.

The advent of deinstitutionalization in the political sixties,brought people with mental illness face-to-face with an unprepared general public. Unless their families could care for them, it generated problems of homelessness with people either living on the streets or committing petty crimes iun order to be accommodated in prison. Although no longer hospitalised, the mentally ill began to see themselves as being members of a rejected, excluded, and oppressed minority groups similar to those traditionally excluded on ethnic, religious, and racial lines. Their negative experiences generated criticism of mental health professionals and the services they provided, and it led their families to join forces to challenge the prevailing assumption that recovery necessarily rested entirely with the medical profession.

For psychiatrists the nadir came in the legal field, in which precedents are much respected, when expert forensic psychiatric opinion was declared 'especially entitled to little or no weight' (Commonwealth v Patskin, 1953), and psychiatric testimony in criminal cases was viewed as 'attempting to cloud our moral standards and to ignore the limits of community tolerance' (Weitzel, 1997). It was accompanied by a growing awareness that the empowerment of patients would be an underlying factor in their recovery (Meagher, 1994; 1995). But after more than a hundred years of patients' rights and consumer rights activity,

[2] The place of ECT remains controversial, despite the use of muscle relaxants, anaesthetics, and improved recovery procedures, because the consequential memory loss causes serious complications for many patients - although the treatment is firmly believed to modify the suicidal risk for others. The treatment was introduced 70 years ago, and it is high time it was properly assessed by clinical researchers.

[3] The relationship having been established first by the Ancient Greeks.

service users are still somewhat disenfranchised. For that reason the deprivation of fundamental rights raises significant issues of social justice and citizenship that need further consideration.

Social Justice and the Mentally Ill

Social justice should ensure fairness and equality, reduce inequalities in wealth and income, and recognize and protect the dignity and self-esteem of all. It should also encourage the participation of the most vulnerable and disadvantaged in society. According to Rawls (1971)

> the 'primary subject of the principles of social justice is the basic structure of society, the arrangement of major social institutions into one scheme of cooperation. These principles govern the assignment of rights and duties in the institutions and they determine the appropriate distribution of benefits and burdens of social life. Institutions have rules that define roles and functions, offices and positions, rights and duties, powers and immunities. Such rules specify certain forms of actions as permissible, others as forbidden; and they provide for certain penalties and defenses'.

The Rawls' conception of justice depends on a society in which a) everyone accepts, and knows that others accept, the same principles of justice, and b) the basic institutions generally satisfy, and are generally known to satisfy, these principles. In fact, his public conception of social justice seems to be the fundamental charter for a well-ordered society. His simple definition reflects the equal distribution of the social values of liberty and opportunity, income and wealth, and the social bases of self respect – unless an unequal distribution might be to the advantage of all (Rawls 1971). He is concerned for the organization of society and its institutions, and with the need to balance them in accordance with the values of equality, liberty, mutualism, cooperation, and community (Gil, 1994).

However, in practice societies are seldom well ordered, because of the prevalence of self-interest, conflicts, and competitiveness. There is disagreement about which principles should define the basic terms of interpersonal associations, and about what the proper distribution of the benefits and burdens of social cooperation should be. The different conceptions and the complexity in balancing competing claims are reflected in government policies, and they often have an unintended impact on groups for which they are designed. In defence, Plant (1999) argued that social justice requires governments 'to work with the grain of the market', implying the acceptance of choice according to the particular theory that prevails at the time decisions are made.

Currently the free market ideology prevails, with an almost exclusive emphasis on individual achievement at the expense of social responsibilities (cf. Taylor, chapter 1 in the present book). It provides yet another rationale for excluding the vulnerable and disadvantaged, especially those with mental health problems (Kelsey 1995; Orovwuje, 2001)). Yet in quite an unexpected way the economic model has brought some positive changes that have affected the quality of treatment. For example the change from 'patient and doctor' to 'consumer and supplier' has removed much of the unequal status that once obtained. It gives consumers a right to be heard, and makes health professionals more responsive and accountable for their practices.

Following this line of argument, mental health has once more become a morally significant issue that calls for redefinition. With this in mind, mental health may be defined as the capacity of individuals and groups to interact with each other and with their environment in ways to promote their subjective well being and optimal development. The redefinition makes clear that mental health is more than the absence of mental illness. It is the fulfilment of human potential shaped by factors such as biological make-up, gender roles, family life, human relationships, work opportunities, educational achievements, and a variety of structural and socio-economic determinants (Commonwealth Department of Health and Aged Care and Australian Institute of Health and Welfare, 1999).

From such an appraisal, mental ill-health can be construed along the spectrum of cognitive, emotional and behavioural disorders that interferes with the lives, wellbeing, and performance of people at home, school, work, and in society at large. It includes the conventional clinical diagnoses of cognitive impairment and disabilities, phobias, panic attacks, drug-related harm, anxiety, post traumatic stress disorder, personality disorders, depressive disorders, schizophrenia and psychoses. Hence the term 'mental disorder' should become a diagnosis requiring liberal and humanitarian remedies – much like the 'clinically recognizable set of symptoms or behaviours associated in most cases with distress and interference with personal functions' as suggested by the .WHO (1992).

However, there is no doubt that mental illness, like physical illness, reflects (without necessarily being caused by) an imbalance in some internal mechanism affecting natural functions. Through evolution these natural functions have had beneficial effects upon the organism's survival (Frances, 1994; Roth and Kroll, 1986; Wakefield, 1992). They derive from interactions with the environment, and should be appraised as a part of that equation rather than apart from it. The exclusive focus on either extreme is ideological and inadequate. On the one hand the organic model of mental illness leaves out the significant ways people structure their world to give meaning to their lives, and it causes unnecessary institutional, pharmacological, and surgical interference, and it constitutes a violation of the integrity of the mentally ill (Ricoeur, 1992). On the other, the exclusive emphasis on psychosocial factors ignores the carefully monitored and moderate treatments that can contribute to the recovery of patients – especially those with either psychosomatic or somatopsychic conditions (depending on the major emphasis of the mental and physical components of the matrix of factors).

Stigma, Stereotypes and Prejudice

Whatever the causative emphasis adopted to account for mental illness, the stigma, stereotypes, and prejudices about it should not be overlooked, because they induce further social isolation, limit further the life chances of those affected, and make them reluctant to seek proper help (Rosenfield 1997). It induces a large percentage of the general population including friends, relatives, neighbours, and fellow workers to avoid them (Angermeyer and Matschinger, 1995). Some mental health professionals are known to make them wait longer for attention at clinics, treat them disrespectfully, do not take their views seriously, and impart the feeling that pharmacological intervention is the standard psychiatric treatment (Schulze and Angermeyer, 2003).

Somewhat similar negative attitudes towards the mentally ill were also evident among a group of university social science students in the 1960's at a time during the revolution in psychiatric care when they might have been expected to be more tolerant. Such negative attitudes remained with little change among comparable groups that were surveyed at regular intervals thereafter (Green, McCormick, Walkey and Taylor, 1987). However, the most recent replication of such studies did show some improvement towards the mentally ill as a general group, but not towards the insane whom students still regarded as more 'cold', dangerous', dirty', 'insincere', and 'worthless' than the other groups with which they were compared (Wilson and Bryson, 2004).

Often the stereotypes have vestigial roots associated with the belief that mental illness is 'sinful, evil, God's punishment, criminal, and demonic' (Rosen, 1969 cited in Perlin 2000, p. 36: Bromberg, 1975, pp.63-64). Whether on religious or pagan grounds, the beliefs perpetuate and reify social, cultural, medical, behavioural, and political myths (Denzin, 1992). They reach beyond the realm of immediate social interaction to the stereotypes of race, gender, ethnicity, economic class, and culture[4]. They have been attributed to the over-representation of minority cultural groups in state psychiatric hospitals, and to the consequent over-estimation of psychopathology in racial and religious minorities (Perlin, 2000). Rosen (2003) argued that the psychiatric stigma 'is culturally applied, sometimes as an artefact of colonization', saying that 'Aboriginal, Torres Strait Islander, and Maori communities where individuals with mental illness frequently have to contend with the "double whammy" in stigmatization and discrimination due to dispossession and devaluing by white society, and by being colonized and controlled by mental health services'. The stigmatization and discrimination continues through imbalances and injustices that exist in social structures, political decision-making, and legal regulations. As Lord and Dufort (1996) suggested in their socio-political analysis, people with serious mental health problems are an oppressed group – but in factwe consider that they might be regarded as a 'multi-oppressed group', with a lack of power and control, facing stigma, poverty, unemployment, and poor housing, with poor quality mental health and community-based services to boot. On several levels the mentally ill are indeed 'prejudged'.

In 1996 the World Health Organisation took heed and laid down 10 basic principles of mental health law relating to the promotion of mental health and prevention of mental disorders. Recently these were reiterated in an authoritative document regarding the best practices for the treatment of disaster trauma (Mollica, Guerra, Bhasin and Lavelle, 2005, pp.22-23). The principles prescribe adequate access to basic mental health care, assessments to be made in accordance with internationally accepted standards, affirm the use of the least restrictive care, encourage self determination, recommend available and automatic review procedures, the use of qualified decision makers, and showing proper respect for patients. If put into practice they should bring a new dawn in the treatment of mental illness, in which all sides might come to share their strengths and skills to maximise the chance of recovery or rehabilitation of the consumers.

---

[4] Yet there is no active academic and professional forum in which the beliefs can be discussed – as Taylor (1975; 1998; 2003) found at different times when trying to engage anthropologists, psychiatrists, and theologians in debates over exorcism and the attribution of adversity.

Questions remain about the historical source of authority that psychiatrists came to have about the treatment of their patients. In considering the answers, it is necessary to make a brief excursion into history of the treatment of mental illness and the rise of psychiatry as a clinical profession (cf. Mora, 1980).

BRIEF EXCURSION INTO THE HISTORY OF PSYCHIATRY

Before the 18th century the mentally ill were left in the community where they experienced periods of fluctuating support and tolerance. During the agrarian and the industrial revolutions, the unproductive were consigned to institutions run like fiefdoms with autocratically layered and controlled communities. There they were promised asylum so long as they were content to fill their allotted roles and functions. There were a few notable exceptions such as the Hospital Bonifazio in Florence, the Quaker Retreat in York, and the Salpétriere in Pari where Vicenzo Chiarugi (1759-1820), William Tuke (1732-1819), and Philippe Pinel (1745-1826) respectively did much to humanize their confinement.

But in many countries the incarceration proceeded apace, with mental hospitals being built away. from the centres of population, out of sight, out of mind. The distance dislocated patients from their families and friends, and made it for difficult for visitors to access. It also kept psychiatrists away from the mainstream of medicine where traditionally 'grand rounds' were practiced every week before a critical professional audience to review patient care and management. Eventually the segregation of patients and staff, and the poor management and treatment regimes, created problems that percolated through to public attention. In the United States the philanthropist and ex-patient Clifford Beers (1876-1943) was one of the first to challenge the psychiatric status quo. But his call for professionals to be accountable for the outcome of their treatment and for them to respect the human rights of their patients was muffled by the patronizing attitudes of professionals towards him – a patient who by definition often was irrational.

To some extent the avoidance of professional responsibility by psychiatrists at that time can be attributed more to their 'on the job' training, than to the quality of their post-graduate academic and scientific studies. Their specialty was late in emerging from medicine, with Wilhelm Griesinger (1817-1868) being the first Professorial appointee in 1864 in Berlin. Although he held office only for a very short period before he died, to his credit he tried to put psychiatry into the general flow of mainstream academic medicine. He also strove to keep the subject abreast of developments in psychology, because he was convinced that psychology had the same relation to psychiatry as physiology to pathology. More than that, he realized that clinicians should pay attention to the adverse effects of social circumstances such as poverty and unemployment in the causation of mental illness. Accordingly he designed a flow of psychiatric services from community support to hospital admissions and follow-up clinics for the treatment of patients. Gradually, other universities established Chairs in psychiatry[5], but not many of the appointees shared Griesinger's vision of the discipline[6].

---

[5] Chairs in Psychiatry were established in Edinbugh in 1879, Melbourne in 1899, Cornell in 1908, and in London as late as 1936.

[6] New Zealand did not establish its first chair in psychiatry until 1953, partly because the country was settled through a treaty partnership only in 1840, but also because of the determined opposition and pragmatism of generations of its leading psychiatrists from Britain and Scotland. The first to promote the case for such an

Like anyone ahead of the field, Griesinger encountered resistance from several quarters (cf. Güse, and Schmacke, 1980). First there was the dogma of his colleagues in the scholastic school of psychiatry who regarded the mentally ill as living witnesses to God's displeasure with a sinful world who could only be saved by punishment. Then came the powerful move from psychiatrists to get their specialty regarded as a science, in the course of which they made unsustainable, if impressive, claims about the causes of mental illness that had devastating consequences. Emil Kraepelin (1856-1929) was in the lead. In keeping with the respectable nosological tradition of the Swedish botanist Carl Linnaeus (1707-1778), he classified 'the abnormal' into the three broad categories of 'physically conditioned psychoses, endogenous psychoses, and insane personalities (psychopaths)' - all of which *ipso facto* were considered reflections of incurable hereditary degeneracy from which society should be protected.

About the same time, either through clinical despair fanned by the nihilistic philosophy of Friedrich Nietzsche, or the spirit of Prussian pride that had united the nation, many psychiatrists in Germany turned to the application of Galtonian dysgenics as the inevitable treatment for their 'biologically defective' and 'incorrigibly inferior' patients, rather than the more positive eugenics adopted in Britain. Again, according to Güse and Schmacke (1980), 'without governmental pressure', a 'whole generation of psychiatrists turned away from the task of developing therapeutic models and conducting exact etiological research, concentrating instead on the purportedly 'prophylactic elimination' of the mentally ill…(*During*) World War 1 at least 50,000 patients were starved to death in German asylums (*and*) 'in the 1920's the demand within the psychiatric profession for the compulsory sterilization of the mentally ill became increasingly pronounced. Concerns about legality were brushed aside, the circle of patients to be sterilized was widened and criteria for the diagnosis of individual illnesses were extended…. (*In the words of*) Hoche, a university professor and psychiatrist of renown, patients were 'empty shells, dead weights, weaklings, and defective human beings with the character of foreign bodies'.

Then in 1933, when the National Socialists assumed power in Germany they passed a law enabling psychiatrists formally to initiate a programme for the compulsory sterilization of over 200,000 of the mentally ill and their relatives[7]. Soon the Nazis brought Jews, gypsies, and Slavonic people under a policy of racial hygiene and political conformity, and, with the cooperation of the medical profession, they established extermination camps in which an estimated number of six millions were killed through starvation, disease, medical experiments, and asphyxiation.

Later when considering the ethical and moral complicity of the medical fraternity in his country, Hanauske-Abel (1986) referred to the courageous stand of a few professors and their students of the 'Red and White Rose' campaigns against the abuse of patients. In recalling their courage he hoped other doctors might be inspired by their anti-Nazi example to stand against the growing threat of nuclear war that was brewing in the 1980's. In a similar vein

academic appointment at the Otago Medical School was Ernest Beaglehole (1950, p.129), a professor of psychology at Victoria University of Wellington – now the country of four million people has four Chairs in Psychiatry in different university settings.

[7] Porter (2002, pp.186/7) reported that between January 1940 and September 1942, 'in what might be seen as a trial run for the 'final solution', 70,723 mental patients were gassed. The patients were chosen from lists of those whose lives were not considered 'worth living' that were drawn up by nine leading professors of psychiatry and thirty-nine top physicians.

Meyer-Lindenberg (1991) documented the actions of Karsten Jasperson who wrote to Count von Galen the Cardinal of Münster and to Adolf Hitler in 1940 about the excesses perpetrated in the name of medicine. Although some Protestnt Church leaders had also gone to extreme lengths to express theoir opposition to the extermination campaign, this particular letter led to an open breach between the Catholic Church and Nazism on this issue, and it brought a temporary cessation to the racial cleansing programme. However in 1942, Hitler revived the extermination of 'undesirables, and he had the medical profession use their diagnostic skills and lethal methods in death camps in Poland.

To continue the saga of injustice against the mentally ill, in the 1930's many countries other than Germany were concerned about the marginal and economically unproductive groups in their industrialized societies[8]. Although they stopped short of the German large-scale 'final solution', some of them created torturers and death squads for political dissents at home, and they trained units to infiltrate and corrupt the political systems of opponents abroad (see the chapter by Sluka in the present volume).

After World War 2 the public exposure of atrocities perpetrated against defenceless victims in the concentration camps, together with the stirring of human rights and the creation of the United Nations Organisation to prevent a recurrence, brought changes to the treatment of the mentally ill. In the United States, under President Kennedy the *Mental Health Study Act* of 1954 led to the seminal publication *Action for mental health 1961* and to the further *Community Mental Health Act* 1963 that established the National Institute for Mental Health. These political efforts were accompanied by a surfeit of powerful theses by critical observers like Goffman (1961); Blatt (1970), Bates (1977), and Fireside (1979) that added to the clamour for reform of treatments for the mentally ill.

Soon the tall, gaunt piles of red brick institutions on the perimeter of big cities in many countries became derelict monuments to human misery. In the now famous words of Enoch Powell in 1961, then the Minister of Health in Britain:

> 'There they stand, isolated, majestic, imperious, brooded over by gigantic water towers and chimney combined, rising unmistakable and daunting out of the countryside – the asylums which our forefather built with such immense solidarity, to express the notions of their day... {But, he added] do not underestimate their powers of resistance to our assault'.

The Minister, being a former Professor of Philosophy, might have had Henri Foucault (1965) in mind, because the Frenchman had gone so far as to describe mental hospitals as the latest in a long line of human repositories from the medieval Lazar Houses established for lepers – all of which had served the undisclosed need of communities to keep out of sight those of its members it considered currently to be marginal or deviant. But signs of change were under way, even in the bastions of conservatism, with pioneers like Maxwell Jones promoting therapeutic groups in Scotland and England, Ronald Laing (1971) emphasising family dynamics and rejecting biological psychiatry, and David Clark (1974) endeavouring to

[8] New Zealand can claim to be a rare exception to the trend, because in 1928 its Parliament rejected a Bill to sterilize the mentally and morally defective that the Government, the Judiciary, the whole psychiatric fraternity, prison administrators, and educational staff had all promoted. However for whatever reason, the country's leading historians have drawn a discreet veil of silence over the extensive debates in which politicians for the affirmative and their advisers paid attention to the research and opinions of Cyril Burt, Charles Davenport, Henry Goddard, Henry Laughlin, Cesare Lombroso, William McDougall (cf. Taylor, 2005).

convert the whole of Fulbourn Hospital near Cambridge into a therapeutic community, with squads of staff visiting ex-patients in their homes in times of emergency, Writing from Canada, the Hungarian psychiatrist Thomas Szasz (1972), challenged the authority of his colleagues to restrict the civil rights of their patients under the 'myth of mental illness'- and his views still resonate in some quarters (cf. Sheppard, 2002).

In Italy, the psychiatrist Franco Basaglia made the boldest move when he created a number of accessible small short-stay centres in local communities for mental patients **before** closing the main hospital for all but the most in need of secure facilities[9]. Then he persuaded the Italian Parliament to approve the extension of the scheme to all provinces (Dell'Acqua, 1985; Robb, 1986). Other countries, including New Zealand, began to follow suit, although invariably the devolution of mental hospitals and the de-institutionalisation of patients was done more speedily than the establishment of community services to provide alternative care (Haines and Abbott, 1985), and there was a distinct lack of central guidance (Brunton, 2001).

In an earlier paper Brunton (1985) had written that for almost a hundred years an 'unwitting six months curability test' had been applied to patients, following which they were regarded as 'lifers: the number of patients so designated between 1873 and 1945 varied from 76% to 60%. A year later in a refreshing frank disclosure to a conference, James Methven (1986), the Chairman of the Australia and New Zealand College of Psychiatrists, admitted that:

> 'Our treatment bag is pitifully small. ...The number of proven treatments at our disposal is small. Constant effort is needed to develop and evaluate new ways of treating the people who come through our doors. Waiting out natural remission is only useful in a limited number of cases. Unfortunately, numbers of our patients are chronic when they arrive and they remain so despite our best efforts. Perhaps that is why fashion in treatment has been so dominant? ... Our treatment procedures are not terribly effective and mostly we don't evaluate them but leave that to overseas people'.

Such disclosures were influential. They corroborated the perceptions of mental health consumers that they were victims of systemic oppression and marginalisation (Gordon and Sheehan, 1986). They galvanised patients in their moves to seek social justice.

Personal Experiences, Frustration and Distress on the New Zealand Scene

In June 1989 the Consumer Advisory Network (CAN) in New Zealand explored the attitudes of consumers and providers to the existing mental health services. As an association of inter-regional psychiatric consumer groups, it wanted to assess the degree of consumer participation in mental health services through their validation, power and information sharing, participatory activities, advocacy, and funding. In some ways the network was not dissimilar to the movements for Civil Rights, Gay Liberation, and feminism (Bassman, 1997).

---

[9] The emphasis is added in bold face, because elsewhere the closure of mental hospitals was often taken as an opportunity to save money rather than to spend it more wisely in reforming the treatment of the mentally.

Although on the one side the Network was not entirely free of preconceptions, and on the other there had been some liberating changes in the provision of clinical services, it still found the treatment regime 'far too controlling, with patients still complaining of being 'over medicated'. It declared that 'nothing is more depressing than being lined up beside the medical model with all its dreary determinism'. Consumers felt they were neglected, not listened to, not tolerated, and perceived by society as unattractive. They described their care as paternalistic and based on the belief that they were incompetent. Those that had been committed involuntarily to hospital felt they had been stripped of their rights; and locked away, with no control over their destiny.

From the results CAN identified various injustices in the mental health system, and it regretted the failure of clinicians to realize that consumers 'think differently'. It considered patients had been subject to tokenism in consumer participation while clinicians payed lip service to them by not sharing power. It believed that non-participation by consumers resulted in the further abuse of power, the lack of clinical and managerial accountability, blockages to consumer self-realization, the lack of trust between consumers and clinicians, insensitivities in care systems, stigmatisation, and discrimination. It also advocated supportive provisions for indigenous Maori because of their double jeopardy within mental health services – i.e. being both patients and being marginalized as members of a minority group that only recently had begun to have equal status with European colonists recognized under the articles of *The Treaty of Waitangi* that their forebears had signed in 1840. Consequently CAN urged mental health consumers to gain acceptance fully as participating citizens in any programme intended to be for their benefit, and to take part in the education of providers and the community (Consumer Advisory Network, 1989).

Meanwhile in response to a fatality caused by a recently discharged mental patient, the Government appointed a formal Committee of Inquiry to review procedures for admission, discharge and other matters related to the adequacy and quality of psychiatric services (The Mason Committee (1988). The Committee responded accordingly, with legislative recommendations that were put immediately into effect. But within a few years the Committee was re-established with a much wider brief, because of the mounting dissatisfaction being expressed publicly about psychiatric services. It found no less than 67 official inquiries were pending at the one time, of which 76% involved the kind of service provided in psychiatric hospitals (The Mason Committee, 1996, p. 19). It described the mental health services as being 'in a state of crisis…in disarray after decades of financial neglect…[the] gradual disintegration of systems, a flight of expertise, a loss of morale by those who remain within the system and a potential loss of confidence by the community' (The Mason Committee, 1996, p.169). It went on to make recommendations for a substantial strengthening of the mental health sector at all levels, particularly in forensic psychiatry, with a substantial allocation of budgetary resources, and a fusillade of impressive policy documents that included proposals for recruiting more trained staff and. for promoting clinical research.

The New Zealand Government responded promptly by setting up a National Mental Health Strategy, followed in 1998 by an independent Mental Health Commission with the authority to address some of the injustices in the care of people with mental illness, complete with a budget to ensure its implementation. The very same year the Mental Health Commission (MHC) (1998) produced a *Blueprint for Mental Health Services in New Zealand* to remedy the faults. At regular intervals since then the Commission has monitored and reported on the progress of the Ministry of Health and of District Health Boards in relation to the aforementioned National Mental Health Strategy.

However, in 2002 the Ministry of Health's briefing to the incoming Minister of Health indicated that the increased funding and efforts in training had not brought the changes desired. The mental health services had not adopted the philosophy of recovery that a) de-emphasized psychopathology and consumer deficits, b) emphasized that persons with psychiatric disabilities can recover even though they might still be symptomatic, c) involved consumer groups actively in the planning and delivery of services, and d) encouraged hope and purposeful management of the condition by the mentally ill that would bring improved functioning across their life domains. It commented that workforce problems and the lack of comprehensive integrated planning put service expansion at risk and created systemic barriers to change. It found 'ignorance and discrimination' affecting the inter-face between mental health and other sectors', and it re-affirmed that discrimination against people with mental illness restricted their access to income, housing, employment, education, social participation, and access to professional help.

The briefing paper also drew attention to the continuing misperception in the community that violent behaviour emanated from mental illness. It noted that some neighbourhoods were trying to prevent people with mental illness from residing in their locality, and were creating pressure for the Government to restore the earlier institutional model of patient care. While acknowledging that consumer advocacy groups had been established, it concluded that the necessary participation of the wider community as a component of a recovery had yet to be achieved.

CONCLUSION

The yearnings of people with mental illness to be recognized as full citizens able to enjoy the same rights as other citizens have yet to be satisfied. Aspects of the historical paradigm of oppression and disenfranchisement still resonate from earlier days, and they dominate institutional behaviour in terms of public relationships, public policies, and clinical management. Social exclusion from the public domain often remains the preferred approach for dealing with mental illness – despite many complaints that are still surfacing about the mismanagement of patients under the previous regime – including the physical abuse of adolescents who are now grown-up and able to challenge their abusers. Clinicians, families/whanau and care-givers wrestle with the stereotypes and issues of disempowerment. In the execution of their duties, law-makers, the media, judicial establishments, and law enforcement agencies reflect the unjustified public expressions of concern.

However, psychiatric treatments have improved, and handbooks are available that attest to the scientific evidence of the treatments proposed (cf. Andrews, Crino, Hunt, Lampe and Page, 1994: Mollica, Guerra, Bhasin and Lavelle, 2005). As the World Health Organization Comparative Studies (1973; 1979) have demonstrated, there is now a far better long-term outcome in the developing for patients with schizophrenia than the developed countries, particularly in rural regions (Rosen, 2003). Explanations to account for the phenomenon are still unclear, but they include the greater social integration of the mentally ill into society, involving the mentally ill in traditional healing rituals, supporting them in work at a lower level of functioning, not isolating the family through social embarrassment, including external kinship systems and communal networks of the menally ill in processes of recovery, diffusing family tensions, and sharing burdens. Other factors in the developing world that promoted greater tolerance and community support for people with serious mental illness include the absence of large scale institutional care from traditional mental health care systems, the rural nature of agrarian society, the strength of extended family systems, explanatory models of illness that place the causes external to the patient, and evidence that symptoms of psychosis are more readily reversible (Leff, Sartorius, Joblensky and Eruberg, 1992)

It remains for strategies to be developed that change negative perceptions and inequities for people with mental illness in the economically more-developed parts of the world. Access to education, welfare benefits, and other opportunities in society should not depend on ethnicity, disability, race, gender, religion, or membership of any group. Paradoxically, problems of inequality can be exacerbated both by treating members of minorities groups the same as members of the majority, as well as by treating them differently (Minow, 1990). Above all the strategies should be underpinned by the inalienable respect for the mentally ill. No matter how similar or how different mental patients might otherwise appear to be from other people in their communities, they are all part of mankind, and they should not be denied their equal share of opportunities to thrive as human beings. There is a moral and ethical requirement for society to respond to the suffering of the innocent (Amato, 1990). It is indeed a matter of recognizing the importance of justice as a basic human need for the mentally ill, as for everyone else.

REFERENCES

Allport, G. W. (1959/1979). *The nature of prejudice*. New York: Doubleday Anchor.

Andrews, G. Crino, R., Hunt, C., Lampe, L., and Page, A. (1994). *The treatment of Anxiety disorders: Clinician's guide and patient's manual.* Cambridge University Press.

Amato, J. (1990). *Victims and values: A history and theory of suffering*. New York: Praeger.

Angermeyer, M. C; and Matschinger, H .V. (1995). Violent attacks on public figures by persons suffering from psychiatric disorder. The effect on social distance towards the mentally ill. *European Archives of Psychiatry and Clinical Neuroscience*, 245, 159-164.

Angermeyer, M. C. and Schulze, B. (2001). *Reinforcing stereotypes: How the focus on forensic cases in news reporting may influence public attitudes towards the mentally ill. International Journal of Law and Psychiatry*, 24, 469-486

Arendt, H. (1958). *The human condition*. Chicago: University of Chicago Press.

Barton, R. (1959). *Institutional neuroses*. London: Wright.

Bassman, R. (1997). The mental health system: experiences from both sides of the locked doors: *Professional Psychology: Research and Practice*, 283, 238-242.

Bates, E.M. (1977). *Models of madness*. St Lucia: University of Queensland Press.

Beaglehole, E. (1950). *Mental health in New Zealand.* Wellington: Price-Milburn.

Blatt, B. (1970). *Exodus from pandemonium: Human abuse and reformation in public policy.* Boston: Allyn and Bacon.

Bracken, P., and Thomas, P. (2001). Post-psychiatry. A new direction for mental health. *British Medical Journal*, 322, 724-727.

Bromberg, W. (1975). *From Shaman to psychotherapist: a history of the treatment of mental illness*. Chicago: H. Regeneracy.

Brunton, W. (1985). Deinstitutionalisation: A romance for all seasons? In H. Haines, and M. Abbott. (Eds.). (1986). *The future of mental health services in New Zealand, Proceedings the Mental Health Foundation of New Zealand Conference.*vol.2. (pp.44-63). Auckland.

Brunton, W. (2001.). *Mental health: The case of deinstitutionalisation.* In P. Davis and T. Ashton. (Eds). *Health and public policy in New Zealand.* (ch. 9). Oxford University Press.

Clark, D.H. (1974). *Social therapy in psychiatry.* Harmondsworth: Penguin.

Cohen, C.I. (2002). Social inequality and health: Will psychiatry assume center stage? http://psychservices.psychiatryonline.org vol53No8.

Commonwealth Department of Health and Aged Care and Australian Institute of Health and Welfare. (1999). *National health priorities areas report: Mental health 1998.* Summary. Canberra: AusInfo.

Commonwealth v Patskin. (1953).100A, 2d 472, 475 Pa.

Consumer Advisory Network. (1989). *Report from the Mental Health Consortium: Consumer participation in mental health services.* Wellington. (Private circulation). pp.20.

Davis, P., Lay-Yee, R., Briant, R., Schug,S., Scott, A., Johnson, S., and Bingley, W. (2001). *Adverse events in New Zealand public hospitals: Principal findings from a national survey.* Wellington: Ministry of Health. Occasional Paper #3. pp.88.

Dell'Acqua, G. (1985). The end of the mental hospital: A review of the psychiatric experience in Trieste. *Acta Psychiatrica Scandanavica*, Supplement 316, 415, 1985.

Denzin, N.K. (Ed.). (1992). *Symbolic interactionism and cultural studies: the politics of interpretation.* Oxford: Blackwell.

Donnelly, J. (1980). Psychosurgery. In H.I. Kaplan, Freedman, A.M., and Sadock, B.J. (Eds.). *Comprehensive textbook of psychiatry /111.* (sec.31.6). Baltimore: Williams and Wilkins.

Drukker, M., and van Os, J. (2003). Mediators of neighbourhood socio-economic deprivation and the quality of life. *Social Psychiatry and Psychiatric Epidemiology*, 38, 698-706.

Fireside, H. (1979). *Soviet psychoprisons.* London: Norton.

Frances, A. (1994). DSM 1V meets philosophy. *Journal of Medicine and Philosophy*, 19, 207-218.

Foucault, M. (1971). *Madness and civilization. A history of insanity in the age of reason.* London: Tavistock.

Frese, F.J. (1997). The mental health consumer's perspective on mandatory treatment. In M.R. Munetz. (Ed.). *Can mandatory treatment be therapeutic? New directions for mental health services*, No. 75. San Francisco: Jossie-Base.

Gil, D. (1994). Confronting social justice and oppression. In F. Reamer (Ed), *The foundations of social work knowledge.* (page numbers?) New York: Columbia University Press.

Goffman, E. (1961). *Asylums.* New York: Doubleday.

Gordon, L., and Sheehan, C. (1986). Consumer perspectives on mental health treatment. In H. Haines, and M. Abbott. (Eds.). (1986). *The future of mental health services in New Zealand, Proceedings the Mental Health Foundation of New Zealand Conference.*vol.2. (pp.44-63). Auckland

Green, D.G., McCormick, I.A., Walkey, F.H., and Taylor, A.J.W. (1987). Community attitudes to mental illness - Twenty-two years on. *Social Science and Medicine*, 24, 5, 417-422.

Güse, H.G., and Schmacke, N. (1980). Psychiatry and the origins of Nazism. *International Journal of Health Services*, 10, 2, 177-198.

Haines, H., and Abbott, M. (Eds.). (1986). *The future of mental health services in New Zealand, Proceedings the Mental Health Foundation of New Zealand Conference.*vol.2. Auckland. Mental Health Foundation.

Hanauske-Abel, H.M. (1986). From Nazi holocaust to nuclear holocaust: A lesson to learn? *The Lancet*, August 2, 271-273.

Henry, G.W. (1941). Mental hospitals. In G. Zilboorg and G.W.Henry. (Eds.). *A history of mental illness.* (ch.14). New York: Norton.

Jacobs, D. (1994). Environmental failure-oppression is the only cause of psycho-pathology. *Journal of Mind and Behavior*, 15, 1 and 2, 1-18.

Johnstone, M. (2001). Stigma, social justice and the rights of the mentally ill: Challenging the status quo. *Australian and New Zealand Journal of Mental Health Nursing*, 10, 200-209.

Kelsey, J. (1995). *The New Zealand experiment.* Auckland: University Press/Bridget Williams Books.

Kierkegaard, S. (1941). *The sickness unto death*. Princeton: Princeton University Press.

Laing, R.D. (1971). *The politics of the family and other essays.* New York: Pantheon.

Leff, J., Sartorius, N., Joblensky, A., and Eruberg, G. (1992). The international pilot study of schizophrenia- Five-year follow-up findings. *Psychological Medicine*, 22, 131-145.

Lord, J., and Dufort, F. (Eds.). (1996). Power and oppression in mental health. *Canadian Journal of Community Mental Health*, 15, 2, 1-185.

Meagher, J. (1994). Empowering consumers. *Open Mind*, Summer.? PAGES.

Meagher, J. (1995). *Partnership or pretence*. Sydney: Psychiatric Rehabilitation Association.

Mental Health Commission. (1998). *Blueprint for mental health services in New Zealand.* Wellington. pp.115.

Mental Health Commission. (2002). *Briefings to the incoming Minister of Health.* Wellington. August. pp.60.

Methven, J. (1986). The middle ground. In H. Haines, and M. Abbott. (eds). (1986). *The future of mental health services in New Zealand, Proceedings the Mental Health Foundation of New Zealand Conference.*vol.2. (pp.111-16). Auckland.

Meyer-Lindenberg, J. (1991). The holocaust and German psychiatry. *British Journal of Psychiatry*, 150, 7-12.

Ministry of Health. (2002). *Doing Better for New Zealanders: Better health Better participation Reduced inequalities: Advice to the incoming Minister.* Wellington. pp.72 available online at http://www.moh.govt.nz/moh.nsf/49ba80c00757b8804c256673001d47d0/d1e2eba61963d020cc256c24007841d4?OpenDocument

Ministry of Health. (2004). *Statement of intent.* Wellington. pp.135. available online at http://www.moh.govt.nz/moh.nsf/0/77F1C4CC86F26A4DCC256B9C000D338B/$File/MinistryofHealthStatementofIntent200405.pdf

Minow, M. (1990). *Making all the difference: inclusion, exclusion, and American law.* London: Cornell University Press.

Mollica, R.F., Guerra, R., Bhasin, R., and Lavelle, J. (Eds.). (2005). *Project 1 billion: Book of best practices: Trauma and the role of Mental Health in post-conflict recovery.* Geneva: WHO.

Mora, G, (1980). Historical and theoretical trends in psychiatry. In H.I. Kaplan, A.M. Freedman, and B.J. Sadock. (Eds.). *Comprehensive textbook of psychiatry/ 111.* (ch.1).Baltimore: Williams and Wilkins.

Nelson, G., Lord, J., and Ochocka, J. (2001). Empowerment and mental health community: narrative of psychiatric consumer/survivor. *Journal of Community and Applied Social Psychology*, 11, 125-142.

New York State Office of Mental Health. (1990). *Final report: Task Force on Stigma and Discrimination.* March 6.

Oruvwuje, P.R. (2001). The business model and social work: A conundrum for social work practice. *Social Work in Health Care*, 34, 1-2, 59-70.

Pearson, A. (2001). Where have we come from, where are we going to? Visioning for people pursuing recovery and partnership after mental illness. Paper presented at 'Forging our future' conference, Sydney: obtainable from Mental Health Commission. P.O. Box 12-479, Wellington, New Zealand.

Perlin, M.L. (2000). *The hidden prejudice: Mental disability on trial.* Washington DC: American Psychological Association.

Plant, R. (1999). Social justice. In R. Walker. (Ed.). *Ending child povert: Popular welfare for the 21st century?* (pp.55-64). Bristol: Policy Press.

Porter, R.A. (1987). *A social history of madness: stories of the insane.* London: Weidenfeld and Nicolson.

Porter, R. A. (2002). *Madness: A brief history.* Oxford University Press.

Rawls, J. (1971) *The theory of justice.* Oxford University Press. *Report of the Committee of Inquiry into procedures at Oakley Hospital and related matters.* (1983). Wellington: Government Printer.

Ricoeur, P. (1992). *Oneself in another.* Chicago: University of Chicago Press.

Robb, J.H. (1986). The Italian Health services: Slow revolution or permanent? *Social Science and Medicine*, 22, 6, 619-627.

Rosen, A. (2003). What developed countries can learn from developing countries in challenging psychiatric stigma. *Australasian Psychiatry*, 11, Supplement 1, s89-s95.

Rosenfield, S. (1997). Labelling mental illness: the effect of received services and perceived stigma on life satisfaction. *American Sociological Review*, 62, 660-672.

Roth, M., and Kroll J. (1986). *The reality of mental illness.* Great Britain: Cambridge University Press.

Schulze, B., and Angermeyer, M.C. (2003). Subjective experiences of stigma: A focus group study of schizophrenic patients, their relatives and mental health professionals. *Social Science and Medicine*, 56, 299-312.

Sheppard, M. (2002). Mental health and social justice: Gender, race and psychological consequencies of unfairness. *British Journal of Social Work*, 32, 779-797.

Szasz, T. (1961). *The myth of mental illness*. New York: Harper and Row.

Taylor, A.J.W. (1975). Possession and dispossession. *Expository Times*, 12, 259-263.

Taylor, A.J.W. (1998). Observations from a cyclone stress/trauma assignment in the Cook Islands. *Traumatology: The International Journal*, 4.1, Article 3. http://www.fsu.edu/~trauma/

Taylor, A.J.W. (2003). The spread of Antarctic and South Pacific research behind the *2002 Hunter Award. New Zealand Journal of Psychology*, 32, 2, 110-122.

Taylor A.J.W. (2005). Sir Thomas Hunter versus the eugenics campaign of the 1920's. *New Zealand Journal of History*, 39, 2, 195-214.

The Mason Committee. (1988). *Report of the Committee of Inquiry into procedures used in certain psychiatric hospitals for the admission, discharge or release on leave of certain classes of patient.* Wellington: Ministry of Health.

The Mason Committee. (1996). Report of the Ministerial Inquiry to the Minister of Health Hon Jenny Shipley: Inquiry under Section 47 of the Health and Disability Services Act 1993 in respect of certain mental health services. Wellington: Ministry of Health.

Valenstein, E.S. (1986). *Great and desperate cures*. New York, Basic Books.

Weitzel, W. (1997). Public skepticism: Forensic psychiatry's albatross. *Bulletin of American Academic Psychiatry and Law*, 5, 459.

Wilson, M., and Bryson, K. (2004). A 20-year follow-up of a 20-year follow-up: Changes in attitudes to mental illness since the 1960's. Victoria University of Wellington, Paper presented at New Zealand Psychological Society Annual Conference.

World Health Organization, (1973). *The international pilot study of schizophrenia.* Vol.1. Geneva.

World Health Organization. (1979). *Schizophrenia. An international follow-up study.* Chichester. Wiley.

Zilboorg, G., and Henry, G.W. (1941). (Eds.). *A history of mental illness.* New York: Norton.

In: Justice as a Basic Human Need
Editor: Anthony Taylor, pp. 113-133
ISBN 1-59454-915-X

Chapter 10

On Common Ground: Justice, Human Rights and Survival

Jeffrey Sluka

'Where there is no justice, there will be violence. We decry the need to resort to violence. Those responsible for violence are not those who must resort to it as a last resort. The responsibility of violence rests upon the souls of those who deny justice'. -- World Council of Indigenous Peoples, 1984 (cited in Burger, 1987:59, emphasis added).

'Justice will only exist where those not affected by injustice are filled with the same amount of indignation as those offended'. -- Plato.

'The greatest challenge, the most difficult truth, to convey - and also the most important one - is that the welfare of the most powerful and privileged of people, and the future of us all, cannot be isolated from that of the poorest, most vulnerable, most wretched of the earth. Contemporary technology has seen to that. We are all in the same frail boat. Human rights and self-interest - social justice and survival - have finally met on common ground'. -- Gerald Berreman (1981).

Abstract

This chapter considers social justice as a cultural universal and fundamental necessity for human survival. It argues that cross-culturally, justice and human rights are inextricably linked, and that their increasing denial is the fundamental cause of growing political violence - including war, state terror, and international terrorism - in the world today. It applies the relative justice theory of political violence to cultural conceptions of justice, and argues that the human experience of injustice is universally experienced as oppression, and that this inevitably leads to resistance and conflict. It concludes that where there is no justice, there will be violence, and that human rights, social justice, and survival have finally met on common ground.

INTRODUCTION

This chapter presents an anthropological perspective on social justice as a cultural universal and fundamental necessity for human survival - that is, as a 'basic human need'. Human rights abuses are universally perceived by their victims as oppression and injustice, and are universally both resented and resisted by those who suffer from them. The usual dictionary definition of 'justice' is that it means moral or absolute rightness, the upholding of what is just, and fair treatment and due reward in accordance with honour, standards, or law. Generally, something is considered 'just' when it is consistent with standards of what is moral and proper, properly due or merited, or legitimate.

Cross-cultural comparison is the hallmark of anthropology, and Gerald Berreman (1981, p.270) has observed:

> It leads us to look at our own society with perhaps an unwontedly jaundiced eye, for we know ours to be only one of many ways of being human, and we know it to have been of but an eye-blinks' duration in the totality of human experience, at least 98% of which has been in small bands of 20 to 150 people, foraging for a living without accumulating goods or power, without elites, without poverty, without soldiers or much in the way of war, with scarcely any occupational differentiation, political domination or economic exploitation. These things we know to have been inventions of the past 10,000 years following from the invention of food production, and to have become predominant only in the last 5,000 years with the development of surplus food production enabling production for accumulation and exchange as well as for use, enabling the origin of cities and the state, the origin of social status based on control of property and labour rather than on family and kinship, and associated with these changes, the appearance for the first time of governments, armies, markets, occupational specialization, social stratification, territorial conquest, ownership of productive resources, human exploitation – and all the rest that we admiringly identify as civilization, exaggerated first arithmetically as technology progressed to the industrial revolution, and then exponentially in the 200 years since. As a result, many of us are sceptical of the word 'progress' and the claims made for it.

Since the Industrial Revolution beginning in the 18th century, very rapid population growth has gone alongside the development and global spread of civilization, with the result that today there are more poor people in the world than ever before. The figures are well-known; in most of the world, the poorest one-third to one-fifth of the population is absolutely and relatively worse off today than was the case in 1945, and out of a global population of 6.3 billion, nearly one-quarter or about 1.5 billion people, live in the desperate state described as 'absolute poverty' in which one or more of their basic survival needs are not being met. Kathleen Gough (1990) has observed that in the three decades from 1960 to 1990, the populations of developed countries shrunk as a percentage of the world population, while the gap in wealth and technology between 'developed' and 'underdeveloped' capitalist states widened alarmingly. In 1960 about 35% of the world's population lived in 'developed' countries, and 65% in 'less developed' ones. Gough reported that the gap in wealth and technology between developed and underdeveloped capitalist states was widening alarmingly, and said 'Today, many more millions of people in the Third world are very poor, and many more are starving, than in 1960'. Four billion people – that is about two-thirds of humankind - now live on less than US$3 (NZ$7) a day (*Dominion*, 23 March 2002), and 40 million children die needlessly each year in the Third (or 'less developed') World, while the developed First World countries do less and less to aid them, and draw more and more of their wealth from these countries.

The gross disparity between the 'haves' and 'have notes' is relevant to the issue of justice, because this massive and expanding global polarization of wealth, power, and privilege is fundamentally related to oppression, the abuse of human rights, and both the objective manifestation and subjective experience of injustice.

Justice, Relativity, and Power[1]

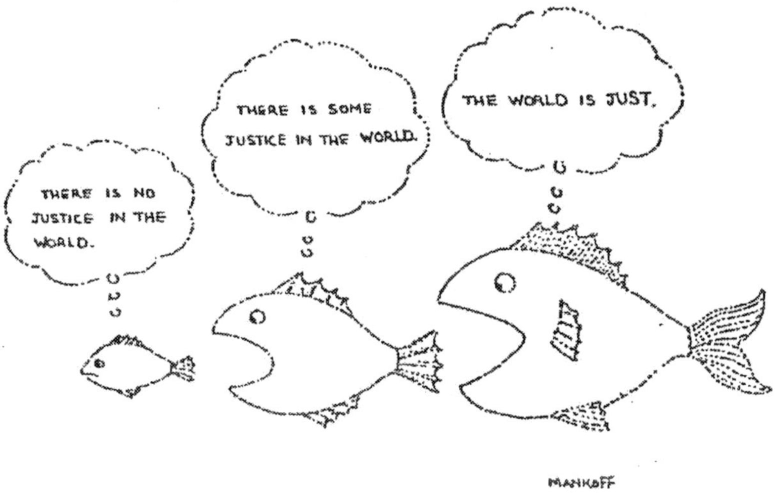

Cultural Relativism and Universal Human Rights

As a result of their cross-culturally comparative perspective, anthropologists have come to believe that justice is both a *universal* and *relative* human experience. Universal, because all of the cultures familiar to anthropologists have had fundamental notions of justice, but along with this culturally variable and relative because people living in different cultures frequently hold significantly different beliefs about what constitutes justice. Another important comparative observation is that at the same time that there are differences or variation, there are also significant similarities, agreement, or sharing among many, if not all, cultures in some basic elements of how justice is defined and enacted. Hence, anthropologists would observe that there are two types of definitions of human rights and justice, the subjective or culturally relative, and the objective or universal.

There are two models available for assessing cultural practices. First, there is an internationally recognised cross-cultural or universal standard, *The United Nations Universal Declaration of Human Rights* 1948. Second, there is the relative deprivation model which

[1] Cartoon credit:Bob Mankoff, *The New Yorker* magazine.

provides a universal, cross-culturally applicable model of the relationship between values – including those about justice – and conflict. Both models are briefly described below.

The United Nations Universal Code of Human Rights

The UN was formed directly following the end of the Second World War as a means of preventing a third world war which would be a thermonuclear holocaust likely to destroy the planet, or at least 'modern civilisation as we know it.' The very idea of the UN was based on the understanding that the only way to prevent war was to work to prevent its causes, and the best way to do this was to work to ensure global human rights and justice. Hence the newly-established UN immediately set to work on the Universal Declaration of Human Rights. The Declaration celebrated its 50th anniversary in 1998, and today it still represents *the greatest single achievement of humankind with respect to issues of human rights.* It was produced both as an expression of hope for a better world, and a practical mechanism for helping to prevent and combat the human rights abuses and fundamental injustices that are widely acknowledged to be the root cause of all of our world conflicts.

Today, there are two main criticisms of the Declaration, both of which revolve around the question of the relationship between *individual* and *group* rights. First, there is an emphasis on individual rights, and a corresponding lack of consideration of basic group rights - for example, the rights of indigenous peoples or 'First Nations' that is currently being addressed in a UN *Draft Code of Indigenous Rights* (see Merrill, 1996). Second, it has come under criticism from countries guilty of severe human rights abuses - particularly China, Indonesia, Singapore, Malaysia, and the Philippines - who have argued that the emphasis on individual rights is a Western bias which is not consistent with 'Asian values,' and that the emphasis in Asian cultures is on individual responsibilities, particularly to the group (for example, the family and nation) rather than on individual rights.

While there is room for criticism of the *Universal Declaration of Human Rights*, it can be and has been amended and improved in response to criticism. It is a mistake to believe that these fundamental principles of universal human rights, civil liberties, and freedom and integrity of the individual have been imposed on other regions or cultures of the world. The loudest critics of the Declaration have been countries with appalling human rights records, which clearly have a vested political interest in diluting international human rights accords. But the document was produced and ratified by all of the countries represented in the UN, who agreed that there were fundamental *universal* human rights that transcend West/East and other cultural differences.

Today, the majority of anthropologists, in full recognizance of the principle of cultural relativity, agree that there are no cultures, religions, or ethical systems that want to tolerate torture, murder, or other grave violations of human rights, and there is no compelling cultural defence, rationalisation, or justification of actions that violate fundamental human rights.[2]

---

[2] Not all anthropologists take this view. A minority have always taken a more extreme or radical interpretation of what might be called *absolute* cultural relativism. They argue that the most fundamental fact is that all cultures are qualitatively or fundamentally unique: hence there are no cultural universals, and no valid or objective judgements can be made about the morality or justice of particular forms of human action. This is an old debate in the discipline that has recently been stimulated by growing concern about how to respond to what Orin Starn (1994) describes as the 'pervasiveness of injustice and terror' in the world today. In recent years, Nancy Scheper-Hughes (1995, p. 409)

Anthropologist Carole Nagengast (1994) summarises the contemporary situation as follows:

> It is perhaps indicative of the crisis of the state that the universality of human rights came under attack at the 1993 UN World Conference on Human Rights, an attack led for the most part by China and other states that have most openly failed to make consensus prevail over coercion and that have records of especially egregious human rights abuses against both individuals and peoples. China's record in suppressing students and Tibetans, for example, needs no rehearsal here. Nonetheless, China, Singapore, and other less well-developed states invoked cultural relativity to justify torture and mistreatment. Cultural relativity is now code in some circles for permission to oppress people and peoples and to maintain women as second and third class citizens in the name of ostensible tradition and lack of cultural equivalence. The world community staved off threats to the universality concept, but the attack suggests the complexity of the terrain faced by anthropologists concerned with many voices and many modalities.

In short, while it is certainly not perfect, the UN *Universal Declaration of Human Rights* represents the most valid and objective universal standard we have against which human rights abuses and injustices may be judged, regardless of cultural differences.

Cultural Relativity, Justice and Deprivation

While different cultures have different values and resulting conceptions of justice and injustice, the relative deprivation theory presents a universal model that applies to all cultural contexts. The relative deprivation model of conflict and violence was developed in the early 1970s by political scientist T.R. Gurr (1972) from the psychological theory of the relationship between frustration and aggression, and he transferred this into the socio-political realm as a general theory of the conditions that determine the likelihood and magnitude of civil violence. He considered that *relative deprivation* and *political violence* were the social analogues of the psychological concepts of individual *frustration* and *aggression*, and his basic premise was that the necessary precondition for civil violence was relative deprivation – the actor's perception of dissonance between their *value expectations* and the socio-political environment's *value capabilities*. Gurr regarded value expectations, which include beliefs about justice and injustice, as the conditions of life that the individual feels justifiably entitled to, and he saw value capabilities as the sociocultural environment, the conditions that determine the 'life chances' available to people, and their chances of attaining their value expectations (i.e., what they feel they are legitimately or justly entitled to).

Gurr (1972, p.35) argued that relative deprivation might be construed as 'systematic frustration' induced by the social system, which causes the social discontent that is the precondition for political violence. He accepted that while the disposition to respond aggressively when frustrated was a universal part of our species' innate biological make-up, but argued that it is not reflexive or instinctive, but *culturally modified*. He considered that what is perceived to be frustrating, modes of aggressive response, inhibition through fear of

has argued that 'cultural relativism read as moral relativism is no longer appropriate to the world in which we live, and anthropology, if it is to be worth anything at all, must be ethically grounded'.

retaliation, and appropriate targets are 'all modified or defined in the learning process, typically but not solely during socialization.'

Deprivation theory holds that relative inequality and injustice between social groups is the basis of political conflict and violence. It presents a structural hypothesis that singles out social conditions – particularly the consequences of social stratification, such as differential access to wealth, power, and status – as the main cause of political violence, and predicts that the sharper the perception of inequity, the more intense or extreme the tactics of protest and/or resistance are likely to be. Berreman (1981, p.290) summarised the consequences of inequality, injustice, and deprivation as follows:

> Deprivation, both absolute and relative, is experienced by its victims as painful, damaging and *unjust* [emphasis added]. Inequality is so experienced by those whom it deprives. Moreover, through the human capacity to comprehend and to empathize, those who are deprived quite consistently resent those who appropriate advantages to themselves at the expense of others. Resentment leads inexorably to resistance in so far as that is possible and practical. Systems of institutionalised inequality carry within them the seeds of their own destruction in the form of the resentment they universally generate – seeds which can remain apparently dormant almost indefinitely, but which await only the proper conditions to suddenly germinate and flourish. Elites have often been unaware of this elementary and repeatedly demonstrated fact, largely because there seem to be so many acquiescent victims among the dispossessed, and also because they have lulled themselves into inattention by self-serving theories and rationalizations endorsing their privilege. But lately such elites have experienced many rude enlightenments on the issue in many parts of the world, as the under-classes have overtly expressed themselves in words and action.

Berreman (1981, p.291) also warned that:

> Deprived people are angry, resentful people. Given the opportunity or provocation – and only *they* can define what constitutes opportunity or provocation – they are sure to act: act to express their anger, to assuage their resentment, to redress their grievances, to right the balance. If descriptions of concentration of wealth, power and privilege fail to evoke outrage in many of us, it is somewhat less than reassuring to recognise that descriptions of terrorism and revolution fail to evoke those emotions in the hearts of millions throughout the world.

Growing State Terror, Declining Human Rights

The major type and source of political violence and terrorism is that practiced by states and their agents and allies against civilians in order to create fear as a political means. Quantitatively it is responsible for far more deaths than terrorism against states is. This is political violence aimed at citizens by their own governments, and is practiced by both governments of the extreme right and extreme left. Despite being quantitatively by far the most important form of political terrorism, state terrorism and the violence of right wing or fascist groups and death squads in support of the state, are often specifically excluded from official definitions of terrorism because these are not considered a direct threat to the status quo. The fact is that even small states have much more power to terrorize their citizens than even the most advanced antistate terrorists have to use against their governments. For example, only state terrorist have weapons of 'mass (civilian) destruction' or the ability to deprive large numbers of people of subsistence requirements and produce hunger, malnutrition, and high infant mortality rates, and other chronic diseases of poverty and neglect, as means of political intimidation and control.

As Herman (1982, p.83) has shown, 'The really massive and significant growth of terrorism since World War II has been that carried out by states'. And as Nagengast (1994) has observed, 'Since 1945, state-sponsored violence toward ethnic and political groups has caused more deaths, injuries, and general human suffering than all other forms of deadly conflict, including international wars and colonial and civil wars'. This rise in state terror is a direct corollary of the alarming rise in the number of authoritarian states during this period - variously characterized in contemporary social sciences literature in terms such as shakedown, strong, fearful, homicidal, outlaw, and rogue states - who routinely employ terrorism and other forms of mass intimidation against segments of their own civilian populations.

In the second half of the twentieth century, military and other authoritarian regimes came to power in virtually all of Central and South America, and in many countries in Asia, Africa, and elsewhere. During this period, terrorism practiced by authoritarian states resulted in a couple of million 'disappearances' and other politically motivated murders, at least several million people tortured, many millions of political refugees, and hundreds of millions of people threatened and intimidated. The massive escalation in terrorism practiced by authoritarian states over the last few decades is evidenced by the re-emergence of torture as a serious world problem, the rising tide of death squad murders, and the use of direct state violence to intimidate millions of people.

Human rights suffered serious setbacks worldwide in the 1970s and 1980s, and the trend continued through the 1990s and into the new century. For many years the UN Commission on Human Rights has reported the increase, particularly in Latin America and Asia. In scores of countries, the most fundamental human rights are being transgressed by government-condoned terrorism involving the harassment, torture, and murder of political opponents of those in power. In its annual global human rights reports, Amnesty International has identified the main forms of state terror as arbitrary detention, unfair trial, and political murder or extrajudicial execution, and it has extensively documented the escalation in state terrorism. Specifically, in their 2002 report Amnesty International recorded that in the previous year there were 151 countries with reported human rights abuses, among which 123 (81%) were guilty of torturing or ill-treating and 71 (47%) of murdering political opponents of those in power.

The use of torture has also grown massively, most notably in the Third World client states of the West. The startling development was highlighted first by Amnesty International in its 1974 *Report on Torture* when it pointed out that torture had suddenly re-emerged and reached 'epidemic proportions'. In the 1970s, about thirty-five countries worldwide practiced torture on an 'administrative basis'. By 1988 Amnesty International was reporting that over half of the world's governments were torturing or otherwise 'mistreating' prisoners, and that torture was increasingly being used not just for interrogation but as a generalized tactic of political intimidation. There were also increasingly widespread reports of torture of children in front of their parents as a method of political intimidation, and of rape being used as a form of mass state terrorism – both of which are still continuing, as Paul Burns indicates in his chapter in the present book.

Along with torture, the proliferation of state-sanctioned extrajudicial killings, 'disappearances,' and death squads were also a hallmark of the massive growth of state terrorism in the last quarter of the twentieth century. During the 1960s and 1970s, death squads emerged in at least ten states in Latin America alone, and like torture and disappearances conducted by regular state forces, they also spread steadily through the Third World in the 1980s and 1990s. Hannah Arendt (cited in Herman, 1982, p.7), in her classic study of the origins of totalitarianism, identified this practice as 'one of the last and most terrible phases in the evolution and degeneration of totalitarian states.' The UN has condemned these disappearances and extrajudicial executions as grave violations of fundamental human rights, and declared that their systematic practice represents 'war crimes against humanity' and 'the acme of despotism.'

Over the last two decades of the last century, between 200,000-300,000 people were 'disappeared' worldwide, and more people 'disappeared' each year in many individual countries than were killed worldwide as a result of 'international terrorism.' Such 'disappearances' are defined as 'cases where individuals are seized by military, paramilitary, or police agents of the state [or their proxies], who secretly murder and dispose of the bodies of their victims, often after torture, always without legal process, and without acknowledgment and admitted responsibility of the state' (Herman, 1982, p.7). The members of these death squads are usually linked directly or indirectly with the regular security forces (police, army, intelligence services), but sometimes they are part of paramilitary 'defence' forces, or civilian right-wing paramilitary groups who kill the people that the state wants to be killed.

For a long time, since at least the 1960s, the message anthropologists have heard from the grass roots in many areas of 'internal conflict' and 'killing fields' around the world, is that the main source of the violence that blights the lives of hundreds of millions of people is the repressive regimes, and those who support them, of the states in which they are citizens.

THE INTERNATIONAL CONTEXT: THE GLOBAL CULTURE OF TERROR

One of the most important observations made by the leading academics who have studied state terrorism over the past two decades is that violent, systematic repression is never an isolated phenomenon. State terrorism in Third World countries is invariably linked at both instrumental and structural levels to militarism (e.g., the arms trade and military assistance) in the countries, particularly the First World ones, with which they have military and economic ties. This system of international as well as domestic terrorism is reinforced through the mutual political, economic, and military interests of the elites in both the First and Third Worlds, and is well-known to political scientists (Stohl and Lopez, 1984). In particular, Michael Stohl (1984) has explored the manner in which the international political system serves as the arena in which state terrorism policies unfold, and he comments that:

> States . . . have been willing in the past decade to help provide other states with the tools of the terror trade . . . the new technologies of repression are widely available and easily distributed. The United States has been an active provider of the instruments of terror and repression to Third World client states to employ on their populations and also in a number of

> cases to train the security services of these societies in the proper employment of these instruments. It is a lucrative trade, and the US government has been an active assistant to the US corporations in the purveyance of their wares. Other Western governments [particularly the UK] similarly assisted their national corporations in this regard . . . [as did] the Soviet Union.

It might not generally be known that the arms or 'security' industry is the largest industry in the world, and a multibillion-dollar international repression trade flourishes in providing not just arms but the whole range of technology and techniques of political control to client dictatorships and other authoritarian states (Klare, 1996).

At the end of the 1970s, at the same time that Amnesty International and other human rights organizations were first beginning to present alarming reports on the existence of the new global 'epidemic' of state torture and murder, the first academic studies on the subject also began to emerge, led by the pioneering work of Noam Chomsky and Edward Herman. In a series of important books (e.g., Chomsky and Herman, 1979; Herman, 1982; Chomsky, 1985, 1986), they reported that the global rise in state terror was concentrated among Third World states in the US 'sphere of influence,' and provided extensive information on the terror occurring in the United States' client states in Latin America. They showed that in the 1970s, all ten of the countries in Latin America in which death squads appeared, and twenty-six (74%) of the thirty-five countries in the world that used torture on an 'administrative basis,' were client states of the United States who received direct military and other assistance enabling them to establish and maintain authoritarian regimes prepared to resort to terror to pursue their interests and stay in power. This led Herman (1982, p.132) to conclude that 'the death squad is a manifestation of US influence. Torture and the death squad are as US-related-American as apple pie'.

In fact, the frontispiece in Edward Herman's *The* Real *Terror Network* (1982) is a citation from a 1982 Council on Hemispheric Affairs report that also specifically linked the rise in state terror to US foreign policy. It says:

> Basic civil liberties, including the right to life, liberty and the freedom of personal and political expression, suffered a drastic setback in 1981. In more than a dozen regional nations, even the most fundamental rights - life and the inviolability of the person - were transgressed by the government-condoned practice of harassing, torturing and murdering political opponents of those in power . . . These reverses can be linked to policies adopted by the Reagan administration . . . [which] has allied the US with the most violent regimes in the hemisphere. He has sanctioned atrocities and human rights abuses by providing those governments with essentially unconditioned US support.

Subsequently in its 1996 report, Amnesty International accused powerful governments of 'trading in terror' by selling arms and other 'security' equipment to countries with bad human rights records, and then denying responsibility when atrocities occurred. Once again, 'the American connection' emerges. In a study of the shifting patterns of the international arms trade since the collapse of the Soviet Union, Michael Klare (1996) showed that a new post-Cold War paradigm of global arms trafficking has emerged, characterized by 'the unrivalled dominance of the USA in the global arms traffic': Between 1987 and 1991, the US provided 21% of arms transfers to the Third World states; between 1991 and 1994 they accounted for 48%.

From the evidence, it is clear that the US has towered above all other countries in arms supply and the training of military and police personnel abroad. The methods of torture first developed in the interrogation centres in South Vietnam have spread throughout the system of US clients, and there is a large body of evidence that US training and aid programs have directly and indirectly encouraged and promoted torture and death squads. The most powerful country on the planet has tended to encourage political torture and murder and, correspondingly, there is a significant positive relationship between US flows of aid and *negative* human rights developments.

Thus, Chomsky's and Herman's basic conclusion, and the thesis they have advanced in their work since then, and which has now been verified by other scholars, is that the global rise in terrorism has been mainly or fundamentally the result of Western – particularly US - foreign policy. Today, Chomsky argues that the United States represents the hegemonic 'culture of terrorism', providing the central model and leading example emulated by every other nation involved in state terror around the world. Their thesis was further supported by Michael McClintock's *The American Connection* (1985), and most recently by Frederick Gareau in *State Terrorism and the United States* (2004), both of which provide additional documentation and analysis of US-backed suppression of political and human rights in the Third World. Between those publications, in 1991 another noteworthy volume was published, *Western State Terrorism*, edited by Alexander George, that was the first to deal substantively with the issue of not just 'the US connection', but the wider context of the Western state-sponsored terrorism which underpins the 'New World Order'. It supported 'the fundamental thesis about terrorism: that its primary manifestations are supported, or directly carried out, by Western governments', and once again stressed the crucial point that 'The plain and painful truth is that on any reasonable definition of terrorism, taken literally, the United States and its friends are the major supporters, sponsors, and perpetrators of terrorist incidents in the world today . . . many, probably most, significant instances of terrorism are supported, if not organized, by the US, its partners, and their client states' (George, 1991, pp.1-2).

However, while the United States leads the way in promoting terrorism, Chomsky (1996), among others, observes that it is not alone in supporting terrorism when it is perceived to be in its politico-economic interests; 'every other power in the world is exactly the same' in their own international spheres of influence, contributing to terror through their support - financial, military, and diplomatic - of Third World regimes founded on violence. From this it is clear that the structures, tactics, and technology of state terrorism have been diffused, in fact aggressively marketed and exported as a form of 'military aid' to developing countries. Individual states which employ terror are encapsulated in a global or international culture of terror within which they are nurtured, and without which they probably could not long survive - that is, they are dependent on international support for their continued existence. They are dependent variables in the equation of global terrorism.

'Death By Government': State Terror and Concentrated Power

In *Death by Government* (1994), his fourth book in a series on genocide and government mass murder - that is, on the state as terrorist - political scientist R.J. Rummell was the first to attempt a thorough accounting of the twentieth century's state-instigated mass murders, starvations, and genocides. He calculated that in total, during the first eighty years of the twentieth century, 'almost one hundred and seventy million men, women and children [were] shot, beaten, tortured, knifed, burned, starved, frozen, crushed, or worked to death; buried alive, drowned, hung, bombed, or killed in any other of the myriad ways governments have inflicted death on unarmed helpless citizens and foreigners'. And this is *conservative* accounting, because it does not include combatants killed in wars; if these were included, the figure would be over 203 million people killed. Rummell (1994, p.9) noted that, because governments have been unwilling to admit such monstrous acts, 'the dead could conceivably be nearly three hundred and sixty million people'. He concluded that no other century has seen a slaughter of such magnitude - and his figures were collected before the massive death tolls in government-inspired genocides and starvations occurred in Bosnia, Somalia, Sudan, Rwanda, and other countries.

Rummell (1994, p.9) considered that 'the sheer lethality of power', and the 'belief in power as a tool' are responsible for the death toll. He said 'It is as though our species has been devastated by a modern Black Plague. And indeed it has, but a plague of Power, not germs'. His central theoretical conclusion stresses the relationship between power and terror: 'as the arbitrary power of a regime increases massively, that is, as we move from democratic through authoritarian to totalitarian regimes, the amount of killing jumps by huge multiples' (p.17). The more concentrated the power of the government, the more deaths; as the arbitrary power of regimes increases, the practice of terror increases:

> The more power a government has, the more it can act arbitrarily according to the whims and desires of the elite, and the more it will make war on others and murder its foreign and domestic subjects. The more constrained the power of governments, the more power is diffused, checked, and balanced, the less it will aggress on others and commit [political mass murder] (pp.1-2).

Rummell (1994, pp.23-24) also argued that where absolute power exists, 'interests become polarized, *a culture of violence develops*, and war and state murder follow. Where, on the other hand, power is limited and accountable, interests are cross-pressured, a culture of non-violence develops, and no wars occur and comparatively few citizens are murdered by the governing elite' (emphasis added). He makes a strong argument for fostering freedom and democracy and restricting and checking the concentration of power as antidotes to state terror or 'death by government', and these go hand in glove with fostering human rights and justice.

GLOBAL CONFLICT: 'THE THIRD WORLD WAR'

Anthropologists of war and conflict have observed that during the second half of the 20th century, along with the development of the potential for global thermonuclear warfare, there were two other major changes in the nature of global conflict. First, that civilians - rather than combatants - emerged as by far the major victims of political violence. During World War I only around 11% of casualties were civilians; by World War II the proportion had risen to 53%; in the wars of the 1960s, 1970s, and 1980s it was 52%, 68%, and 76% respectively; and in current conflicts the estimate is 90% civilian casualties (Zulaika and Douglass, 1996, p.128). Second, that wars within states rather than between them have emerged as by far the major form of armed conflict.

In an important study published in 1987, political geographer Bernard Nietschmann argued that the Third World War had already started, and that the nature and geography of global war had changed. He showed that there were more armed conflicts in the world than ever before, that they were concentrated in the Third World, and that they were mainly internal wars between states and 'nation peoples' – that is, indigenous and other national groups. Of the 120 armed conflicts or wars going on at that time, he found that the vast majority – 72% (86) – were internal wars between states and oppressed 'nation-peoples' (indigenous peoples, ethnic and religious groups, and minorities) within their boundaries, and that these wars accounted for 'the longest modern conflicts, huge numbers of casualties and the majority of refugees, human rights violations, genocide and "terrorists"'(p.11). He also predicted that this Third World War 'will not end in your lifetime', and 'is now being fought on every continent except Antarctica. It has produced millions of casualties and massive forced dislocations of nation peoples who make up the majority of the world's refugees. *It encompasses most of the peoples and groups who are accused of being terrorists*. Each year it involves new areas, states and nations' (p.1, emphasis added). In another article published in 1994, Nietschmann updated his statistics on global armed conflict, and reported that there were 122 wars or 'armed conflict' in the world, of which 79.5% (79.5%) were internal conflicts between states and 'nation peoples' within their own boundaries.

Nietschmann (1987) also highlighted two major characteristics of these internal wars - that the indigenous or nation fighters are always misidentified by the states fighting them as 'terrorists', and that they tend to be vicious 'dirty wars'. He made an important point about armed resistance by nation peoples and 'terrorism,' which has become even more important since the '9/11' terrorist attacks in the US in 2001:

> When a state is militarily invaded or economically attacked it may declare war, but when the same things happen to a nation and it resists, it will be accused of declaring terrorism. By state definition, state combatants conduct war, counterinsurgency and 'police actions' and maintain law and order; nation combatants conduct terrorism. *Every nation people that has resisted state invasion has been accused of being terrorists*: Karen (all 5 million), Miskitos, Kurds, Palestinians, Basques, Irish, Oromo, Tamils, and so on (p.15, emphasis added).

In the same article, Nietschmann (1987) went on to observe that oppressive states fighting internal wars against indigenous or other nation peoples refer to this as 'counterinsurgency' (or one of its newer euphemisms like 'low-intensity conflict,' 'irregular war,' or 'asymmetrical warfare') and 'counterterrorism', and all try to defeat the nation fighters and crush their civilian support by employing terrorism or 'dirty war' tactics. He said:

> War against the state is outlawed. No rules limit how state armies and security forces may act against nation combatants or insurgents and their civilian supporters. Unshackled, state armies use genocidal tactics to stamp out resistance to state control: destruction of food supplies, eradication of communities, dislocation of populations into state camps or into refugee camps in other states, killing of captured prisoners and wounded combatants, arbitrary and systematic arrest, imprisonment and torture to instil fear and submission, and imposed military rule over entire regions and nations. Regular genocide is often the state's antidote to 'irregular warfare'.

In 2004 a Canadian Red Cross report confirmed that there were more armed conflicts in the world than at any time since World War Two, that war dominated life in more than 80 countries, and that more people were affected by war than ever before in the past. At the same time, there were dozens of examples of the abuse of the epithet 'terrorism' being applied to legitimate armed resistance movements. Prominent contemporary examples included all of the major hot spots of political violence in the world; the Russian government claims that Chechen rebels are 'terrorists', the Israeli government claims that the PLO are 'terrorists', the Chinese government claims that Uigher and Tibetan separatists are 'terrorists', the Indonesian government claims that the Free Papua Movement (OPM) and Free Aceh Movement (GAM) are 'terrorists', the Sri Lanka government claims that the Tamil Tigers (LTTE) are 'terrorists', the Spanish government claims that the Basque ETA are 'terrorists', the British government claims that the IRA in Northern Ireland are 'terrorists', the Burmese junta claims that the Chin, Karen, Kachin, Mon, Karenni, Shan, Wa, and other ethnic rebels in the highlands are all 'terrorists', the Indian government claims that the indigenous rebels in Kashmir are 'terrorists,' the Colombian and US governments claim that the FARC guerrillas in Colombia are 'terrorists'. And so the list grows day by day. But because in all these cases many well-informed people might be inclined to believe that the causes are just, these governments have tried to convince the world that their opponents are all terrorists, and to create the impression that the solution need not involve political concessions but merely vicious 'counter-terrorism' (really counterinsurgency) campaigns.

HUMAN RIGHTS AND JUSTICE

So far in this chapter, I have argued that justice is intimately related to power, inequality, and human rights, and asserted that nearly all of the political violence in the world today is fuelled or caused by serious violations of fundamental human rights. Earlier, we saw that during the 1970s and 1980s state terrorism massively escalated, and as a consequence human rights suffered serious setbacks globally. The trend continued through the 1990s and into the present century, and the figures have yet to include the global impact on human rights of the '9/11' terrorist attacks on the US in 2001 that stimulated an even greater decline in the safeguarding of human rights. Worldwide, the most significant correlation with the growth of both state terrorism and anti-state terrorism is the growth in abuse of human rights. The increase in global inequality and state terror over the past thirty years has resulted in a massive decline in human rights. It is the fundamental cause of the spiral of political violence, war and resistance now termed 'terrorism' and the new global 'war on terrorism' being led by the US and UK.

Since the '9/11' terrorist attacks on the US, human rights organizations have expressed growing concern that the masses of new anti-terrorism legislation enacted by governments around the world has produced a rapid rolling back of civil liberties. Both Irene Khan, the Secretary General of Amnesty International, and Mary Robinson, the United Nations High Commissioner for Human Rights, issued strong condemnations of and warnings about this development. In her forward to the 2002 *Amnesty International Report* (p.5) Khan observed that:

> Undoubtedly, the environment for human rights activism changed sharply after 11 September in some parts of the world, setting back the gains of many years. . . As the 'war against terrorism' dominated world news, governments increasingly portrayed human rights as an obstacle to security, and human rights activists as romantic idealists at best, 'defenders of terrorists' at worst. But precisely because of these pressures, the role of human rights activists, far from diminishing, gained new urgency and importance . . . The readiness of governments to trade human rights in the interest of security is nothing new. . . The doctrine of national security has been used frequently in the past to deny human rights. The difference this time lay in the uneasy realization that it was not autocratic regimes but established democracies that took the lead in introducing draconian laws to restrict civil liberties in the name of public security. . . The dichotomy between security and human rights is false.

She went on to argue that:

> We must turn the debate about security and human rights on its head - human rights are not an obstacle to security and prosperity, they are the key to achieving these goals. Human security comes only with human rights and the rule of law. . . The past year has shown more clearly than ever that if human rights are sacrificed in the search for peace and security, there will be no peace and no security. The challenge to states therefore is not security versus human rights, bur rather to ensure respect for the full range of human rights (p.6).

Similarly, Robinson ended her term in September 2002 with a bleak assessment of the state of human rights around the world, and a strong condemnation of governments for using terrorism as an excuse to trample human rights. She accused governments of rushing through laws giving themselves emergency powers with little regard for human rights, and echoed the warning issued by Amnesty International, saying that the US-led 'war on terrorism' was threatening civil liberties and human rights around the world, and that 'there has been a tendency to ride roughshod over or at least to set on one side established principles of international human rights and humanitarian law'. She singled out the US, explaining that it was necessary to criticize Washington's policies first and foremost, because when she censured other countries for their human rights records, 'they say, look at what is happening in the United States' (*SUNS,* 2002).

Social Inequality and Justice

Social stratification is the central feature of the state and civilization. Morton Fried (1967), John Bodley (1976), Gerald Berreman (1977; 1981) and other like-minded anthropologists have identified it as the most dangerous and problem-causing feature of contemporary society. It leads to such conflict-inducing factors as the market economy; ethnic, religious, and ideological discrimination; socioeconomic deprivation; political inequality and its correlates such as infringement of rights, injustice, and oppression; the absence of effective channels of peaceful or systemic resolution of grievances and conflicts; exploitation and alienation; state terror to maintain and defend the order of stratification against challenges to elite rule and the social, economic, and political status quo; and antistate resistance, including the use of terrorism.

Fried (1967, p.235) has defined the state as 'a collection of specialized institutions and agencies that maintain an order of stratification', and Bodley (1976) argues that social stratification, the most fundamental characteristic of civilization, is linked to all of our major contemporary human problems such as inequality, over-population, over-consumption and other symptoms of the environmental crises, and is clearly linked to poverty, war, crime, and many personal crises. Berreman (1977, p.229) has argued that systems of social stratification are 'everywhere characterised by conformity rather than consensus, by conflict rather than tranquillity, by enforcement rather than by endorsement, by resentment rather than by contentment,' and what he observed over a quarter-century ago seems to be even more true today, i.e.:

> Naked power is being resorted to more unabashedly as the conflict becomes more evident. . . the incidence, the likelihood and the impact of overt conflict between individuals is increasing both within and between societies and nations . . . Present trends suggest a worldwide polarisation in access to power, privilege and resources - the gap between the 'haves' and the 'have nots' increases with a diminishing willingness among the poor to continue to suffer deprivation, and among the wealthy to ameliorate it (p.236).

The gap between the rich and poor, between developed nations and developing ones, is growing ever wider, and all of our major world problems are growing at an accelerated rate.

Berreman (1981, p.8), the world's leading authority on the study of systems of social inequality, went on to argue that 'stratification and the state are one in origin; one in function – creation, protection and continuation of the powerful and privileged at the expense of the rest'. Berreman states that 'social stratification refers to the fact that some categories of people get more of the valued things in life and others get less; a few get most, and most get the rest. Some live well and long; some live poorly and briefly. There is a ranking, in other words, of access to goods, services and experiences - to what the social theorist Max Weber called "life chances". There are national elites and international elites; the national poor and international poor. There are rich nations and poor nations' (pp. 285-286).

But physical power alone is not sufficient to integrate a state. Integration must be based on legitimacy, not just force. The crisis of the state is that as social inequality grows, the ideological basis of state legitimacy breaks down. Increasing numbers of people become politically alienated, and when popular legitimacy cannot be maintained by ideological means, the elites in the power structure rely on force – on terror – to protect and advance their interests: i.e. when consensus fails, coercion rules.

However, the anthropologists cited above, along with power conflict and deprivation theorists in other disciplines, have emphasized social inequality because they believe it is the most dangerous feature of contemporary society, and the root cause of most of the injustice experienced by people in the world today. Berreman (1981, p.286) also reminds us that social equality is worth focusing upon because:

> It is an entirely cultural, man-made phenomenon which could be drastically reduced or eliminated, were people to decide to do that (which I doubt that they will). If it is not, the animosities it arouses may well be the end of us. The ultimate cause may be the pattern of nation states, of accumulation, territoriality, bureaucracy, poverty and accumulation which define or accompany stratification, but the proximal cause is surely the greed and envy, excess

and suffering that inequality causes, especially that kind of inequality among entire categories of people which we call stratification.

POWER, INEQUALITY AND THE SPIRAL OF VIOLENCE

Both the power of those C. Wright Mills (1963) termed 'the power elite' and the degree of social inequality grew by leaps and bounds in the last quarter of the 20th century. It strikes me that the steady growth in political violence is fundamentally linked to the continuing growth in the concentration of power in the hands of the elite and the increase in social inequality – the ever-widening gap between rich and poor, within countries and between countries, that every social observer has noted as among the main characteristics of the of the global scene since the rise of the New Right in the West in the 1970's. In fact there appears to be a direct correlation between the increasing power and wealth of the elite, the steadily increasing gap between rich and poor, the decline in human rights, and the growth of state terror and resistance to it - perhaps the four most obvious global characteristics of the last quarter of the twentieth century. It suggests that political violence - including war, state terror and anti-state terrorism - is a dependent variable in the equation of inequality, not the independent variable that many elites, governments, and academic defenders of the state claim it to be.

The gap between the rich and poor, powerful and powerless, is immense and continues to widen at an alarming rate. Power conflict theory, which focuses on the operation of elites within a global system of social stratification, argues that this inequality leads to violence and terrorism. The concentration of wealth and power has lead to increasing exploitation and oppression, and the globalisation of market forces has greatly increased inequality in the world. In 2004:

- The wealth of the world's 225 richest individuals equalled that of the poorest 47% of the world's population.
- The richest 20% of the world's population received 83% of the world's income, while the poorest 60% of the world's people received just 5.6% of the world's income.
- The richest 20% of the world's population in northern industrial countries used 70% of the world's energy, 75% of the world's metals, 85% of the world's wood, and 60% of the world's food. This 20% minority was also responsible for producing about 75% of the world's environmental pollution.
- At the same time, 1.5 billion people, about a quarter of the world population, lived in 'absolute poverty' without access to basic subsistence resources – food, water, clothing, shelter, and essential health care.

It appears that poverty is the one thing that is truly being 'globalised' (Chossudovsky, 1997; 2000). It has stimulated increasing resistance and anti-state protests, violence, and terrorism, which has in turn further stimulated state repression and terrorism, thereby producing the upward spiral of violence we find ourselves in today.

Therefore it is no coincidence that the global decline in human rights and rise in state terror corresponds with the rise of the New Right in the West and the emergent global hegemony of economic neoliberalism - particularly through the Reagan and Thatcher governments and their successors in the United States and the United Kingdom and their combined influence on their Third World client states. Starting in the early 1980s, these governments abandoned any previous emphasis in international relations on human righs and replaced it with an emphasis on combating 'terrorism', and it is with the propaganda of 'fighting terrorism' that states who employ terror themselves most frequently justify their actions.

CONCLUSION

Is justice then a 'need,' merely a desire, or even a luxury? In the 1950s, when the eminent psychologist Abraham Maslow (1954) developed his pioneering theory of basic human needs essential for healthy human development, he did not include justice on his list of what he thought were the needs. But he did describe it as 'almost' one. I and other like-minded anthropologists agree with psychologist A.J.W. Taylor's (2003) conclusion that justice is of such paramount importance as to deserve elevation to Maslow's list of basic needs. As the World Council of Indigenous Peoples declared in 1984, '*Where there is no justice, there will be violence'* (cited in Burger, 1987, p.59, emphasis added), and without peace the prognosis for the future of civilization and humankind is bleak.

Berreman (1981, p. 291) has argued that people resist injustice publicly 'when they believe the chances for redress or revenge are worth the risk, *or* when things can be reasonably expected to change under pressure and when the means to a successful application of pressure – namely power - are thought to be at hand, *or* when the *status quo* is thought to be bad enough that even slight odds are worth a gamble, *or* when things are so bad that any resistance, any revenge is thought worth any price. Anyone who reads the papers, or history, is aware of the phenomena. The means employed range from the ballot box to the media to the barrel of a gun or the devastation of a bomb'.

Technological development has proven to be a two-edged sword, and modern technology – in particular weapons of mass destruction – is no longer reserved for the rich and powerful. The 'globalisation' of access to 'high technology' allows the poor and relatively powerless access to new and frightening forms, means, and tactics of fighting for their human rights against what they experience and perceive as fundamental and intolerable injustice. Now, in the service of those who feel themselves to be the victims of oppression, exploitation, and injustice, the technology provides a counterbalance to the old constraints of economic and political power.

Again Berreman (1981, p.291) warned nearly a quarter century ago that 'Guns, explosives, getaway cars, hideaways, even *planes* and nuclear devices are now exclusive properties of nobody: of no nation, no ethnic group, no class, no individual, proponents of no single political philosophy, economic philosophy, religion, or technology. They are in the international public domain' (emphasis added). The warning was dramatically driven home to the whole world in 2001 by the '9/11' terrorist attacks against the US.

But even a half-century earlier Franklin Delano Roosevelt, in his second inaugural address in 1937, warned that 'The test of our progress is not whether we add more to the abundance of those who have much; it is whether we provide enough for those who have little'. We have failed this test, and now those who have little – those described by Franz Fanon (1963) in his classic study of Third World politics as 'the wretched of the earth' – have acquired the technology to redress or avenge their grievances against those who have much but have thus far declined to share it with them. Today, President Roosevelt's prescription is not only a test of progress; *it is a prerequisite for survival.*

Contemporary events have validated Berreman's (1981, p.297) conclusion that 'human rights, justice, and survival have finally met on common ground'. I argue that justice should be considered a basic human need simply because without it our survival is doubtful. While there is a paucity of scholarship and empirical studies relating specifically to the concept of justice, in recent years social scientists have begun to pay more attention to the issue of justice in contemporary human affairs. For example, psychologist Tony Taylor (2003, p.11) has suggested that 'Were psychologists to take up the intellectual challenge, simultaneously they would be able to build a more realistic picture of the complex framework within which people live, pay attention to the effect of the deprivation of justice as well as to its fulfilment, and join forces with other scientists and scholars to validate the concept, consider the remedies for injustice, and so help to bring about a more just society for the greater good of all'. Anthropologists are prepared to accept this challenge.

Postscript

In the months between writing this chapter and awaiting its publication, the international political situation deteriorated significantly. The 'war on terror' has already lasted longer than World War Two, and the Bush administration has used the '9/11' terrorist attacks in 2001 as an excuse to launch a massive assault on the human rights of people throughout the world. In 2005, four years after '9/11,' Amnesty International reports that human rights continue to be in retreat worldwide, and for that the US bears most of the responsibility. From Afghanistan to Zimbabwe, the picture is bleak. Governments are increasingly rolling back the rule of law, taking their cue from the US-led 'war on terror'. Secretary General Irene Kahn states in the forward to Amnesty International's 2005 annual report that 'When the most powerful country in the world thumbs its nose at the rule of law and human rights, it grants license to others to commit abuse with immunity'.

Documented evidence shows that, in pursuing the 'war on terror' the US military has itself engaged in dozens of cases of abuse, torture, and even murder of prisoners. Thus the US has joined the ranks of the growing number of 'torture states'. Amnesty charges that Washington has emerged as a leading purveyor and practitioner of torture and ill-treatment, and it has described the US prison camp at Guananamo Bay as 'the gulag of our times' (2005). In May 2005, a US Army report confirmed that several prisoners were tortured to death in Afghanistan in 2002; that American guards brutalized and sexually humiliated Iraqi prisoners at Abu Ghraib prison as a matter of routine to soften them up for interrogation; and that US guards at Guantanamo Detention Centre have terrified prisoners with vicious dogs and mocked their religious beliefs.

The US has also added a new word to the political vocabulary of state terror – 'rendering' - despite US laws that ban expelling or extraditing individuals to countries where torture occurs. Under that policy, between 2001 and 2005 some 150 people were flown to Egypt, Morocco, Syria, Jordan, and other countries known to use torture during interrogations. By legal standards, the US has now 'disappeared' at least eleven al Qaeda suspects.

Thus, as this volume goes to press, the US - the world's only 'superpower,' the acknowledged global *hegemon* and proclaimed leader of the 'free world', has proven itself to be guilty of torture and murder, including the 'disappearances' of its political enemies, and the killing of detainees in secret jails. Since, as noted earlier in this chapter, such actions are the generally recognized hallmarks of 'state terror', the US can no longer avoid the accusation that it is itself a terrorist state. President Bush has chosen to engage in a mass campaign of state terrorism in order to fight terrorism. Unfortunately, since state terror, oppression, and injustice are the root causes of political terrorism, adopting these practices as a means of reducing terrorism is analogous to trying to extinguish a fire by pouring petrol on the flames. The outlook for global justice looks increasingly bleak: 'Where there is no justice, there will be no peace.'

References

Amnesty International (1974). *Report on Torture*. London: Amnesty International.

Amnesty International (1988). *Amnesty International Report*. London: Amnesty International.

Amnesty International (1996). *Amnesty International Report*. London: Amnesty International.

Amnesty International (2002). *Amnesty International Report*. London: Amnesty International.

Berreman, G, D. (1977). Social Barriers: Caste, Class and Race in Cross-cultural Perspective. *Papers in Anthropology*, 18:2, 217-242.

Berreman, G, D. (1981). Is the Consideration of Human Rights Merely a Politicised Luxury in the World Today? In G. D. Berreman (ed.), *The Politics of Truth: Essays in Critical Anthropology* (pp.268-298). New Delhi: South Asian Publishers.

Bodley, J. (1976). *Anthropology and Contemporary Human Problems*. Menlo Park: Cummings.

Burger, J. (1987). *Report From the Frontier: The State of the World's Indigenous Peoples*. London: Zed Books.

Canadian Red Cross (2004). *Even Wars Have Limits*. Accessed 9/9/04 from http://www.redcross.ca/article.asp?id=001738andtid=006.

Chomsky, N. (1985). *Turning the Tide: US Intervention in Central America and the Struggle for Peace*. Boston: South End Press.

Chomsky, N. (1986). *Pirates and Emperors: International Terrorism in the Real World*. Claremont: Black Rose.

Chomsky, N. (1987). *The Culture of Terrorism*. London: Pluto Press.

Chomsky, N. (1996). Enduring Truths, Changing Markets. *Covert Action Quarterly*, 56, p.46.

Chomsky, N. and Herman, E. (1979). *The Washington Connection and Third world Fascism (The Political Economy of Human Rights, Vol. 1)*. Nottingham: Spokesman.

Chossudovsky, M. (1997). *The Globalisation of Poverty: Impacts of IMF and World Bank Reforms*. Boston: Common Courage Press.

Chossudovsky, M. (2003). *The Globalisation of Poverty and the New World Order*. Oakland, CA: Global Outlook.

Fanon, F. (1963). *The Wretched of the Earth*. Harmondsworth: Penguin.

Fried, M. (1967). *The Evolution of Political Society: An Essay in Political Anthropology*. New York: Random House.

Gareau, F. (2004). *State Terrorism and the United States: From Counter-insurgency to the War on Terrorism*. London: Zed Books.

George, A. (ed.) (1991). *Western State Terrorism*. Cambridge: Polity Press.

Gough, K. (1990). 'Anthropology and Imperialism' Revisited. *Economic and Political Weekly*, 25:31, 1705-1708.

Gurr, T. R. (1972). Psychological Factors in Civil Violence. In I. Feierabend, R. Feierabend and T. Gurr (eds.), *Anger, Violence, and Politics: Theories and Research* (pp.31-57). Englewood Cliffs: Prentice-Hall.

Herman, E. S. (1982). *The* Real *Terror Network: Terrorism in Fact and Propaganda*. Boston: South End Press.

Khan, I. (2002). Countering the Backlash. Foreword in *Amnesty International Report 2002* (pp.55-58). London: Amnesty International.

Klare, M.T. (1996). The Arms Trade in the 1990s: Changing Patterns, Rising Dangers. *Third World Quarterly*, 17:5, 857-874.

Maslow, A. (1954). *Motivation and Personality*. New York: Harper.

McCamant, J. (1984). Governance Without Blood: Social Science's Antiseptic View of Rule, or the Neglect of Political Repression. In M. Stohl and D. Lopez. (eds.), *The State as Terrorist* (pp.11-42). Westport: Greenwood.

McClintock, M. (1985). *The American Connection, Volume One: State Terror and Popular Resistance in El Salvador*. London: Zed Books.

Merrill, R. (1996). Theory and Progress of Human Rights: The UN Declaration and the Rights of Indigenous Peoples. In L. Foerstel (ed.), *Creating Surplus Populations: The Effects of Military and Corporate Policies on Indigenous Peoples* (pp.249-267). Washington, DC: Maisonneuve Press.

Mills, C. Wright (1963). *The Power Elite*. New York. Oxford University Press.

Nagengast, C. (1994). Violence, Terror, and the Crisis of the State. *Annual Review of Anthropology*, 23, 109-136.

Nietschmann, B. (1987). The Third World War. *Cultural Survival Quarterly*, 11:3, 1-16.

Nietschmann, B. (1994). The Fourth World: Nations Versus States. In G. Demko (ed.), *Reordering the World: Geopolitical Perspectives on the World* (pp.225-242). Boulder: Westview Press.

Rummel, R. J. (1994). *Death by Government*. New Brunswick: Transaction Books.

Scheper-Hughes, N. (1995). The Primacy of the Ethical: Propositions for a Militant Anthropology. *Current Anthropology*, 36:3, 409-420.

Sluka, J. A. (2000). Introduction: State Terror and Anthropology. In J. Sluka (ed.), *Death Squad: The Anthropology of State Terror* (pp.1-45). Philadelphia: University of Pennsylvania Press.

Starn, O. (1994). Rethinking the Politics of Anthropology: The Case of the Andes. *Current Anthropology*, 35:1, 13-38.

Stohl, M. (1984). International Dimensions of State Terrorism. In M. Stohl and G. Lopez (eds.), *The State as Terrorist* (pp.43-58). Westport: Greenwood Press.

Stohl, M. and Lopez, G. (eds.) (1984). *The State as Terrorist: The Dynamics of Governmental Violence and Repression*. Westport: Greenwood Press.

SUNS (South-North Development Monitor) (2002). United Nations: Robinson Departs Repeating Criticisms Against US. #5189, 12 September, email edition. No page numbers. Accessed 30/9/2002 from http://www.sunsonline.org.

Taylor, A. J. W. (2002). Justice as a Basic Human Need. *New Ideas in Psychology*, 21:3, 209-219.

Zulaika, J. and Douglass, W. (1994). *Terror and Taboo: The Follies, Fables, and Faces of Terrorism*. New York: Routledge.

In: Justice as a Basic Human Need
Editor: Anthony Taylor, pp. 135-157
ISBN 1-59454-915-X

Chapter 11

JUSTICE, TORTURE AND RESTORATION

Paul Burns

'Not one out of a million witches would be accused or punished if regular legal procedures were followed.' Jean Bodin, Professor of Law, in his book of 1580, *De La Démonomanie Des Sorciers*. (Quoted in Quaife, 1987, p140)

ABSTRACT

The continuing and widespread use of torture by governments and agencies is a matter of growing clinical, humanitarian, political, and social concern. The practice is defined, put in historical and social context, and presented as a process with sequential phases outlined from direct clinical experience with survivors. Attention is paid to the long lasting cognitive and emotional effects of torture, as well as to testimony therapy and elements of a restorative model of intervention that have been found helpful in easing the burden of survivors. Underlying the whole deplorable phenomenon is the neglect of justice as a basic human need.

N.B.: in this chapter 'Medical Foundation' is the short name used for the Medical Foundation for the Care of Victims of Torture, 'victim' for a person still exposed to direct torture, and 'survivor' for a person who is beyond the immediate risk of further torture.

INTRODUCTION

In his history of torture Peters (1985) has named a chapter after Goya's sketch called 'The Sleep of Reason Begets Monsters' that, like others published in *Los Caprichos* (Goya, 1799), scorned the Inquisition and the superstition that gave rise to the persecution of suspected witches. Later Goya depicted 'The Fatal Consequences of the Bloody War in Spain Against Bonaparte', showing gruesome scenes of torture such as castration during interrogation (Wyndham Lewis, 1968, p.162). These images were brought to mind in 2004 by events in Iraq when other shocking pictures came to prominence. 'How,' many citizens of the

USA and the UK asked, 'could our soldiers who brought down a regime notorious for torture add to the atrocities? How did Abu Ghraib prison so quickly become again a centre for systematic torture? (*New Scientist*, 10 May 2004) 'How have we begot such monsters?'

But people who monitor human rights were not altogether surprised by the abuses perpetrated by the occupying forces in Iraq. They knew that many detainees at Special Interrogation Centres in Northern Ireland had reported the use of violence, psychological and physical stress, and forced confessions by the Royal Ulster Constabulary that amounted to torture (Amnesty International, 1997: Gudjonsson, 2003, p. 44). More recently the Commissioner of the London Metropolitan Police found that the Northern Ireland security forces were guilty of a 'wilful failure to keep records, the absence of accountability, the withholding of intelligence and evidence, and the extreme of agents being involved in murder'. He went on to say that 'These serious acts and omissions have meant that people have been killed or seriously injured' (*Stevens Enquiry*, 2003).

According to the *Human Rights Watch Americas Overview* (1997), the USA has long supported regimes with appalling human rights records, with training manuals used at the US based School of the Americas confirming allegations that foreign military officers were taught methods there of assassination and torture: an investigation by the Organization of American States found that Guatemalan government agents were implicated directly in the 1989 abduction, rape, and torture of Sister Dianna Ortiz at a military camp, where she spoke with a man who appeared to be a US advisor (Ortiz and Davis, 2002).

Torture, the monstrous practice considered here, has long been an instrument of war. In some countries it has been handed down from one generation to the next, and sometimes been adopted by people who themselves had been victims. For example the French troops used methods in Algeria that the Nazis had used throughout Europe, and when General Aussaresses publicised the details, his superiors chided him for the disclosure rather than for perpetrating the abuse. (Daley, 2001). In turn, the politically independent Algeria that emerged came to be recognised for its brutality after its military junta cancelled elections in 1992, and it won the 1998 'Alternative World Cup' for its ignominious record for torture and 80,000 extrajudicial killings (*The Observer*, 1998).

For a long time dominant countries used torture to subjugate their colonial dependencies, and during the post-colonial era they often relied on the brutality of client regimes to avoid nationalistic reactions, international opprobrium, and possibly a nuclear standoff. Hence, both the USA and USSR created and supported tyrants like Mbutu, Pinochet, Mengistu and Ceausescu, while the UK, France and China courted Idi Amin, 'Emperor' Bokassa and Pol Pot. Then after the collapse of the Soviet Union and the emergence of the 'International War on Terrorism' governments with scandalous disregard for human rights were recruited for the campaigns against the Taliban, Al Qaeda, and Chechen separatists. This toleration of one form of terrorism to fight another again promoted the unregulated abuse of power, and became our era's 'Sleep of Reason'.

The purported justification of torture is to gather intelligence. However, as the maltreatment of captives in Abu Ghraib prison by the US military has shown, this is only one of the reasons. The behaviour of individual guards, while fostered by the demands for intelligence, resulted from not expecting that they would have to answer for abuse. They had no effective independent inspection and were deterred neither by witnesses not taking part in the torture nor by the possibility of medical examinations drawing attention to mistreatment.

Human rights organisations expressed concern about the legal basis for detention at Guantánamo Bay and in Afghanistan, and the harsh treatment of prisoners in these places (*Human Rights Watch*, 2004a). But at least until photos of abuses at Abu Ghraib were distributed, the US government appeared disinclined to alter policy and practices (cf. *Freedom House Report on the USA* 2003). Afterwards the US suggested that abuses in Iraq were isolated and not the result of policy – despite the evidence from eight Pentagon documents between October 2002 and April 2003 outlining the practices that might be permitted during interrogation (*Human Rights Watch*, 19 August 2004).

Further concern about US connivance with torture stems from 'rendition', the practice of sending suspects to countries where torture is readily used. Apprehension for rendition sometimes involves the compliance of another state, and at other times it involves abduction. After one such 'disappearance', an Italian Judge issued a warrant for the arrest of 13 of those suspected of involvement in a US Central Intelligence Agency led kidnapping of a man who was subsequently flown to Egypt (*The Guardian,* 25 June 2005).

Without going into detail, it can be said that whatever the legal standards in place, there will be some in authority who ignore them. Consequently the lack of effective inspection at places of detention like Guantánamo, and reports of 'ghost detainees' who did not appear in any records at Abu Ghraib are of great concern (Washington Post, 11 March 2005). The conclusion to be drawn is that citizens in every country need to be vigilant and active in their opposition to torture to ensure that their political leaders and government advisors observe basic human rights. When none is accountable the rule of law has ended.

The remainder of this chapter sets out international legal agreements concerning torture, considers the actions of participating professionals, and the historical and social aspects of the practice. It goes on to review the profound psychological effects of torture, and the stages from pre-arrest through to post-discharge that contribute to the overall harm that ensues. Finally it describes Testimony Therapy and support that helps survivors to move towards a more tolerable existence.

Legal Responses to Torture

The UN Convention Against Torture and Other Cruel, Inhuman or Degrading Treatment or Punishment (1984) prohibits 'an act by which severe pain or suffering, whether physical or mental, is intentionally inflicted on a person, for a purpose such as obtaining information or a confession, punishment, intimidation or coercion, or for any reason based on discrimination of any kind'. The convention focuses on torture by government agents acting with official sanction, and establishes the responsibility of the state for an act of torture inflicted 'with the consent or acquiescence of a public official', and for ensuring that in its legal system 'the victim of an act of torture obtains redress and has an enforceable right to fair and adequate compensation, including the means for as full rehabilitation as possible'. Subsequently the *UN Optional Protocol to the Convention Against Torture* (2002) sought to eliminate torture and to improve prison conditions, but it still needs ratification from twenty countries before it comes into effect - as of January 2006 only 16 had either acceded to or ratified it.

Torture is proscribed under other international agreements such as Article 7 of the *International Covenant on Civil and Political Rights* (1966) and the *Rome Statute of the*

International Criminal Court (1998) that lists torture under crimes against humanity. Yet today the world community is shamed by the extent of torture and the suppression of those who oppose it – and this includes the city that lent its name to *The Istanbul Protocol* (1999) that documented methods for investigating torture and proceeding against suspected torturers. In Istanbul, for instance, Gulbahar Gunduz complained of being tortured and raped by four men identifying themselves as police officers, and the police reportedly used tear gas and beatings to break up a demonstration by 300 women supporting her (*Country Reports on Human Rights Practices – Turkey*, 2003).

Human rights organisations have long recognised as torture the use of sexual enslavement, rape and other sexual assault for reasons related to political oppression (Amnesty International, 2003), and their stance has now been vindicated by decisions of Human Rights courts. As a Rwandan Tribunal stated, 'Like torture, rape is used for such purposes as intimidation, degradation, humiliation, discrimination, punishment, control or destruction of a person. Like torture, rape is a violation of personal dignity, and rape in fact constitutes torture when inflicted by or at the instigation of, or with the consent and acquiescence of a public official or other person acting in an official capacity' (Prosecutor v. Akayesu, 1998).

Sadly, there are still countries where the courts are not a defence against terror but instigators of it. For example, the Human Rights Watch Report (2004b), *Torture, Detention, and the Crushing of Dissent in Iran*, concluded that, 'The Iranian judiciary is at the centre of the human rights violations documented in this report. A small group of judges accountable only to the Leader has shut down public dissent. They have used various tools for repression: including plain-clothes militia, various intelligence services, prisons and detention centers, and courtrooms'. And following recent terrorist attacks in the USA, calls have arisen in that country for the introduction of torture within the law. In support of the proposition Dershowitz, a professor of law, cited the findings of Israel's *The Landau Commission* (1987). This Commission stated that a moderate degree of physical pressure could not be avoided in responding to terrorism – while accepting that state agents had used violent interrogation methods routinely on Palestinian detainees for at least 16 years and had perjured themselves in court by denying such practices. Deshowitz (2003, p277) in response to critics of 'torture warrants' replied:

> 'I am generally against torture as a normative matter, and I would like to see its use minimized. I believe that at least moderate forms of non-lethal torture are in fact being used by the United States and some of its allies today. I think that if we ever confronted an actual case of imminent mass terrorism that could be prevented by the infliction of torture we would use torture, (even lethal torture), and the public would favor its use.'

The Landau Commission's justification for allowing force was that a predisposition of Palestinians for terrorism limited their right to legal protection, that the security service operated morally in protecting Israeli national security, and that the interrogation methods *per se* did not constitute torture. But there is evidence that since the publication of that report in 1987 the Israeli authorities continued to interrogate immoderately. In the words of Cohen and Golan (1991, p.86), 'Although methods of collecting information are not always reliable, these reports show beyond reasonable doubt that practices definable as ill-treatment or torture have been used against Palestinian detainees. We draw particular attention to the cases of death under suspicious circumstances during interrogation (five in the last three years)'. Another observer, Hajjar (2004), linked the Landau acceptance of 'moderate force' back to British torture in Northern Ireland but noted,

> 'the Landau report adds a distinctive wrinkle...(*by embracing the*) majority decision by the European Court of Human Rights that the five techniques (wall standing, hooding, subjection to noise, sleep deprivation, and deprivation of food and drink) do not amount to 'torture' but to the lesser - and also prohibited - category of 'inhumane and degrading treatment'...... Thus was born the euphemization of 'moderate physical pressure' as 'not torture'.

In 2004 two out of three UK Court of Appeal judges ruled that evidence obtained through torture could be used in a British court, provided that the state itself had not procured or connived at the mistreatment (*The Guardian*, 12 August 2004). Given what happened with the European Court of Human Rights ruling, it is likely that the Court of Appeal decision will be used in other jurisdictions to justify the use of torture.

OTHER PROFESSIONAL PARTICIPANTS

Politicians and lawyers are not alone in being explicit or implicit accomplices to torture. Deahl (2002) expressed concerns about the practices of psychiatrists in China resembling the abuses by Soviet psychiatrists, and Lifton (2004), commenting on the failings of doctors and nurses at Abu Ghraib prison mentioned previously, wrote,

> 'Physicians have served as actual torturers in Chile and elsewhere; have surgically removed ears as punishment for desertion in Saddam Hussein's Iraq; have incarcerated political dissenters in mental hospitals, notably in the Soviet Union; have, as whites in South Africa, falsified medical reports on blacks who were tortured or killed; and have, as Americans associated with the Central Intelligence Agency, conducted harmful, sometimes fatal, experiments involving drugs and mind control.'

A UN report on Guantánamo referred to treatment amounting to torture 'as it inflicts severe pain or suffering on the victims for the purpose of intimidation and/or punishment'. Speaking of the role of medical personnel the report referred to assertions 'many confirmed by investigations of the United States military, that health professionals in Guantánamo Bay have systematically violated widely accepted ethical standards...' The alleged violations included 'breaching confidentiality by...disclosing health information for purposes of interrogation, participating in, providing advice for or being present during interrogations; and being present during or engaging in non-consensual treatment, including drugging and force-feeding.' (Situation of Detainees at Guantánamo Bay, 2006 Pp 26 & 33)

Psychologists are also not beyond reproach. Hendrik Verwoerd (1901-1966) was previously a professor of social psychology who wrote his PhD thesis on 'The blunting of the emotions' long before leading South Africa into the brutality of apartheid (Verwoerd, 1924). Other psychologists participated in the use of torture in Chile, and in Cuba they assisted the secret police by conducting psychological tests and developing techniques of torture (Suedfeld, 1990). Uruguayan psychologists were also accused of training torturers and of using psychological methods systematically 'to induce fear, disorientation, depressions, and nervous breakdowns in the political prisoners. They directed guards to the particularly sensitive areas and/or psychological weaknesses of the prisoners, and had prisoners placed with aggressive psychotics' (Lucas and Pross, 1995, p109-110).

Such complicity by people in the 'helping professions' with special responsibilities is a reminder that status, education, and professional ethics are at times no match for the identification with a group or ideology that disregards human rights to promote actual or perceived self-interest.

THE HISTORICAL AND SOCIAL CONTEXT OF TORTURE

The reluctance of the authorities to eliminate torture can be explained partly because it has long been an integral part of the legal process for determining guilt or obtaining information, and at times even some independent judiciaries have accepted the extraction of confessions and the installation of terror as a normal part of government activities (Foucault, 1995). Amnesty International's (2000) global survey into patterns of torture found that most commonly the victims were suspected and convicted criminals for whom there was little sympathy. There were also insufficient numbers of police trained as investigators, the under-reporting of torture, a failure both by criminal suspects and the perpetrators to recognize routine beating as torture, and a lack of opportunity to seek redress for complaints. Even today, most of the world's population resides in countries where the use and threat of torture prevails (*Freedom in the World*, 2003)[1]. According to Mollica's estimate (2004) some 60 percent of asylum-seekers in the United States have previously been tortured.

As well as protecting the interests of temporal rulers, torture has been used in the past by religious powers to suppress heresy, stifle minority faiths, deal with suspected witches, force people to convert and, as in the case of Galileo, to suppress scientific advance. Catholics, unnerved by the Renaissance and Reformation, attempted to preserve their power through the infamous Inquisition that became synonymous with torture, yet only recently has a Pope apologised for its excesses (John Paul II, 2004). Then the Protestants reproduced some of the most repressive features of the Inquisition (cf. Webster, 1990), with Luther imprisoning and killing Catholics, and Calvin, having unsuccessfully denounced the theologian Servetus to the Catholic Inquisition, had him tried for heresy and blasphemy and sentenced to death. Similarly Henry VIII executed clerics to establish the Church of England, and Cromwell slaughtered Catholics in Ireland to subjugate the country.

Yet there have been periods when the authorities showed greater humanity. In the hundred years after Sweden gave the lead in 1734, torture was prohibited in much of Europe, but it remained acceptable for use in colonisation, slavery, and the discipline of soldiers and sailors. According to Peters (1985), the partial revulsion can be attributed to a combination of the philosophy of the enlightenment and reactions to the excesses of the American and French revolutions. But in the 20th century the rise of fascism, communism, and other dictatorships undid many of the gains, and torture flourished once more.

1 This publication, providing information on human rights, shows torture to have been reported in 14 out of the world's 20 most populous countries. Between them the 14 countries had over 3,845 million people, i.e. more than half the total of the planet.

PSYCHOLOGICAL IMPACT OF TORTURE

The Istanbul Protocol (1999) listed the symptoms commonly presented by torture survivors. These included sexual dysfunction, dissociation, depersonalisation, and psychosis. Clinicians like Graessner, Gurris and Pross (2001, pp.222-223) also mentioned 'persistent depression, panic attacks, compulsive behaviour, psychogenic eating disorders, suicide risk, alcohol and medication abuse, addictive behavior in general and somatization (transposition of feelings and emotions into psychosomatic pain and psychosomatic illnesses)' – with Mollica (2004) noting the particular tendency following torture for depression in some cultural groups to be expressed somatically. Kira (2002) noted the cumulative cognitive effects on victims who were subject to repeated torture. Certainly it is well known that repeated blows to the head cause brain injury, especially when victims are blindfolded or restrained and unable to reduce the impact, and that electric shocks, violent shaking, and near asphyxiation carry similar risks. The effects of brain injury, as listed by Khan, Baguley, and Cameron (2003), include memory impairment, difficulty with new learning, reduced attention and concentration, reduced speed and flexibility of thought processing; impaired problem-solving skills, problems in planning, organising, and making decisions, language problems and impaired judgement.

Posttraumatic Stress Disorder is also commonly diagnosed in torture victims. It has been recognised by both the World Health Organisation (ICD-10, 1992) and the American Psychiatric Association (DSM IV 1994), An associated ICD-10 classification is 'Enduring Change to Personality After Catastrophic Experiences', such as 'concentration camp experiences, torture *and* hostage situations', when survivors exhibit symptoms of permanent hostility and distrust, social withdrawal, feelings of emptiness and hopelessness, increased dependency, problems with modulation of aggression, hypervigilance, irritability, and feelings of alienation. A comparable alternative DSM diagnosis for more severe reactions to extreme events, but lacking full recognition, is Disorders of Extreme Stress Not Otherwise Specified (DESNOS) (cf. Luxenberg, Spinazzola, and van der Kolk, 2001).

As Ehlers (2000, p. 766) pointed out, a high rate of Posttraumatic Stress Disorder (PTSD) (*DSM*, IV 1994) among torture survivors is to be expected, given that the diagnosis is linked to threats to life and autonomy, loss of control, and that torturers deliberately instil massive fear, self-doubt, self-loathing and despair through what Schlapobersky and Bamber described in 1988 as a perverted form of intimacy. One defining feature is the persistent avoidance of stimuli associated with the trauma. The evocative stimuli might be an innocuous object such as a manila folder, or an authoritarian manner, a uniformed official, and being questioned in a facility resembling a prison or cell. One of my clients went hungry rather than eat the meals provided at his hostel because queuing for the food reminded him of the place in which he was tortured. In some circumstances survivors might be aware of sudden and apparently inexplicable surges in anxiety without immediately being able to make a connection to a past experience. Others have found themselves reliving the horror in flashbacks that typically were disjointed and fragmentary (cf. Brewin and Holmes, 2003). Fear of triggering further flashbacks could precipitate incapacitating anxiety in survivors making them reticent to disclose the details of torture, a reticence often reinforced by deep feelings of shame, for example from sexual humiliation or for yielding information.

Most people acknowledge some discomfort when under public scrutiny (Rosenbaum Biederman, Pollock, and Hirshfeld, 1994), and for some 2 to 5% of adults the experience becomes a phobic condition (den Boer, 1997). Victims with an already high level of anxiety are made more anxious by the thought of possible consequences of not being able to answer questions posed by their interrogators. Under torture they also strain against despair and face fresh anxieties about what they might become should they survive captivity, and what meaning their lives could have. Turner and Gorst-Unsworth (1993) considered this Existential Dilemma as the most important of the four psychological sequelae of torture – the others being Incomplete Emotional and Cognitive Processing, Depressive Reactions and Life Events, and Somatic Symptoms - and they thought it the most difficult to conceptualize in medical terms, saying that 'Survivors face a double dilemma, coming to terms with the full reality of torture in their world and not succumbing to the insidious pressure of the torturer to change.'

TORTURE AS A PROCESS

To understand more of the subjective impact, it is helpful to regard torture as a process with several stages that often begins before arrest within a general climate of repression and lasts well beyond imprisonment wherever the survivor might try to settle. Not every victim will experience all the stages. For example, a demonstrator beaten up and left for dead on the street may never have been imprisoned.

Pre-Seizure

People living in communities in which torture is practised are apprehensive long before being physically assaulted or detained. Historically, knowledge of persecution in their community will have affected their basic need for psychological security and grossly distorted their childhood development, as also would the experience of civil war, invasion, lasting poverty, famine and other kinds of disaster. In many of these circumstances children have to hold their tongues, learn not to question their fathers returning from the police station battered and bruised, nor to ask what happened to their mothers after soldiers took them away. In some cultures even when all or most of a group were raped, none will speak of it. Guilt, shame, and fear of retribution reinforce the silence.

Adults who try to protect themselves from violence by avoiding activities that invite unwelcome attention, might live with self-reproach for their cowardice - witnessing and hearing stories of repeated injustice, and feeling unable to challenge those in authority, creates a sense of being trapped and powerless. Even covert challenges to the powerful provoke anxiety and guilt because of the risk to self and consequences for the family. Mildly dissenting talk of politics at home carries dangers because of pressure that the authorities could bring to bear on anyone present. The perception of the risks is heightened if the individual already has been treated brutally either in or out of prison, or has known others who suffered or have disappeared.

In societies where the authorities use psychiatric diagnoses to portray dissidents as insane, seeking professional help also carries the risk of being locked in a hospital ward and subjected to the unethical use of mind-numbing drugs.

Seizure

Often the potential victims of torture are subject to shock tactics such as pre-dawn raids, the wilful destruction of property, and rough handling, if not actual beating. There is often the use of painful restraints or uncomfortable postures, blindfolds, gags or hoods made more dreadful by the stench of vomit or blood from previous captives. For adult victims the distress during such raids is compounded when, even without overt violence, children present become distraught with fear because they are old enough to know what is happening and likely to follow for the prime target. Families suffer not just through dreading the fate of loved ones but also from the consequences for those not seized such as becoming isolated, losing income, possessions and homes, and being forced to flee to safety. In particular the impact of such disruption on children cannot be minimised.

Detention

Depending on the type of conveyance and the time it takes to travel to a centre for torture, there could be harsh exposure to the elements, the denial of food, drink, medical treatment, and use of toilet facilities: even after arrival such necessities are not guaranteed, and frequently their absence is a deliberate part of the ill treatment. Captives unable to see during the journey to the detention centre are disoriented on arrival, and the guards on reception might aggravate this by walking them blindfolded around complicated routes, accompanied by blows, tripping, pushing into walls or even down flights of stairs.

Even for people with no reason to expect torture, incarceration often comes as a shock. Jail conditions are never luxurious, but for those facing torture they are likely to be particularly bad. Survivors describe one-person cells so small that they were unable to lie down or to stand without bending, or being crammed into a larger room with too little space for the number they contain. Their cells are often either below ground or windowless by design, with limited sanitation, poor ventilation and the pervasive smell of urine, faeces, vomit or blood. They are often denied medical treatment and essential medication for any pre-existing medical condition. They have to cope with the consequences of poor hygiene and unsafe drinking water, and at times the deliberate introduction of infection that causes great pain or discomfort. Then in places where brutality is the norm, the financial exploitation of prisoners and their families is common, with captives in some places being obliged to pay guards to bring food. Speaking with fellow political prisoners, if allowed, needs caution because of informers or the authorities forcing a confidant to disclose. Criminals, if allowed access to political prisoners, might abuse them either to gain favour from the jailers or for other reasons, including sexual gratification.

Underlying all, the political prisoners feel guilty for not providing for their dependents and for adding to their dangers, and they wonder whether their families will be allowed access to their remains or even learn of their death.

Preliminary Acts

Many torturers use 'softening up' techniques on their victims or what has been called facetiously 'torture lite' after reduced calorie products. Despite the euphemisms, the deliberate infliction of suffering is part of the definition of torture prohibited by the 1984 UN Convention. The preliminaries might include sleep or sensory deprivation techniques, extended isolation, overly bright lights, excessive noise, unwelcome music, mind-altering drugs, repeated exercise beyond the point of pain, excruciating restraint and body positions, smearing with ordure, being forced to swallow contaminated food or drink urine, intimidation by dogs, and sexual humiliation. In the preliminaries the torturers note the cruelties that victims find most disturbing, and then increase their frequency and severity accordingly.

For victims, being threatened or forewarned of torture by the guards creates additional stress, as does exposure to the sight and sound of others being tortured (particularly if they involve family members), being told of executions, made to watch them, or forced to undergo mock executions - but there is nothing 'mock' about the terror that comes from having a revolver placed against the temple and waiting to learn if the chamber is loaded. After such an experience one client could not listen to a cassette tape because the noise at the end of the reel resembled the sound of a trigger clicking, and it evoked panic.

Denial of Communication

Captors give few victims the opportunity to speak to a lawyer, and if they do it is very likely to be when any obvious evidence of assault has disappeared. But in any case the victims fear that their communications are not privileged, that being honest will invite reprisal, and even that their lawyers might be tortured either for information or for being diligent in their defence. Lack of trustworthy or effective representation adds to the sense of being beyond justice.

Major Physical Attacks

Grievous assaults, especially when repeated, are likely to leave lifelong physical injuries – commonly these include musculo-skeletal pain, damaged kidneys, burns that limit movement, reduced vision and hearing, brain damage and severe headaches. The enduring pain and disfigurement remind survivors of their terrible past, sometimes in very vivid and frightening ways. Sexual assaults also raise questions in their minds about self-worth, gender identity, and the effects of breaking cultural taboos (no matter how involuntarily). Such assaults also interfere in other ways with libido and the ability to enjoy intimacy. Rape, which may occur frequently over weeks or years, can cause infections including HIV, with dire prospects if no treatment is available. One client raped by his guards in a country where AIDS is a major killer, lived in the UK for years convinced that he was doomed before being persuaded to be tested. His relief was enormous after tests showed no sign of HIV, despite confirming Hepatitis B.

With repeated torture, victims have difficulty in retaining a sense of time. They might have no clues as to whether it is day or night or how long they have been detained, and are even likely to register time by the frequency of sessions of physical torture. But they can never be sure when the next session will begin, how far it will go, or how long it will last. Should they try to provide their interrogators with information to avoid further sessions of torture, they might arouse suspicion that the information is either misleading or that there is more to be had, and so invite further punishment. The oppressors exploit concessions as they think fit.

Further Detention

After the desired information or confession has been extracted, or after the torturer has given up for whatever reason, prisoners might continue to be detained under a harsh regime but without further physical torture. With no release date or mechanism for review and family contact still barred or very infrequent, survivors suffering the effects of torture, malnutrition, and disease, have little support to help them counter their despair and promote psychological healing. A combination of stoicism, machismo, and lessons learned earlier in life might deter them from speaking to each other of the horrors endured. Some have to bribe officials for opportunities to escape or to obtain their release.

Post Detention

For torture survivors, sanctioned release from prison is likely to be the start of new problems unless the political regime in society at large has changed. On discharge they might remain under surveillance, and be required to report regularly to hostile authorities and/or be visited by them. They might be sent into internal exile, banned from certain occupations and activities, and required to take jobs in which no one will risk associating with them. At home their feelings of guilt will be compounded by awareness of the suffering the family has endured. Relatives might find that despite their best efforts, they can do little to revive the spirits of the home-comers, and they are at a loss as to where they should turn to find help, because governments relying on torture are unlikely to assist the rehabilitation of survivors.

Continuing persecution often forces survivors and their families to flee. The flight could use up much of an extended family's reserves with bribes to secure documents and safe-passage. If caught, the punishments can be severe for most and fatal for some. In transit the fugitives present ready targets for exploiters. Their journeys can involve physical dangers over snow-covered mountains, along arid trails, the use of ramshackle transport and overloaded boats. Their survival might bring further psychological burdens for all members of the family – such as the guilt of a parent who nearly suffocated a young child to keep it quiet and avoid being detected, and the anxiety instilled in everyone as the escape progresses. Most of them have worries about leaving the elderly and other members of the extended family behind, with the constant fear that anyone there could be made to suffer for being suspected or blamed for their disappearance.

Often their sense of relief on arrival at their destination is short lived, and major crises follow as they await decisions from the authorities about being allowed to stay. As refugees they lose status, often have their skills, learning, and heritage undervalued by the people of the host country, and they might be subject to verbal or physical attacks by local xenophobes.

They might continue to suffer trauma that is tantamount to torture by proxy, as news filters through of the continuing oppression in their country of origin, with images of violence such as those commonly shown on TV stirring up their guilt and despair. One survivor fled with his wife and children to the UK after several months of systematic torture. There he learned that a close relative had been arrested and was in the same prison where he had been held. Another refugee whose torture included rape, had to leave behind daughters whom she believed were in danger of being treated similarly if they were identified by the regime.

SURVIVORS AND LEGAL PROCESSES

In some jurisdictions cases of torture might only come before judges because a detainee had died from injuries. In such cases the emphasis tends to be on determining the cause of death and identifying those responsible. In cases of non-fatal torture, the legal focus still tends to be on major physical assaults, because they offer objective data. Yet even severe torture might leave no lasting physical trace, and when there is a scar it is not always possible for it to be attributed to deliberate mistreatment (cf. *Examining Asylum Seekers, A Health Professionals' Guide to Medical and Psychological Evaluation of Torture,* 2001). Therefore because of the difficulty in assessing the reliability of the subjective evidence the incorporation of psychological injury presents a challenge to those who draft legislation and administer the law (cf. Courts, 2001). Consequently those investigating, prosecuting and sentencing torturers tend to be guarded when adducing evidence about the extent of psychological damage to victims. Also, to ensure justice for those accused of torture, judges are often obliged to rule out as inadmissible or legally irrelevant some hurtful experiences of survivors, and they have to pay more attention to procedural issues such as retrospectivity, double criminality, extradition, double jeopardy, witness protection and disclosure (Woolf, 2000).

Even for petitioners in the general population, establishing that a single incident resulted in legally significant psychological symptoms presents problems (cf. Echeburúa, de Corral, and Amor, 2002). As described above in *Torture as Process*, multiple trauma might arise for victims before, during, and after their detention, so that, for example, survivors could be required to establish that their psychiatric symptoms arose during their detention alone. And those in countries racked by civil war with atrocities committed on both sides, have to explain why they attributed their psychiatric condition to being tortured by one army, rather than to having witnessed the atrocities committed by the other.

Consequently as *The Istanbul Protocol* (1999) indicated, there is not only a need for separate legislation against torture, but for those investigating, prosecuting and sentencing torturers to be made fully aware of the extent of the psychological damage that torture has inflicted on the survivors. Specifically it noted that one of the central aims of torture 'is to reduce the individual to a position of extreme helplessness and distress that can lead to a deterioration of cognitive, emotional and behavioral functions. Thus, torture can be a means of attacking the individual's fundamental modes of psychological and social functioning. Under such circumstances, the torturer strives not only for physical incapacitation of the victim, but for the disintegration of the individual's personality… to destroy the victim's sense of being.' (p. 43).

Even when totalitarian regimes are replaced and democracy begins to take root, powerful forces can remain to deter legal action being taken within a country and sometimes beyond - as happened with Pinochet avoidance of prosecution in Chile and in Europe. Even a new government with a strong will to tackle past abuses might lack enough jail and court facilities for dealing with all of those accused of practising torture, and it might fear that instability would follow the arraignment of even the few most responsible for human rights abuses. At the time of writing, Slobodan Milosevic is in the sixth year of his trial at the International Court in the Hague, charged with responsibility for unlawful confinement, imprisonment, torture, wilfully causing great suffering, and other inhumane acts. A Balkan survivor, prompted by the news that the hearing might be brought to an earlier close than expected, complained about the hundreds of other Serbian killers and rapists lower down the hierarchy who are able to go about their lives unchallenged. He wanted the prosecutions extended to all the major abusers, not just confined to the political leadership and senior military officers. Knowing that many face no sanctions and are able even to draw pensions for their brutal work, increased his anguish and bought back the intense feelings of powerless, capriciousness and gross injustice associated with his experience of torture. The Balkan man accepted that the international criminal court brought an essential degree of impartiality and expertise to a bitter and contentious matter, but he wanted Serbia specifically to acknowledge the scale of its war crimes and to apologise for them.

The transfer of a hearing to a court in another country raises other questions about the axiom of justice needing to be seen to be done. *Human Rights Watch* (2004c, p. 207) commented that such relocations abroad were 'less accessible to victims... These trials sometimes lack the visibility in the country where the crimes occurred that a local trial would have'. At the very least, when trials are held further afield, arrangements should be made to ensure that survivors, whether or not remaining in the country where the crimes took place, are kept informed. This could mean not just having designated media representatives in the courtroom, but independent journalists with the responsibility for spreading information about the proceedings more widely.

Where the full legal process is seen as impractical or impossible, one option might be to have public procedures akin to those initiated by the *Truth and Reconciliation Commission* (TRC) *of South Africa* (2002) that offered amnesty in return for confessing horrendous crimes. However Fullard (2004) noted that many of the victims who went before the TRC, with the hope that their case would be investigated, felt let down and no closer to the truth than before they publicly told of their suffering. He said 'Irrespective of the feasibility of investigating every case, victims' high expectations of the TRC have been dashed, and in their eyes, this has undermined its credibility'.

The typical political survivor of torture, like other parties in restorative justice procedures of the kind mentioned by Maxwell and Morris in the present book, wants to have injustice remedied. The remedy fulfils a basic need, and it makes a difference to the ability of victims to move on in their lives. It is not simply a matter of seeking punishment and reparation – although as Cullinane (2001) found, research has to be undertaken with different cultural groups to determine their wishes in the matter. Rather, as Summerfield (2000) argued, it concerns respect for ethnic cultures, minority groups, social justice and economic development, saying,

> 'In Guatemala, restitution of Mayan identity is central to both personal and social recovery after cultural assault. In Mozambique, the actual physical work of reconstruction building houses and planting fields is considered by ex-refugees to be particularly crucial. Nevertheless, people do not necessarily aim to restore everything to its pre-war state; many recognise that some things have changed and they must adjust. Ultimately a population recovers from war not as recipients of aid or as patients but as active citizens. Structural poverty, landlessness, and lack of viable jobs too often retard this rebuilding of lives'.

The *Istanbul Protocol* (1999, pp. 27-28) also acknowledged that it is common for victims who have been traumatised either to omit or be unable to recall significant details of their shocking experience. Ehlers (2000, p763) said the same of the general population with PTSD, noting that patients have 'relatively poor intentional recall of the traumatic event. Their narratives tend to be fragmented and disorganized.' Obviously the gaps and inconsistencies in recall present problems for courts, and they raise doubts about the credibility of asylum seekers when details that were not mentioned in initial interviews are disclosed later. But the authorities need to recognise the multiple factors that often contribute to the poor recall of important facts.

It follows that interviewers seeking accurate histories need training to ensure that they cause minimal distress, assist accurate recall, and know when they should seek the advice of health professionals skilled at interviewing traumatised people. Officials might not be aware of the effects on memory of altered states of consciousness, avoidance, cognitive deficits, performance and social anxiety, classical conditioning, the psychological effects of brain injury, and the adverse effects of such medication as sedatives prescribed for psychological and neurological conditions, and of street drugs and alcohol taken to dull awareness and overcome poor sleep. Then other factors like poor interpreting, cultural differences, severe pain, and the physical and emotional exhaustion that might accompany an asylum seeker's arrival in another country might complicate responses to interviews.

Given that survivors willing to support legal action often find it painful to recount their experiences no matter what the setting, they should have recourse to measures such as screens to prevent eye contact with the accused, and video testimony to minimise the emotional impact of cross-examination – consistent with David Wexler's wider appeal for therapeutic jurisprudence that he made in the present book. But in preparing survivors who wish to make an initial statement of complaint, the technique of Testimony Therapy should be considered.

TESTIMONY THERAPY

Elizabeth Lira and Eugenia Weinstein[2] developed Testimony Therapy as a response to the brutality of the Pinochet regime. It is a form of history taking in which the therapist looks to the client's preferences and welfare in creating a written record of events. As Blackburn (2003) denotes, a typical record would include information about:

- The informant's background - age, country of origin, social data, important political cultural or religious aspects

- Situation up to the traumatic event
- The trauma story in detail – dates, hours, places
- Description of torture methods used and the reaction to them
- Examples of daily life in prison
- The flight - how and why the client escaped
- Life in exile
- Dreams, hopes for the future and realistic possibilities
- A final statement where the client declares this is a true account
- Signatures - the client if she or he is willing to go public, the therapist or others, such as interpreters, who witnessed the giving of testimony

Survivors might also sketch details or add comments to relevant photographs and drawings that others have made. With client agreement some therapists tape testimony sessions from which they provide transcripts, while others rely on note taking before typing drafts. The process continues until a survivor is satisfied with the accuracy and truth of the account. The aim of the therapists, taking care not resemble interrogators, is to bring out useful details without leading with questions that suggest answers. They often begin at some less fraught stage of personal history, and proceed at a speed that is appropriate for engaging the client. Once completed, the witness still has an absolute right to decide if and how the testimony is to be made available to others. Some survivors find it sufficiently beneficial to unlock and share their memories without taking the matter further. As with Narrative Therapy, a later development used in the general population for the assimilation of traumatic experience, Testimony Therapy involves restructuring the trauma story, rebuilding shattered assumptions, seeking completion, acknowledging and working through memories, reconstructing the self and providing new perspectives about the past, developing new meaning, a theory of healing and their own voice to avoid repeating that of the perpetrator (Meichenbaum, 2000).

Such therapeutic concerns mean that lawyers should not expect every client who begins Testimony Therapy to hand over a document, nor that all accounts delivered will meet the standards of legal proceedings. However, Testimony Therapy does have some important lessons for the legal profession and the immigration authorities. It shows that in the right circumstances torture survivors will provide far more detail of the atrocities to which they have been subjected than otherwise, and that this can be done in a way that helps rather than harms them while overcoming the problems of memory described above.

But Testimony Therapy does not suit all survivors of torture. As well as the 'persistent avoidance of stimuli associated with the trauma' mentioned above, some survivors fear that testimony might bring further repercussions for themselves and their families. So great was the fear of one Iraqi client for his relatives that it was only after the fall of Baghdad that he resumed his real name and spoke more freely. Others might not want to share the details of what happened, perhaps from shame or a suspicion that they will not be believed. Some feel it too soon to revisit the horror, and others might wish to keep a fragile emotional distance from the trauma of their past. Blackwell (1988) also pointed out that testimony might be prompted more by the survivors' desperate need to avoid deportation than by a desire for wider justice.

[2] For their personal security this work appeared under pseudonyms, and it is listed here under Cienfuegos & Monelli (1983).

Cunningham and Silove (1993, p756) warned that survivors might interpret as persecutory even their most subtle pressures to elicit stories.

ELEMENTS OF A MODEL FOR RESTORATION

The Medical Foundation has a number of strengths, one of which derives from its assembly of staff and volunteers with varied backgrounds and skills. The personnel contribute to the restoration of survivors through activities as diverse as horticultural therapy, creative writing, a chess club, and a befriending scheme. The treatment and support advocated below also draw on visits to other centres for survivors, conferences on trauma, and organisational theory. Its elements are presented under the headings of Passion and Dispassion, Integrated Services, Acknowledging the Stress of the Work, Providing Better Service, and Ending Isolation and Silence.

Passion and Dispassion

As McIvor and Turner (1995) indicated, supporters need to look deeper and harder in interviews to understand the significance of what transpires. They need constantly to ask themselves what patterns of behaviour perhaps are being repeated? What value or meaning might be attached to particular events and symbols? What else might have happened that is as yet unspeakable or overlooked, perhaps because it was thought obvious to the supporter? Are there any current fears or pressures, such as the threat of deportation or poverty, that might also prompt the concealment or distortion of information? One client was particularly slow to reveal the details and accept the significance of his torture, because beating prisoners was so commonplace and he had grown up in a community where no one spoke about what happened in prison. Another survivor 'forgot' for almost two years of group meetings that he had been rammed head first into a wall, despite reporting frequent excruciating headaches and a diagnosis of traumatic epilepsy.

McIvor and Turner (1995, p708) also thought that contrary to normal practice in which psychotherapists need to be more neutral, those working with torture victims 'should be prepared to declare an open commitment to supporting human rights, while at the same time remaining objective'. Such an affirmation by individuals and the organisation offering a service makes it easier for survivors to reveal and express views for which previously they were punished. But strong emotions can be stirred simply by demeanour or the visible signs of injuries, even before details of torture and other tragedies emerge. While such feelings of identification are part of being fully human, in the interests of clients it is important for them to be put to one side and dealt with later. Supporters need to monitor their own emotional reactions to ensure that they do not impair their ability to carry out the work.

Helpers also need to be emotionally aware and dispassionate to avoid the 'silencing response' that knowingly or inadvertently reduces their own discomfort (Baranowksy, 2002). The 'silencing' involves redirecting clients to less fraught topics for the helper's benefit, and minimizing and neglecting discussions of the horrors they have experienced. The helper might rationalise the avoidance with thoughts of protecting the client', or thinking that the statement cannot be true. Mollica (2004) noted how survivors and supporters have even conspired to avoid the discussion of trauma. By way of illustration he reported that a woman who had an excellent relationship with her doctor for nine years, gave him no reason to think that she had been tortured. But after the doctor had attended a training session on treating the effects of terrorism, he asked the patient for the first time whether she had undergone extreme violence, and was told of the horrors she had experienced in Cambodia and being the victim of a violent crime since arriving in the US.

Obviously helpers have also to be good listeners, but good listening is an art and a time consuming process. Belton (1998) called his biography of Helen Bamber, the founder of the Medical Foundation, *The Good Listener* in recognition of her ability to listen anew and patiently to each survivor. He also commented on the healing quality of her attention. Like many good listeners, Helen had no formal training but her commitment to eliciting so many complete and horrifying stories is exceptional, and it has inspired many professionals to pay more attention to refugees and others likely to have been exposed to torture.

Integrated Services

Some survivors will be wary of anything that might be seen to suggest that they have a mental illness. Therefore it is useful for supporters who are not mental health professionals to be able to explain and encourage survivors to consider the services available. Classes or activity groups dedicated to survivors and refugees also do much to help them realise they are not alone in their symptoms, perhaps making it easier for them to accept a more explicitly therapeutic approach. But it must be understood that survivors have many needs other than the psychological that supporters should recognize and try to remedy. Therapy cannot succeed while clients are overwhelmed by current anxieties and unmet practical needs. Therefore clinicians need to identify and find resources or other agents to address such issues as suitable housing, access to utilities, and having adequate income. Attending to such needs blurs traditional boundaries. For example, a doctor might identify not just physical needs but other kinds and refer to a lawyer and a welfare advisor. Or a counsellor might refer a survivor to English classes or get forms from the Red Cross to begin a search for missing relatives.

Acknowledging the Stress of the Work

Exposure to survivors' stories and contact with those beginning to deal with their experiences is likely to assail the individual supporters, the team of helpers, the wider organisation including receptionists. As Taylor and Frazer (1981) reported from their study of personnel involved with the recovery and identification of human remains after an aircrash, the stress affects not just front-line workers but support staff of all kinds. It makes them generally less efficient, less able to meet the needs of clients and more likely to engage in activities that disrupt the organisation and add to the stress of others. Countering it should begin with an induction that makes clear the work is seen to carry certain risks, and outlines the organisational plans to minimise them. Staff and volunteers should be made to understand that part of their commitment is to monitor themselves and take appropriate action to recognise and address the early symptoms of stress. Non-clinical staff, in addition to regular reviews with the line manager about what impact the work is having on them personally, should be offered outside supervision.

Providing a Better Service

Many survivors are refugees who initially lack command of the local language. For this reason those who provide services ideally should have not only a survivor's first language but also a good understanding of the culture from which particular refugees have come. Should this be impossible, helpers should use interpreters who are bilingual, bicultural, and able to work with emotionally challenging content of interviews. Soon such interpreters develop into cultural brokers, proactively working to promote two-way understanding and extending the range of services between survivors and supporters in a culturally sensitive manner. Access should also be arranged to groups in the wider community with particular religious, philosophical and political beliefs that might help survivors to express themselves and so assist their recovery. For example, finding a congregation that worships in the client's language can provide valuable spiritual and social support.

Supporters working with women survivors need to be aware of the possibility of gender being a significant factor on the expression of inhibition of sensitive matters - not just those relating to humiliation and the disclosure of sexual assaults, but for other extreme events such as genital mutilation, imposed sterilisation or abortion, enforced marriages, threats or actual assault for trying to escape or avoid an unwanted relationship (Amnesty International, 2001). Hence women survivors might often have a preference if not a need to work with women supporters. Similarly men who have been raped might have a gender preference in selecting their supporters, with some finding it easier to talk with a woman while others might feel able only to speak of such topics with another man. In particular children who are either survivors or are in the families of survivors require supporters with the experience and insights of those specially trained to help them (Melzak, 1992).

Clinical experience shows that supporters need to be therapeutically versatile, because no single approach to working with survivors can be seen as universally the best. As Pope and Garcia-Peltoniemi (1991, p274) noted, 'practitioners and researchers will find it less useful to search for the most effective treatment model for torture victims than to attempt to find what model works best under what circumstances for what person with what cognitive and related coping styles'. Interventions often need to draw on the survivors' distant experiences to re-activate, perhaps forgotten resources. At other times it is a case of helping people to realise that learning from one area of their life can be relevant to current needs.

Ending Isolation and Silence

Sometimes the easiest way to help survivors who have been seriously hurt is not through formal therapy but through largely non-verbal activities such art, gardening and crafts, educational classes, social activities, community publishing, video making, displays, and cultural events, especially when there is someone skilled to facilitate the discovery of wider meanings, encourage greater exploration and rebuild confidence. The experience can reactivate old learning as well as provide new opportunities for the expression of latent talent.

One of the most touching scenes I have witnessed involved two devout survivors from very different backgrounds. One was torn between mourning his lost family and keeping alive the hope they might have survived genocide, and the other was grieving for the family he was prevented from seeing. They, along with others in the group which included men of lapsed or no faith, increased their ability to survive by becoming brothers through sharing their past, their current struggles and beginning to voice hope for the future. After some months of weekly meetings the two pious men responded to each other's difficulties by saying 'I will pray for you'- gestures that were warmly received despite one being Christian and the other Muslim.

Supporters and their organisations should consider how to encourage involvement in the community, such as securing employment. Work helps the alienated to organise their daily activities, develop their skills, and become more financially independent. It also provides social benefits through contacts and activities with other employees, and it gives refugees something else to think about other than painful ruminations of the past. But the current ban in the UK on asylum seekers working in paid employment not only promotes poverty and unnecessary reliance on the state, but it is also an obstacle to forming friendly contacts. Many survivors would welcome the social benefits of work and the demands of a job.

Kindness is important for those who have been so cruelly treated, and I end this section with one example. The Medical Foundation arranges for individuals and families to have a holiday with people who welcome survivors. The hosts are briefed both about the needs of survivors in general and the specific needs of any guest they are about to receive. A treasured photo shows a client on holiday in Scotland, standing under a blossoming tree in highland outfit, including a kilt. The dressing up was just one in a week full of activities arranged by his hosts, from playing golf at St Andrews, to visiting the Edinburgh Festival, to learning very practical cooking in the family kitchen. For a man who had lost all of his relatives, being received in this way was momentous. The man's smile in the photograph, and again when we met in London two weeks after the holiday, spoke volumes about the healing contributions made by people with good will who were also generous with their time.

Conclusion

While the nature of the torturer has yet to be clearly identified and addressed, and the sinister means of their organisations fully exposed, there can be no doubt that their practice is one of the most pernicious and unconscionable that any human being can use against another. Torture exemplifies extreme injustice, strikes at the heart of positive personality growth of the victims and the harmonious development of communities and – although they might think otherwise – it works to the detriment of those who practice or condone it. Those working to help the tortured cope with their burdens can only hope that a sufficient number of people with goodwill in society at large might deal with the social and political issues to help to create a world in which humankind displays more virtuous than vicious behaviour. The hope is that justice might eventually prevail, and that the better side of mankind will flourish to the benefit of all concerned.

REFERENCES

Amnesty International. (1997). *Response to UN Special Rapporteur on the independence of judges and lawyers in the United Kingdom of Great Britain and Northern Ireland.* - accessed at http://web.amnesty.org/library/index/ENGEUR450061998

Amnesty International. (2000). *Amnesty International Torture worldwide: An affront to human dignity.* New York: Amnesty International Publications - accessed from www.amnestyusa.org/stoptorture/tortureworldwide.pdf

Amnesty International. (2001). *Broken bodies, shattered minds*; *Torture and ill-treatment of women.* – accessed from
http://web.amnesty.org/library/Index/engACT400012001?OpenDocumentandof=THEMES%5CWOMEN

Amnesty International. (2003). *Combating torture: a manual for action.* London: Amnesty International Publications.

Baranowsky, A.B. (2002). The silencing response in clinical practice: On the road to dialogue. In C.R. Figley. (Ed.). *Treating Compassion Fatigue.* (pp. 155-170). New York: Brunner Mazel.

Belton, N. (1998). *The Good Listener: Helen Bamber: A life against cruelty*, London: Weidenfeld and Nicholson.

Blackburn, P. (2003). Handout for a staff development meeting at the *Traumatic Stress Clinic.* London. (private circulation).

Blackwell, R. (1988). *Testimony and psychotherapy: A comment on Buss and Agger*: he Testimony Method. Refugee Participation Network, No.3 - accessed at http://www.torturecare.org.uk/publications/Archive/Black_4.rtf

Brewin, C.R., and Holmes, E.A. (2003). Psychological theories of posttraumatic stress disorder. *Clinical Psychology Review*, 23, 339-376.

Cienfuegos, A.J., and Monelli, C. (1983). The testimony of political repression as a therapeutic instrument. *American Journal of Orthopsychiatry*, 53, 43-51.

Cohen, S. and Golan, D. (1991). *The Interrogation of Palestinians during the Intifada: Ill-treatment, 'moderate physical pressure' or torture ?* Jerusalem: B'Tselem - The Israeli Information Center for Human Rights in the Occupied Territories- accessed from http://www.btselem.org/Download/1991_Interrogation_Eng.doc

Courts, R. (2001). Wider Still and Wider? *The history of the law of psychiatric damage, and options for reform,* – accessed at http://www.courts.fsnet.co.uk/widerstill.htm

Country Reports on Human Rights Practices - Turkey 2003, U.S. Department of State, the Bureau of Democracy, Human Rights, and Labor, released on February 25, 2004- accessed from
http://us.politinfo.com/Information/Human_Rights/country_report_2003_125.html

Cullinane, S. (2001). *Torture survivor's perceptions of reparation: Preliminary survey.* London: Redress Trust.

Cunningham, M., and Silove, D. (1993). Principles of treatment and service development for torture and trauma survivors. In J. P. Wilson, and B. Raphael. (Eds.). *International Handbook of Traumatic Stress Syndromes.* (pp. 751–762). New York: Plenum.

Daley, S. (2001). *France is seeking a fine in trial of Algerian War General.* New York Times, 29 November.

Deahl, M. (2002). Commentary: The alleged abuses of human rights in Chinese psychiatry. *Psychiatric Bulletin*, 26: 445-446.

den Boer, J. A. (1997). Social phobia: epidemiology, recognition, and treatment. *British Medical Journal,* 315, 796-800.

Dershowitz, A.M. (2003). The torture warrant: A response to Professor Strauss. New York *Law School Law Review*, 48, 278-294.

DSM IV, *Diagnostic and statistical manual of mental disorders*. (IV edn.). (1994). Washington DC: American Psychiatric Association

Echeburúa, E., de Corral, P., and Amor, P.J. (2002*). Evaluation of psychological harm in the victims of violent crime. Psychology in Spain*, 6, 10-18. Available in English at http://www.psychologyinspain.com/content/full/2003/full.asp?id=7002

Ehlers, A. (2000). Posttraumatic stress disorder. In M.G. Gelder, J. Lopez-Ibor and N.C. Andreasen (Eds.). *New Oxford Textbook of Psychiatry*. Vol. 1. (pp. 758-771). Oxford: Oxford University Press.

Examining Asylum Seekers, *A Health Professionals' Guide to Medical and Psychological Evaluation of Torture*. (2001). Boston: Physicians for Human Rights.

Freedom House Report on the USA 2003, Freedom House–accessed from http://www.freedomhouse.org/research/freeworld/2003/countryratings/usa.htm

Freedom in the World. (2003). – accessed from. www.freedomhouse.org

Fullard, M. (2004). *Displacing Race: The South African Truth and Reconciliation Commission (TRC) and Interpretations of Violence. Race and Citizenship in Transition Series*, Centre for the Study of Violence and Reconciliation, Johannesburg. available at http://www.csvr.org.za/papers/paprctp3.htm

Foucault, M. (1995). Discipline and Punishment: the birth of the prison. New York; Vintage Books.

Goya, D.F. (1799) *Los Caprichos*. Madrid: Self-Published.

Graessner, S., Gurris, N., and Pross, C. (2001). *At the side of torture survivors: Treating a terrible assault on human dignity*. Baltimore: John Hopkins University Press. First published in German in 1996.

Gudjonsson, G.H. (2003). *The psychology of interrogation and confessions*: A handbook. Chichester: Wiley.

Hajjar, L. (2004). *Torture and the future*. Interventions: A Middle East report online - accessed from http://www.merip.org/mero/interventions/hajjar_interv.html

Human Rights Watch Americas Overview. (1997) Accessed from http://www.hrw.org/reports/1997/WR97/AMERICAS.htm

Human Rights Watch. (2004a). Lawyers' statement on Bush Administration's Torture Memos, 4 August - accessed from http://www.hrw.org/pub/2004/lawyers-statement.pdf

Human Rights Watch Report. (2004b). Like the dead in their coffins: Torture, detention, and the crushing of dissent in Iran- accessed at
http://hrw.org/reports/2004/iran0604/iran0604.pdf

Human Rights Watch World Report (2004c). New York: Human Rights Watch.

Human Rights Watch Background Briefing (19 August 2004). Interrogation Techniques for Guantánamo Detainees - accessed from
http://hrw.org/english/docs/2004/08/19/usdom9248.htm

ICD-10. (1992). *Internati*onal classification of diseases: Clinical descriptions and Diagnostic guidelines: 10th Revision. Geneva: World Health Organisation,

International Covenant on Civil and Political Rights (1966). G.A. res. 2200A (XXI), 21 U.N. GAOR Supp. (No. 16) at 52, U.N. Doc. A/6316 (1966), 999 U.N.T.S. 171, entered into force Mar. 23, 1976.

John Paul II. (2004). Letter to Cardinal Roger Etchegaray on the occasion of the presentation of the volume L'inquisizione - accessed from
http://www.vatican.va/holy_father/john_paul_ii/letters/2004/documents/hf_jp-ii_let_20040615_simposio-inquisizione_en.html

Khan, F., Baguley, I.J., and Cameron, I.D. (2003). Rehabilitation after traumatic brain injury. *Medical Journal of Australia*, 178 , 6, 290-295.

Kira, I. (2002). Torture, assessment and treatment. *Traumatology,* 8, 2, 61-89.

Landau, M. (1987*). Report of the Commission of Inquiry into the Methods of Investigation of the General Security Service Regarding Hostile Terrorist Activity*, Report. English translation issued by the Israel Government Press Office, Jerusalem.

Lifton R. J. (2004). Doctors and torture. *The New England Journal of Medicine*, 351, 5, 415-416.

Lucas, T. and Pross, C. (1995). Caught between conscience and complicity: Human rights violations and health professionals. *Medicine and Global Survival*; 2, 2, 106-114.- accessed from http://www.ippnw.org/MGS/V2N2Lucas.html

Luxenberg, T., Spinazzola, J., and van der Kolk, B. A. (2001). *Complex Trauma and Disorders of Extreme Stress* (DESNOS) Diagnosis, Part I: Assessment. Directions in Psychiatry, 21, 373-393. – accessed from http://www.traumacenter.org/DESNOS.pdf

Margarion, C. J. (1982). Hyperventilation syndromes: Infrequently recognized common expressions of anxiety and stress. *Medicine*, 61, 219-236.

McIvor, R., and Turner, S.W. (1995) Assessment and treatment approaches for survivors of torture. *British Journal of Psychiatry*. 166, 705-711.

Meichenbaum, D. (2000). Treating patients with PTSD: A constructive narrative approach. Clinical Quarterly, *National Centre for Posttraumatic Stress Disorder*, Fall 9, 55-59. accessed from http://www.ncptsd.org

Melzak , M. (1992). *Secrecy, privacy, survival, repressive regimes, and growing up. Bulletin, Anna Freud Centre,* 15, 205 - accessed from
http://www.torturecare.org.uk/publications/Archive/Melz_2.rtf

Mollica, R. F. (2004). Surviving torture. *New England Journal of Medicine*, 351, 1, 5-7.

New Scientist. (2004). *Abuse of Iraqis well thought through.* 10 May.

Ortiz, D., and Davis, P. (2002). *The blindfold's eyes; My journey from torture to truth: Maryknoll,* NY: Orbis Books.

Peters, E. (1985). *Torture*. Oxford: Basil Blackwell.

Pope, K.S., and Garcia-Peltoniemi, R.E. (1991). Responding to victims of torture: Clinical issues, professional responsibilities, and useful resources. *Professional Psychology, Research and Practice,* 22, 269-276.

Prosecutor v. Akayesu (1998) Case No. ICTR-96-4-T, 2 September, para 687. *Discussed, in End Impunity: Justice for the victims of torture.* (pp. 45-48). London: Amnesty International Publications, 2001.

Quaife, G.R. (1987) *Godly zeal and furious rage*. Beckenham, Kent: Croom Helm.

Rome Statute of the International Criminal Court. (1998). U.N. Doc. A/CONF.183/9*.

Rosenbaum, J.F., Biederman, J., Pollock, R.A., and Hirshfeld, D.R. (1994). The etiology of social phobia. *Journal of Clinical Psychiatry*, 55 (suppl. 6), 10-6.

Schlapobersky, J., and Bamber, H (1988), Rehabilitation with victims of torture. In D. Miserez. (Ed.) *Refugees - The trauma of exile.* (pp. 206-222). Dordrecht: Martinus Nijhoff.

Situation of Detainees at Guantánamo Bay (2006) United Nations Commission On Human Rights – accessed from http://www.ohchr.org/english/bodies/chr/docs/62chr/E.CN.4.2006.120_.pdf

Stevens Enquiry: *Overview and Recommendations.* (2003) - accessed from http://news.bbc.co.uk/1/shared/spl/hi/northern_ireland/03/stephens_inquiry/pdf/stephens_inquiry.pdf

Suedfeld, P. (1990) Psychologists as victims, administrators and designers of torture. In P Suedfeld. (Ed.): *Psychology and torture.* (pp.101-114). New York: Hemisphere Publishing.

Summerfield, D. (2000). War and mental health: a brief overview *British Medical Journal,* 321:232-235.

Taylor, A.J.W. and Frazer, A.G. (1981). *Psychological sequalae of Operation Overdue following the DC10 air crash in Antarctica.* Wellington: Victoria University, pp. 72.

The Istanbul Protocol: Manual on the Effective Investigation and Documentation of Torture and Other Cruel, Inhuman or Degrading Treatment or Punishment. (1999). Geneva: United Nations Publications (Professional Training Series No. 8). - accessed fropm http://www.phrusa.org/research/istanbul_protocol/ist_prot.pdf

The Observer. (1998). *This is the World Cup that no country wants to win.* 28 June, London.

Truth and Reconciliation Commission of South Africa. (2002). Report Vol. 7, Cape Town: Juta.

Turner, S.W., and Gorst-Unsworth, C. (1993). Psychological sequelae of torture. In J. P. Wilson, and B. Raphael. (Eds.). *International handbook of traumatic stress syndromes.* (pp.703-713). New York: Plenum. Chapter available at http://www.torturecare.org.uk/publications/Archive/Turn_2.rtf

Turner, S.W., and Hough, A. (1993). Hyperventilation as a reaction to torture. In J. P. Wilson, and B. Raphael. (Eds.). *International handbook of traumatic stress syndromes.* (pp. 725-732). New York: Plenum. Chapter available at http://www.torturecare.org.uk/publications/Archive/Turn_1.rtf

UN Convention Against Torture and Other Cruel, Inhuman or Degrading Treatment or Punishment (1984). *UN General Assembly Resolution* 39/46 of 10 December 1984. Entry into force 26 June 1987.

UN Optional Protocol to the Convention Against Torture and Other Cruel, Inhuman Or Degrading Treatment Or Punishment (2002) *Adopted by the UN General Assembly* 57/1999.

Verwoerd, H.F. (1924). Die Afstomping van die Gemoedsaandoeninge. (The blunting of the emotions). *Doctoral Dissertation.* Stellenbosch University.

Webster, R. (1990) *A brief history of blasphemy: Liberalism, censorship and the Satanic Verses*. Southwold: The Orwell Press.

Woolf, M. (2000). Challenging impunity for torture: A manual for bringing criminal and civil proceedings in England and Wales for torture committed abroad. London: Redress Trust. accessed from www.redress.org/publications/CHA.pdf

Wyndham Lewis, D.B. (1968). *The world of Goya.* London: Michael Joseph.

In: Justice as a Basic Human Need
Editor: Anthony Taylor, pp. 159-175

ISBN 1-59454-915-X

Chapter 12

THE INTERNATIONAL BILL OF RIGHTS AND HUMAN NATURE

Andrew Ladley[*]

ABSTRACT

This chapter is exploratory and argumentative, because it asks what the striving to establish an International Bill of Human Rights tells us about ourselves and about human nature? In seeking the answer it argues around two related questions:

(1) Why does humanity need an International Bill of Rights to achieve something so apparently unarguable as the statement that humans have the right to live in dignity?
(2) Why is it that out of some of the greatest wrongs of the human story have come some of the noblest ideals?

In the end it suggests a simple thesis– that the search for a common humanity, a common code, is the key to the avoidance of the personal and inter-group competition, so often accompanied by violence, is what I call 'the human story'. In this sense, internationalized standards of human rights are not optional extras. Neither is the implementation of 'universal human rights' some sort of moral western neo-colonialism. Put simply, the argument is that some form of universality is the only way forward, in a Darwinian sense: it is either 'common humanity', or the endless repetition of group struggle, discrimination, and violence. Human beings, in other words, *need* universalism

INTRODUCTION

The detailed content of the various international documents on human rights has been discussed at length by many people. So have other aspects of this vast subject, such as the notions of universality versus western legal imperialism in human rights, the failure of all

[*]Whilst I take responsibility for the product of course, I wish to acknowledge and thank my colleagues who commented on drafts, and our IPS graduate researchers Chloe Davenport and Jessie Williams.

those noble documents to effectively make any difference to the realities of abuse and deprivation in so many countries, and the important differences between the different 'classes' of rights.[1] I will touch on some of these debates, without engaging with them substantially. My purpose here is to reflect on the continuing need of people in different parts of the world to establish the framework for human rights, usually after periods of disaster that although producing exhaustion, often lay the foundation for social and political change.

The thesis does not in any way suggest a 'western' harmony/superiority as opposed to a 'developing country' conflict/inferiority. Actually there is no 'moral high ground' in the historical record, because most of the better-documented examples of group conflict are western. My argument is that the potential for doing harm to others is, alas, universal. So, it follows, must be the remedy, if there is one. In fact, all human beings, in all cultures, have very good historical reason for being nervous about other human beings, as Solzhenitsyn (cited in Katz, 1993) lamented:

> If only there were evil people somewhere, insidiously committing evil deeds, and it were necessary only to separate *them* from the rest of *us* and destroy *them*. But the line dividing good and evil cuts through the heart of every human being. And who is willing to destroy a piece of his own heart? (emphasis on *us* and *them* added).

THE INTERNATIONAL BILL OF RIGHTS (IBR)

The IBR originates from the United Nations Charter (UNC) (1945) and the Universal Declaration on Human Rights (UNDHR) (1948). The UDHR was later elaborated into the two major international treaties, known as Covenants: the first on *Economic, Social and Cultural Rights*, and the second on *Civil and Political Rights*. The three documents (UDHR, ICESCR and ICCPR) are commonly known as the 'International Bill of Human Rights'. However, for the purposes of this chapter, I include a wider set of treaties, even though they are mostly elaborations of what is in the core three, because a) they all are in some way mentioned in the UDHR and the two main Covenants, b) they are virtually universally accepted, and c) their titles and contents assist the arguments of this chapter.

So, in this discussion the IBR is regarded as comprising the following documents and their relevant Protocols and supplementary conventions:

[1] One key difference between 'economic, social and cultural' rights, and 'civil and political' rights is the notion that the former might envisage "positive" state action, for example in ensuring that all people have adequate shelter, or health care. The latter, in contrast, are generally regarded as protecting people *from* state action, such as the prohibition on the state from arbitrary arrest. A great deal of scholarly ink, pop-political philosophy and international diplomacy has been exhausted over whether these two categories should both be regarded as of equal status. In general, the ideological camps united the socialist and developing world in arguing that only they cared for the basics of human existence (the economic, social and cultural rights), whereas the 'west' seemed obsessed by the civil and political rights that more clearly reflect western philosophy and law. All this mightily occupied the minds of those attending the World Conference of Human Rights held in Vienna in 1993, where desperate diplomacy resulted in a Final Declaration that prevented any major split along 'north-south' lines. The wording reveals the issues: 'All human rights are universal, indivisible and interdependent and interrelated...(however)... the significance of national and regional particularities and various historical, cultural and religious backgrounds must be borne in mind...' (United Nations General Assembly, A.CONF.157/23, 12 July 1993, *Vienna Declaration and Programme of Action,* para 5).

- United Nations Charter 1945 (selected parts)
- *Universal* Declaration of Human Rights 1948
- International *Covenant* on Economic, Social and Cultural Rights (1966)
- International *Covenant* on Civil and Political Rights (1966)
- Convention on the Prevention and Punishment of the Crime of Genocide (1948)
- International Convention on the Elimination of all forms of Racial Discrimination (1965)
- Convention on the Elimination of all forms of Discrimination Against Women (1979)
- Slavery Convention (1926 and the 1957 Supplementary Convention)
- Convention Against Torture and Other Cruel, Inhuman and Degrading Treatment or Punishment (1984)
- Convention on the Rights of the Child (1994)

Even thus expanded, this selection does not include all relevant human rights documents in the ever-evolving international human rights framework, such as the Rome Statute on the International Criminal Court (1998).[2] Nor is there space to discuss the regional human rights treaties, covering Europe, the Americas and Africa.

As regards the titles in the core IBR, it is useful to note the words 'Universal' and 'Covenant' in the three key documents. In 1948, the assertion of universality in the Universal Declaration was breathtaking, given the complexity of social form known in the middle of the twentieth century. Professor Mary Ann Glendon (2000), examining the key role played by Eleanor Roosevelt in drafting the UDHR and securing its unopposed passage through the General Assembly in 1948, noted that the main achievement of the Declaration was to remove the individual from the total control of the state, by the assertion of universality and international 'supra-state' standards. The terminology attracted almost a religious air, and the notions were construed as applying to all of humanity.[3] Notably the ICCPR and ICESCR secured those rights as a 'covenant', that most solemn of promises, usually associated with the Biblical pact between God and the Israelites. But for the purposes of this Chapter, the combination of the UN Charter and the UDHR is taken as the post World War 11 genesis of the IBR and, following Abrams (2001) its emergence from the 'ashes of Auschwitz and the testimony at Nuremberg' accepted as its immediate driving force.

---

[2] The Rome Statute of the International Criminal Court on 17 July 1998 was adopted by 120 States participating in the 'United Nations Diplomatic Conference of Plenipotentiaries on the Establishment of an International Criminal Court'. This is the first ever permanent, treaty based, international criminal court established to promote the rule of law and ensure that the gravest international crimes do not go unpunished. The Statute sets out the Court's jurisdiction, structure and functions and it provides for its entry into force 60 days after 60 States have ratified or acceded to it. The 60th instrument of ratification was deposited with the Secretary General on 11 April 2002, when 10 countries simultaneously deposited their instruments of ratification. Accordingly, the Statute entered into force on 1 July 2002. Anyone who commits any of the crimes under the Statute after this date will be liable for prosecution by the Court. http://www.icc-cpi.int/ataglance/whatistheicc/history.html

[3] Criticising the proclaimed universalism as 'shameless presumption' by the West, Professor Makau Mutua (2000) thought it 'inappropriate for the document to announce itself as a kind of Magna Carta or bible of the good society...(saying that) the Declaration seems to be premised on the notion that political democracy is sufficient to achieve human dignity, and accordingly, it wrongly equates the containment of state despotism with the attainment of human dignity'

Question 1: Why does humanity need an International Bill of Rights to achieve something so apparently unarguable as the statement that humans have the right to live in dignity?

As the titles to the human rights documents indicate, each elaborates protections in a particular sphere. Collectively, and trying to squeeze their purpose into a single word, they envisage humans living with each other in 'dignity'. I argue that dignity in this sense has the two main threads associated with living standards and security. Here I do not discuss whether the 'economic, social and cultural rights' that feature in the ICESCR should be regarded as 'rights' as compared with 'civil and political rights' as in the ICCPR. My purpose is to illustrate the intertwined nature of human dignity that both Covenants envisage. Whatever the background, starvation is undignified, so is homelessness; torture is not dignity, and neither is being a victim of discrimination.

The first thread of dignity deals with 'living standards': access to the basics of food, shelter and health. The second thread of 'security' deals mostly with protecting people from each other – particularly from the organized form of society known as the State. Actually, the bulk of the standards in the IBR are focused on this second thread, including such rights as freedom from torture and freedom of expression. Security here, then, is not about food – it is about fear. The source of the fear, mostly, is the capacity of the State to threaten. But closer examination suggestions that it is more accurate to see this potential as yet another example of group conflict. The 'State' is not some disaggregated mythical creature, but an organization staffed by people whose collective behaviour is similar to that of any tribal or ethnic groups, a point we return to shortly.

Following the view that human beings live in the collective, rather than as individuals seeking self-expression in splendid isolation, I do not think that there is a first order set of needs here – such as Maslow's basics of security, shelter, food, followed by higher order notions of self-actualisation. And I certainly do not think that the one is more important than the other - I argue here, are intertwined[4].

The State might be the current dominant form of that collective for the purposes of order and governance, but it is obviously not the first or last form of human collectivity. And the State certainly has not escaped from being yet another 'them or us'. Whatever the exact ethnic composition of power, rulers have long seen challenges to their rule in terms remarkably similar to the 'in and out' groups which define racism, tribalism, religious competition, or indeed any other form of the same phenomenon. For their part, subjects and citizens have done the same from the other side. They express alienation from the state, from politicians, 'capital cities' ('the Wellington/Washington/London/Abuja/Waigani view…'). Sometimes, citizens see the State in outright hostility, justifying violence and war. This categorization has, wherever it is used, supported the claim of 'them' (the state, officials, police, tax collectors) being less human that 'us'. The state-subject divide as 'them-us' is, I believe, not different conceptually from any tendency for individuals in their development to form groups. State-subject categorisation is the same phenomenon as Catholic-Protestant, Muslim-Hindu, Jew-Palestinian, Tamil-Singhala, Red-White Russian, worker-capitalist, Montague-Capulet, tribe-tribe, wherever. In saying so, I make no comment on who is right or wrong. It is the

[4] For a fuller discussion of the strengths and limitations of Maslow's theory in relation to human development see the concluding chapter by Taylor in the present volume.

phenomenon of 'in' and 'out' groups that is the point - and this is played out in the modern state, just as in religion or tribe.

It can be asked whether what I call 'groupism', (the banding together into groups, both for mutual protection and for attack on others), is the real *universal* in human society? Probably. If one thinks of human beings struggling for survival across the millennia that our genes were formed, it would not surprise me if one day we were to discover that humans evolved to favour groups - meaning that just as we have genes enabling language, so we probably have genes for banding together. As Pinker (2002 p.viii) speculates:

> 'The idea that nature and nurture interact to shape some part of the mind might turn out to be wrong, but it is not wishy-washy on unexceptionable, even in the twenty-first century, thousands of years after the issue was framed. When it comes to explaining human thought and behavior, the possibility that heredity plays any role at all still has the power to shock. To acknowledge human nature, many think, is to endorse racism, sexism, war, greed, genocide, nihilism, reactional politics, and neglect of children and the disadvantaged. Any claim that the mind has an innate organisation strikes people not as a hypothesis that might turn out to be incorrect but as a thought it is immoral to think.'

I pause to make the critical point that I do not suggest facile conclusions can be drawn because humans may be both biologically and socially programmed to form groups - such that racism is somehow 'natural' (hence 'acceptable'). My point is that for some reason group behaviour persists, with potential for both good and bad in its expression. The evil of racism can and must be avoided, and one way is to redefine the 'group' to include all humanity – this is precisely the central argument of the International Bill of Rights, and indeed this chapter.

The argument is that to understand the intertwining of the threads of dignity in the IBR ('living standards' and 'security') it is essential to recognise human needs in the *collective* as being primary rather than secondary. Group identity (e.g. by association, or worship) has been the *means* by which across all history humans found food, took shelter, protected themselves from (and threatened) the *other*, and established working frameworks for their lives.

But the complexity of many societies today blurs older and simpler notions of what constitutes a 'group', and in most discussions about rights there seems to be a curious unwillingness to accept the obvious group elements of human society. I am not here referring to the debates about 'communal/collective versus individual' human rights, and the related suggestion that African or Asian societies (and hence their people's rights) are somehow different from the Western versions.[5] My argument is that we need to understand *why* it is necessary to assert the right to dignity at all. The obvious answer is because the UDHR recognises the deprivation of such dignity, everywhere.

In other words, the mere assertion of universal values in the international bill of rights is itself testament to what I call here 'the human story'- i.e. the shorthand term for a story of inter-group struggle. I do not suggest that the struggle erupted in violence at every point of human history. Nor that the struggle derives inevitably from a genetic characteristic of humanity – though genes may actually be much more important than many acknowledge or

[5] See, for example, Makau Mutua (2000) who comments that the Universal Declaration on Human Rights has an 'unremitting emphasis on the individual as the center of the moral universe'. He says that the idea has deep roots in Western philosophy and culture, and that many non-European cultures, including African cultures, do not give the individual primacy over the community'.

are comfortable with. My argument here is that reduced to its essence, the human story is one of the struggle for survival against the elements, animals and disease *and against other human beings* – all as part of communal groups.

This picture of the human story does not suggest that *inside* a group all was cuddles and mutual support – and that the only conflict was with *outside* groups. A critical part of the group dimension is that challenges from *inside* are often regarded by members as being much the same as those from *outside* (i.e. those from deviants, heretics, revisionists, subversives, dissidents, leftists, liberals, terrorists – it is a chilling list). The pre-history logic is clear, namely that unity was essential for survival, and hence internal divisions justified repression. Viewed thus, it is easy to see how the group dimension helps also to explain the abuse of 'deviants' by challenged 'rulers' across history. Having threatened unity, 'deviants' lost the quality of 'in-group' (and hence human) membership. It is a small slide from burning witches to 'disappearing' subversives, from stoning adulterers to torturing Steve Biko.

If 'in and out' groups can be created by social or political behaviour, they are even more likely to exist where there is an obvious aspect of 'difference' stemming from the simple biology of being male or female. Hence, amongst the oldest and most enduring aspects of the group dimension concerns women. A gendered pattern persists across all societies of systemic disadvantage and discrimination. As Nussbaum (2003, p1) summarises:

> 'Women in much of the world lack support for fundamental functions of a human life. They are less well nourished than men, less healthy, and more vulnerable to physical violence... women have fewer opportunities than men to live free from fear and to enjoy rewarding types of love – especially when, as often happens, they are married without choice in childhood and have no recourse from bad marriages. In all these ways, unequal social and political circumstances give women unequal human capabilities'.

Given women's reproductive biology, these issues are deeply ingrained in all societies. But like all other aspects of biology, it is also clear that social rules frame and reframe the deeper biological facts, including what constitutes 'marriage' and 'family'. It is of course no coincidence that the UN Charter and the UNDR affirm the equal rights of women and men, and that so much energy is devoted by movements for human development as well as for human rights in trying to revise the social rules that put female at a disadvantage.

Nussbaum's approach stresses a formulation of human capabilities that encompass all aspects of physical and emotional life, and particularly engages the role of family which is so central to many women's lives but often omitted from discussions of the principles of justice. Reviewing Nussbaum's work, Turiel (2003, p. 366) comments that her 'writings pose challenges to the psychological study of morality and culture via her assertion that the approach is "full" universalist. She discounts as implausible the proposition that a non-Western nation like India... does not value the ideas of political liberty, sex equality and nondiscrimination. Those ideas, which are in the Indian Constitution, were fought for by the founders of an Independent India'.

The call for gender fairness also shows why it is necessary to protect children as another easily-identifiable category – like the disabled, and many others. The repetition of the story *is* the story.

There are many testaments to the group dimension of discrimination in anthropology, religion, military action, politics and archaeology. But the simplest testament is all around us, every day, in our neighbourhoods, in the dramas on our television screens, and in the annual reports of organizations like Amnesty International and Human Rights Watch.

This rather dismal categorization of the human story is of course contestable, and it reflects an old debate about whether humans are naturally 'warlike', or simply were corrupted by 'civilisation'. Here John Dryden's 1670 poem comes to mind in which he was the first to coin the term the 'noble savage':

> 'I am as free as Nature first made man,
> Ere the base laws of servitude began,
> When wild in woods the noble savage ran'.

His romanticism of the noble savage being in a 'state of nature' contrasted with Thomas Hobbes'(1651-1957. pp 185-6.)[6] contemporaneous and oft-repeated idea of a harshly competitive humanity that sounds like inner-city suburbia in some states today, or Robert Kaplan's depiction of Sierra Leone (1994):

> *'Hereby it is manifest, that during the time men live without a common power to keep them all in awe, they are in that condition which is called war; and such a war as is of every man against every man... and, which is worst of all, continual fear, and danger of violent death; and the life of man, solitary, poor, nasty, brutish, and short'.*

Which then is accurate of the human story: the 'noble savage' living in dignity before 17th century slavery and the corruption of humanity by the then dominant states of Europe, or every man against every man in continual war? This is not the place to argue the issue fully. But suffice to say that surely no serious historian, much less an anthropologist, would support either of these formulations as being accurate for all societies at all times. Hobbes described a war of individual against individual that might have a place in a temporarily 'lawless' city. But the real competitiveness in the human story has always been in the group dimension, France against Spain, England against Scotland, Catholic against Protestant, and so on. And similarly, it is trite to say that that within a group, *cooperation* was a key aspect of communal survival – hence the treatment of the un-cooperative. Thus the 'noble savage' of one part of the Pacific that welcomed travelers, was matched by nearby groups where cannibalism and warfare were staple affairs. So in making their extreme statements both Hobbes and Dryden (and Rousseau after him) miss the point: societies can be noble or brutish, depending on whether one is perceived as belonging either to 'them' or to 'us'.

Hence, the pattern that has emerged from the last few centuries of European history, for example, is of group cooperation as well as of competition. Cooperation between England and other European allies defeated Napoleon; competition between national groups saw his rise and conquest of much of Europe. Group competition has, alas, very often been through violence, most dramatically illustrated by World War II. And the same can be said about any other society. Humanity can indeed be 'noble' in its cooperative stability – but it also makes life nasty and brutish for 'outsiders' (and insider 'deviants').

Asserting a right to dignity, then, does not seem such a tall order. Which group, religion or culture, which democratic leader, which individual, would disagree with the proposition that we should all live in dignity? This seems so obvious that in the IBR, the standards elaborating dignity are styled as 'rights'. The rights framework is of course an argument that these standards are inherent to the quality of being human. Hence, no-one, be it government or other claimed authority – should be able to deprive us of such 'rights arbitrarily; hence the construction not only of the standards, but of complex processes for protection of the 'rights' as against each other, and primarily as represented by the organized collective of the modern state.

Seen this way, the IBR immediately tells us two things about human beings. First, it speaks to a human history in which 'dignity' has not been the universal experience – just the contrary. Second, the IBR speaks to 'process' – the peculiar business of writing rules and then trying to ensure that they are enforced by institutions.

The stress on process is of course historically linked with the relatively recent rise of the modern constitutional state from about the 16th century onwards in Europe and thence elsewhere as a major organizing form of the human collective. In that sense, one can indeed speak of processes that are obviously 'foreign' in origin. The links between the rule of law, government by consent, the assertion of limits on government in constitutions, and so on, are clearly tied to the creation, export, internationalization, and local adaptations of the western experience. As Mutua (2002) recently characterized, the whole human rights movement was 'part of the European colonial project... The white human rights zealot joins the unbroken chain that connects him to the colonial administrator, the Bible-wielding missionary, and the merchant of free enterprise[7].

However, the adaptation between 'outside' forms of social and political organization (or anything else, such as technology) and domestic culture is hardly new, and it serves little purpose to keep calling something 'foreign' when it so obviously has become part of the domestic order. It is silly, for example, to regard Japan's law, cabinet process and constitution as somehow 'western', even accepting the borrowings from the German civil code, the Westminster parliamentary monarchy, and USA constitutionalism. These aspects of governance have become part of the Japanese political and social order.

To give another example, the same can be said of the adaptations that created Papua New Guinea's current constitutional structure on top of what is probably the world's most complex set of communal structures with more than 700 separate languages and communities in the state. In my view, most Papua New Guineans would laugh at the suggestion that their democracy is 'foreign' – it is theirs, they work within it daily, they vote ('early and often') in vast numbers in the political competition that has blended with the underlying communalism. That said, few Papua New Guineans would say that they are happy with the current state of the transplant. They are constantly making changes to the political structure as it takes root in PNG soil, adapting it to local conditions and pressures. It would be surprising were it any other way, after only 20 years of independence. PNG is thus building its own constitutionalism. Importing processes and structures to deal with governance in a country *changes* the domestic social and political situation, as well as the imports. This is hardly new – witness the new institutions that arose in Britain after 1066, or in the USA after its revolution. So, whatever the historical origins in western constitutionalism of 'process', it

[6] Both of the quotes are used in Steven Pinker (2002, pp 6-7).

[7] Later in the paper, Mutua (2002, p.11) criticised the use of the term Female Genital Mutilation as one which 'decontextualises the cultural foundation of the practice and promotes the stereotype of barbaric, machete-wielding natives only too eager to inflict pain on women in their own societies. It is a view that is racist...'

makes little sense today to regard such as forever 'western' in those societies that have taken the forms into their constitutional, political and social orders.

The stress on 'process' in the International Bill of Rights thus clearly has its origins in the western experience of trying to limit the power of monarchs. John Locke (1632-1704) built his founding conceptions of the limited state on the struggle against the Stuart monarchs' despotism (Carpenter, 1924). But it is also directly reflective of the competition between groups. The notion that it makes sense to limit state power, or to provide some process for decisions to be 'checked by independent authority' to avoid abuse is not just western legality. Saddam Hussein centralized power, neutralized the judiciary, faked elections and executed his opponents. In modern Zimbabwe, Robert Mugabe is doing much the same. One does not have to parrot the western tradition to see similarities with John Locke. There is abundant evidence that the concentration of power can, and will, be abused, everywhere – especially against 'deviants' or 'outsiders' (or some unlucky enough to be both, as the Kurds in Iraq found). Obviously, different cultures and social orders might have different ways of guaranteeing order and preventing the abuse of power. But the form of state that emerged from the western struggle with the group dimension has been exported, and a central part of that export is the requirement of 'process' to limit the abuse of human rights.

To return to the question: why the need to elaborate a code of rights (and processes) to secure human dignity? The answer is surely that our biggest need is, and has always been, for protection from the group phenomenon. And the more organized the society, the bigger is the promise of protection for those on the 'inside' and the bigger the danger to the 'outside'. Standing together to defeat a common enemy may of course be illusory in building dignity for a people 'inside' a group. Hitler's post World War I popular rise in Germany as part of the rebuilding of German pride and strength is the supreme example. It was at once popular within the 'in-group' to the point of fanaticism, a massive threat to neighbouring states, and a genocidal threat to insiders who could be reclassified as outsiders, such as Jews, or indeed anyone who questioned the political path on which the government was bent.

Alongside the 'final solution', there is a vast literature[8] on how the Gestapo saw various groups as enemies of the state and sought to humiliate and subdue them. For one of the more sobering papers, see Bruno Bettleheim's account (1943) of the year he spent as a prisoner in German concentration camps at Dachau and Buchenwald. His experience led him to conclude that:

> 'an institution was needed to threaten the opponents of the system. To imprison all of these would have interrupted the functioning of industrial production. Many Germans were dissatisfied with the system. Therefore, if a group of the population got fed up with the Nazi regime, a selected few members of the group were brought into the concentration camp. If lawyers, for instance, became restless, a few hundred lawyers were sent to the camp. The Gestapo called such group punishments "actions." During the first of them, only the leaders of the opposing group were punished. That led to the feeling that to belong to a rebellious group only as a member was not dangerous. Soon, the Gestapo revised its system and punished a cross section of the different strata of the group. This procedure had not only the advantage of

[8] For a recent work related to the themes of this chapter, see Zygmunt Bauman's body of work, especially his *Modernity and the Holocaust* (1989), examining the question of whether cruelty still persists in the 'postmodern' era and the legacy of the Holocaust.

spreading terror among all members of the group, but made it possible to destroy the group without necessarily touching the leader, if that was for some reason inopportune'.

To suggest that humans are our own biggest threats – and have always been so - might sound counter-intuitive if one pictures a cave-humanity pre-historical struggle to survive. But the record of group competition, often by violence, suggests that facing nature has mostly been easier than facing one's rivals, neighbours, or the bands that appeared out of the sea. Hugh Thomas (1994, p.xiii) captures this precisely, reflecting on the story by which the Spanish conquistadors conquered the extraordinarily powerful Mexica empire ruled by Montezuma:

> 'Neither Cortes nor Columbus, nor any other conquistador, entered a static, timeless and peaceful world of innocents. The Tainos whom Columbus encountered seemed happy enough. But they had themselves once come to the Caribbean islands as conquerors and had driven out, or rather had driven into the west end of Cuba, the primitive inhabitants, the so-called Guanahatebeys... They themselves were menaced by the Caribs who, coming from the South American mainland, had been fighting their way up the lesser Antilles. The Caribs had already conquered the so-called Igneri culture in what are now called the Windward Islands, and were beginning to threaten the Leewards... The Mayas ... whom Cortes and his fellow conquistators visited, and whom expeditions led by the Montejo family eventually conquered, have now been shown to have been warlike even during their golden age. The Mexica were the successors of several warrior peoples who had ruled in the Valley of Mexico. Their own empire had been established by military conquest. The Spaniards in their opposition to old Mexico were given decisive support by Indian allies, who hated the Mexica. The Spanish were, of course, conquerors, as were, in their day, the Vikings, the Goths, the Romans (whom they admired), the Arabs, the Macedonian Greeks, the Persians, to mention only a few of those who preceded them; or the English, the Dutch, the French, the Germans and the Russians, to mention some who followed them'.

However tempting it is to regard 'nature' as humanity's principal enemy (disease, food, climate) the record suggests a threat closer to home. As regards disease, the war between human biology and microbe is of course unending. Unhappily, some of the easiest areas of the planet for humans to find food and shelter, the tropics, also welcomed parasites, bacteria and viruses in competitive quantity. Putting aside new diseases (variants of the micro-warriors), technology has in some measure started to tip the competitive balance in favour of humans. But even if a technological solution to some of the major remaining micro-competitors is found – like immunization against AIDS or mosquito-borne diseases – it would still require a human infrastructure to make it work. Human conflict makes technological solutions hard to deliver. So we keep coming back to the same point: our biggest threat is from ourselves, especially as we constantly reframe 'in' and 'out' groups.

As regards the struggle for food and shelter, it might also be that humans (currently) are winning that battle in the cycle of revolutions that saw humanity conquer the planet. For example the agricultural revolution introduced large-scale food production and the accumulation of vast food surpluses that brought the capacity to live in urban conglomerates, with new building materials, methods of construction, and different kinds of habitat, across to the green revolution from the need to control pesticides and waste-disposal. With all these changes in food production and shelter technology, it seems that across all known history, but especially across the last five thousand years, humans mostly adapted to find sufficient food and shelter in adequate quantities. This is, after all, an abundant planet, apparently able to support ever-increasing billions of people, and ever-decreasing other species. The modern ethnographic record supports this in studies of small-scale societies not markedly affected by the industrial revolution and nature's hostility. For example, the Khoisan people (sometimes known as Bushmen) adapted to the deserts of southern Africa to eke out an existence with almost no rainfall;[9] and the Innuit (Eskimo) thrived in the frozen Arctic.

Even accepting that humans have always battled for survival in some measure against the rest of nature, it still seems that by far the biggest danger to human existence always came from other humans. The Khoisan people did not migrate to live in waterless deserts for modern lifestyle reasons, like choosing a five-acre plot on the edge of a city, but to avoid being wiped out by their physically larger human neighbours. Their first predators were the Bantu people of Southern Africa who swept down from central Africa colonizing and warring as they trekked South, driving other peoples before them. And then a few centuries later, the surviving Khoisan (and some of the Bantu tribes) had then to face the European settlers who swept up from the South into the interior of southern Africa, escaping domination from other European groups and colonizing and warring as they trekked North.

There are examples everywhere of that story, not limited to the particular phenomenon of European colonialism that began in the seventeenth century. It is the story of the movement of peoples, everywhere, at all times. Peoples moved, they encountered other groups (or redefined their own), and (mostly) they fought. The castles of Europe are not architectural testaments, but stone records of this story. The Great Wall of China is similar monument. The Pacific offers its own examples, though in oral and earth records rather than stone buildings. The great stories of Maori migration to New Zealand are of clashes between warriors and lineages; the counterpart to castle is the fortified *pa*; the counterpart to European nationalism is Maori tribalism in the pursuit of *mana* (status), land, and conquest across the Pacific. To the extent that the Bible reflects aspects of human history, the same story is replayed in the flight of the Israelites from the Egyptian Pharaoh to survive, as well as to live by their own religion. From ancient to modern history, human conflict threatened far more than the natural disasters of drought, earthquake, or flood – or at least they made survival against nature significantly harder.

Jumping to the present, television screens bring us pictures of sudden catastrophe (earthquake, drought, flood) or third world images of countless numbers scrambling for limited resources. But these struggles, harsh as may be, are really human disasters (Taylor, 2003), often magnified by human conflict. The terrible famines in Biafra in the 1960s were caused by an attempted secession from Nigeria. The Horn of Africa famines a generation later were all massively exacerbated by human conflict. In Cambodia, apart from the several thousands executed by the AK47, malaria and starvation killed nearly a million people in that country between 1975 and 1979. But it was the Khmer Rouge administration that really caused the problems and destroyed the entire market and social structure, and hence capacity of the people to live off their fertile fields or survive against malaria. The story of the 'killing fields' is really the destruction of an entire agricultural economy, not only in the paranoia of executing deviants from the vision of Brother Number One. Similarly the struggle of the poor

[9] There is a considerable literature on the Khoisan. See for example the text and references at: http://www.museums.org.za/sam/resource/arch/khoisan.htm.

in India to survive is indeed harsh – but it is harshest for those belonging to 'out' groups, like the 'untouchables'.[10]

The answer to the first question is thus relatively simple: the international assertion of a universal human right to dignity is an eloquent statement to the lack of that dignity across all human societies and across history.

Question 2: Why is it that out of some of the greatest wrongs of the human story have come some of the noblest ideals?

According to Grandin (2001, p.26).

> 'At the close of every great and violent conflict comes due a bill of rights. Following the barbarism of World War II, the United Nations' 1948 Universal declaration of Human Rights, along with the Nuremberg trials, overturned the doctrine which held sway among Western nations, that there are no rights other than those conferred by states. Individual liberty and the guarantee of a decent and secure life, the declaration proclaimed, were rights bestowed not by blood or borders but by universal human dignity...From the terrors of the cold war came the hope that the promise of the UN declaration would be fulfilled, that resources consumed by the superpower contest would be put towards human needs, and that repression would no longer be tolerated in the name of national security or sovereignty.'

There is a certain perversity in this notion, if true. Does it take a great wrong to make a right? Clearly the UN Charter and Universal Declaration was a combined attempt to acknowledge the great wrongs evidence in WWII and prevent any reoccurrence. But as regards human dignity, the world outside of the Atlantic Charter has good reason to argue that the attempt was at best of limited success. After 1945, most of Eastern Europe and the Soviet Union were tightly held in Stalin's Iron Fist. In 1949, China fell to the Communists and its people awaited Mao's Cultural Revolution and Great Leap Forward. After the liberating wave of independence, much of Africa struggled with dictatorship of varying degrees, as did Central and South America, and certainly with ever-grinding poverty and disease. In South East Asia, millions died, were persecuted or simply fled as refugees in the unfolding of the 'domino theory' of progressive Communist expansion down through the Malaysian archipelago. Perhaps the grossest example was the murderous Khmer Rouge in Cambodia between 1975 and 1979, although the massacre of around a million ethnic Chinese in Indonesia in the 1960s was more systematic in its savagery. In Europe, it was not until the mid-1970s that Spain and Portugal returned to democratic government, but Greece returned briefly to a military dictatorship. In Central Europe the 1990s Yugoslavia disintegrated bloodily, and in Africa Rwanda decentralised killing to a level that it is hard to comprehend. And in all this, struggles for self-determination of various sorts were accompanied by substantial violence and repression.

Did any of those post-WWII 'wrongs' produce their own crop of noble ideals? The 1992 international conference to produce a comprehensive settlement of the problem of Cambodia

[10] For a general summary of the issues, see http://magma.nationalgeographic.com/ngm/0306/feature1/; Narula, Smita. Broken People: Caste Violence Against India's "Untouchables." Human Rights Watch, 1999. Available online at www.hrw.org/reports/1999/india/.

promised much. Out of Yugoslavia and Rwanda came the International Tribunals to try people for Crimes against Humanity, and finally, stepping hesitatingly onto the world stage, but with the same idealism, the International Criminal Court. After Idi Amin's fall in Uganda in 1986and the subsequent devastating civil war when former President Obote thought he could return to his own form of pre-Amin repression, there was a sense of 'never again'. In South Africa, the determination that the country would never again fall victim to the form of discrimination known as apartheid is enshrined in a noble 1995 constitution packed with human rights standards and new structures for enforcement. It led South Africa to produce a Truth and Reconciliation Commission whose report attempts both to document the wrongs and to create a culture to prevent any such repetition. Indeed, from the traumas of the 1960s to the 1980s in different coluntries came dozens of such Commissions, each seeking outcomes in balancing justice, truth, and reconciliation. The most recent, and still functioning Commission, is in Timor Leste that followed the Indonesian-controlled killing, rape, destruction of property, and the mass-displacement of more than half the population in 1999.

These post WWII examples reflect a pattern that has very deep resonance in the human psyche. Consider briefly Christianity's foundation narrative of injustice, sacrifice, and suffering - followed by the expression of hope for a better life to come. It exemplifies the argument that great wrong and suffering lead to the articulation of noble ideals in a deep-rooted, compelling, normative framework of rules of conduct.

The pattern is evident in the law, especially in the western tradition. The Magna Carta of 1215 recites the oppressive deeds that preceded it and the remedies it promises. So does the Bill of Rights of 1688, beginning with a lamentation of the actions of the Stuart Kings, and followed by the remedies. In political analysis, Karl Marx (1848) bitterly denounced the evils of the early industrial revolution, war, class war, and the suffering and injustice of working people. His vision of a classless, conflict-free, and just society emerged from that suffering too – and it promised a better world. In bloodier, but equally grizzly terms, Henry Dunant (1862) wrote powerfully of the inhumanity and suffering after Battle of Solferino in 1859. From that suffering emerged the International Committee of the Red Cross, and the hope that human suffering in war could be reduced. If there was to be conflict, let it be fought in reasonably humane terms with predetermined *rules* to be followed by all.

The principles of International Humanitarian Law thus have their foundations in great suffering. The pattern of 'great wrong' followed by the assertion of 'right' had many other forms preceding the Universal Declaration in 1948, including the Virginia Declaration of Rights (1776), the United States Declaration of Independence (1776), and the French Declaration of the Rights of Man and of the Citizen (1789).

And so we come to the 1945 United Nations Charter that emerged from World War II and the Holocaust. The Charters' opening words capture the argument:

> We the peoples of the United Nations, determined to save succeeding generations from the scourge of war that twice in our lifetimes has devastated humanity, and to reaffirm faith in fundamental human rights, in the dignity and worth of the human person, in the equal rights of men and women and nations large and small… (amongst the founding objectives are the achievement of) international cooperation… in promoting and encouraging respect for human rights and for fundamental freedoms for all without distinctions as to race, sex, language, or religion…'

The theme is picked up in the opening articles of the Universal Declaration (1948), a few of which are worth quoting in full:

> *Whereas* recognition of the inherent dignity and of the equal and inalienable rights of all members of the human family is the foundation of freedom, justice and peace in the world,
> *Whereas* disregard and contempt for human rights have resulted in barbarous acts which have outrages the conscience of mankind, and the advent of a world in which human beings shall enjoy freedom of speech and believe and freedom from fear and want has been proclaimed as the highest aspiration of the common people,
> *Whereas* it is essential, if man is not to be compelled to have recourse, as a last resort, to rebellion against tyranny and oppression, that human rights should be protected by the rule of law…
>
> Article 1. All human beings are born free and equal in dignity and rights. They are endowed with reason and conscience and should act towards one another in a spirit of brotherhood.
> Article 2. Everyone is entitled to all the rights and freedoms set forth in this Declaration, without distinction of any kind, such as race, colour, sex, language, religion, political or other opinion, national or social origin, property, birth or other status…
> Article 3. Everyone has the right to life, liberty and security of the person.
> Article 4. No one shall be held in slavery or servitude…
> Article 5. No one shall be subjected to torture or to cruel, inhuman or degrading treatment or punishment.
> Article 7. All are equal before the law and are entitled without any discrimination to equal protection of the law…
> Article 8. Everyone has the right to an effective remedy by the competent national tribunals for acts violating the fundamental rights granted him by the constitution or by law'.

As with the UN Charter's opening lines, the immediate message is powerful un noble ideals arising from great wrongs. But note also that the stress is on equal dignity and rights for all, without discrimination. The notion of discrimination underlines the group dimension, and points to group conflict as a fundamental cause of the 'barbarous acts which have outraged the conscience of mankind'. Such barbarism included slavery, genocide and other mass murder, torture (and cruel, inhuman and degrading punishment) - and the denial of any effective remedy for those who suffered.

It is not possible here to explore different historical tradition further. Suffice to say that logic suggests that the recitation of a wrong, and the articulation of a remedy is a common pattern. Why? I think the answer lies deep in the human psyche, both for individuals and for groups. My view is that building 'it must never happen again' standards and processes are part of the response to trauma. After the 'wrong', the goal for survivors is somehow to move forward. For individuals, counsellors speak not so much of 'closure', but of creating mechanisms that allow people to get on with life, to learn lessons, to avoid repetition (Hamber, 1999a and1999b; Hamber, and Wilson, 1999).[11] This was clearly a central purpose of the International Bill of Rights. In other words, it may be that the assertion of idealism is

[11] The issues are well-explored in the paper presented by Brandon Hamber and Richard Wilson at the Traumatic Stress in South Africa Conference hosted by the Centre for the Study of Violence and Reconciliation in association with the African Society for Traumatic Stress Studies, Johannesburg, South Africa, 27-29 January 1999.

central to the healing process after great wrong. This has profound implications for the question of what the IBR tells us about 'who we are'.

To return to the title of this chapter, what, then, does the International Bill of Rights tell us about human nature? Having explored the other questions, the answer can now be brief. I argue that the key message in the written documentation is acceptance of the danger that humans pose to each other. What does it say that one has to write down that genocide – the deliberate destruction of another group – is unlawful? Imagine needing to write into a document that people should not be tortured? Why does the international community at large have to spell out that people should not be held in slavery, or subject to racial discrimination? Is it really necessary to state the people should have reasonable shelter, water, food, the right to marry, the right to worship? That these have to be stated is the message. We human beings do not only emerge from the noble catalogue of rights with some pride, but also with considerable nervousness about each other.

In my view, the assertion of universality in the International Bill of Rights' is, in the end, profoundly illustrative of the biggest problem, and paradoxically of the only solution. The problem is that humans appear to band together in groups for survival, however expressed. In grouping lie the roots both of cooperation and violence. Groups are mostly socially constructed, because they are no longer divided constantly along any single feature (such as descent). Common humanity, and indeed common standards of dignity, cut across at least one key part of the 'them or us' that has been what I have here called the 'human story'. If we are all 'us', there is no 'them', at least not in the sense that 'they' are neighbours who can be killed with machetes, or 'subversives' who can be 'disappeared' by death squads, or 'gooks', or 'pigs', or any other form of labeled abuse of 'them' that lies at the heart of adverse group behaviour, racism, and its companions.

After centuries of essentially racist clan warfare in Europe, the assertion of a common European humanity, backed by common standards of human rights, has made all the bloody and desperate struggles just so meaningless. Is this really just a 'western' thing? I think not. My view is that having become so enmeshed in group conflict, including two world wars, western Europe simply reached exhaustion from which came the recognition of common humanity. In time, this will surely also happen where other regions and fighters reach their own points of no-return. What else will solve the Israeli and Palestinian divide, other that the shared recognition of their common humanity and the building of common standards of human dignity?

When the time is right, an extremely simple formula will allow the warring peoples (and sug-groups) to preserve their identity, but as part of a broader human family. With luck, and persistence in re-framing social rules, it will not be necessary to reach the same point of exhaustion in relation to other aspects of this phenomenon, such as discrimination against women, or children. And as each society genuinely seeks to come to terms with the group dimension, it will have also to confront the apparently endless numbers of groups that will seek recognition and protection. Nobody said this was going to be easy.[12]

But the alternative to seeking recognition of group identity *within* a stressed common humanity is to carry on with the same story. Darwin might suggest that we have run out of planetary room to keep moving, like the Israelites away from Egypt, the sailors of the Pacific

[12] Nancy Fraser (1997), for example, explores the explosion of demands for 'group recognition of difference' after the collapse of the 'class' paradigm.

on the winds for other islands, or the Khoisan, into the deserts. Either we adapt and build our common humanity, or we can anticipate more Rwandas and Bosnias, more refugees, and a sorry continuation of the treatment of women, children, the aged and the disabled in so many societies, to name but four groups which incidentally constitute a significant majority of humanity.

The message from the International Bill of Rights is thus simple: we *know* what we are, what we have done, and what we might do again. We *know* it can be stopped, and that it is only by re-framing the group dimension. No society, no culture, no history, and probably no single individual, is exempt. Like other needs, the fundamental value of human dignity becomes clearest when it is deprived. Viewed thus, *non-discriminatory justice* (in the framework of *universal human rights)* is not only a human need, it is critical to human development in a complex, multi-grouped and ever-regrouping world.

References

Abrams. E. (2001). *Human Rights and Mrs Roosevelt: First things*. 114, June/July: 45 http://print/firsttings.com/ftissues/ft0106/reviews/abrams.html

Bauman, Z. (1989). *Modernity and the holocaust*. Ithaca NY: Cornell.

Bettelheim, B. (1943). Individual and mass behaviour in extreme situations. *Journal of Abnormal and Social Psychology*, 38, 417-452. The extract used in this chapter was taken from http://www.psy.dmu.ac.uk/brown/dmulib/BET.htm.

Carpenter W S. (Ed.). (1924). *Two treatises of civil government*. London: New York.

Dunant, H. (1862). *Un Souvenir de Solferino (A Memory of Solferino)*. Geneva: Jules-Guillaume Fick.

Dryden, J. (1978) Works of John Dryden Vol. I, Plays : The Conquest of Granada, Part One and Two, Marriage A-LA Mode, and the Assignation-Or, Love in a Nunnery Los Angeles, University of California Press.

Fraser, N. (1997). *Justice Interruptus*. London: Routledge, Taylor and Francis Books.

Glendon, M.A. (2000). *A world made new: Eleanor Roosevelt and the Universal Declaration of Human Rights*. New York: Random House.

Grandin, G. (2001). Toward a Global New Deal. *The Nation*, Oct 8, 273, 10, http://web2.infotrac.galegroup.com/itw/infomark/786/407/49454825w2/purl=rcl_EAI

Hamber, B. (1999a). *Do sleeping dogs lie? The psychological implications of the Truth and Reconciliation Commission in South Africa*. http://www.csvr.org.za/papersldog.htm

Hamber, B. (1999b). *Dealing with the past and the psychology of reconciliation* http://www.csvr.org.za/papdlpst.htm

Hamber, B. and Wilson R. (1999). *Symbolic closure through memory, reparation and revenge in post-conflict societies'*. Paper presented at the Traumatic Stress in South Africa Conference http://www.csvr.org.za/papers/papbhandrw.htm

Hobbes, T. (1651, 1957). *Leviathan*. New York: Oxford University Press.

Kaplan, R. (1994). The Coming Anarchy. *Atlantic Monthly*, February, 273, 2, 44-65.

Katz, F. E. (1993). *Ordinary people and Extraordinary Evil – a Report on the Beguilings of Evil*. New York: State University of NY Press.

Marx, K. and Engels, F. (1848, 1948). *The Communist Manifesto.* London, Lawrence and Wishart.

Mutua, M. (2000). Assessing the Universal Declaration. *Harvard Law Bulletin*, Spring, Article 5. http://www.law.harvard.edu/alumni/bulleting/backissues/spri2000/article5.html

Mutua, M. (2002). *'The complexity of universalism in human rights'*. Paper presented to the 10th Annual conference on 'The Individual versus the State', Central European University, Budapest, 14-16 June 2002.

Pinker, S. (2002). *The bank slate.* New York: Penguin.

Taylor, A.J.W. (2003). Bringing 'complex terrorism' and 'corporate malfeasance' into a classification schema for disasters. *Australian Journal of Emergency Management*, 18, 1, 27-34.

Thomas, H. (1994). *The Conquest of Mexico.* London: Pimlico.

In: Justice as a Basic Human Need
Editor: Anthony Taylor, pp. 177-199
ISBN 1-59454-915-X

Chapter 13

DOVETAILING JUSTICE INTO AN EXISTING FRAMEWORK OF NEEDS

A. J. W. Taylor

ABSTRACT

Having made an appeal in the present book for justice in all its forms to be recognised as essential for the all-round enjoyment of a civilised existence, it remains to consider into which of the existing theories of motivation it might fit. Towards that end, this final chapter considers the major theories that have stood the test of time and might accommodate the new proposition. It concludes by favouring the humanitarian schema created by Maslow, but argues that the case cannot rest without being exposed to proper scrutiny from researchers in different domains - including those with a cross-cultural frame of reference. It declares that the real reward will depend on the fruits of the application.

INTRODUCTION

Contributors to this book have demonstrated the importance of justice as it underlies moral philosophy, religious awareness, human development, criminal behaviour, the functioning of the criminal courts, the purpose of punishment, the care and management of the mentally ill, the treatment of offenders, the adverse effects of the global economic system, and social cohesion. They have also addressed the use of torture, the operation of government death squads, and opened the realm of human rights. Others involved in the care and management of neglected children, the elderly, displaced persons in refugee camps, prisoners of all kinds and their victims, could have illustrated the theme, but the selection is enough to show the relevance of justice for individuals as well as their local, national, and international communities. To my mind there can be no doubt that justice is a vibrant and ubiquitous force affecting all of mankind separately and collectively.

It remains now to select a theory of human motivation into which the concept might appropriately be lodged. Put simply, the argument is not for justice to be recognised as an essential precondition for human existence and given solitary status as a theoretical construct, nor for it to be regarded as supreme among a group of other basic needs. Rather it is for justice to be acknowledged and included in the established ranks of other needs. The parsimony, together with the 'interrelatedness of concepts, objectifiability, measurability, and modifiability', appears in the list of criteria for a good theory that Whyte (1969) presented and Alderfer reaffirmed (1972, p.154).

After that the proposition would have to comply with the semantics, syntactics, and pragmatics of theory construction, because:

> 'good theories must be accountable for and sensitive to observations. That is, if they seem to contradict observations, intuitions, or even common sense, their adherents should be able to say why, ... (*and they*) should have heuristic value, suggesting both theoretical development and empirical observations that test predictions of the theory,...(*and be*) aesthetic in their simplicity' (Marx and Cronan-Hillix, 1987, ch.9).

However, the synthetic methods used in the experimental laboratory should not necessarily be considered the *sine qua non* for researchers to adopt with participants in the real word. The domains are quite different, as also are the limits to which researchers might go in pursuit of results (cf. Milgram, 1974). Therefore while some applied researchers like Lizt, Gray, Bryant, and Adler (2002) might continue to advocate the adoption of the *gold standard* in research design, with the use of clinically and psychometrically robust methods in the assessment of specific conditions, randomly allocated trial and control groups, well defined dependent and independent variables, and independently applied follow-up procedures, others must be free to compromise according to the 'non-laboratory' circumstances of their clinical, developmental, epidemiological, and observational studies (cf. Hayes, 1997: Cox, 2002).

More than that, as Jones and Hughes (2003) pointed out succinctly, questions arise about the changing shift in the intellectual climate has created 'a rushing torrent of exploration.... about the nature of reality'. The process began four centuries ago with the onset of the Age of Enlightenment that spurred objectivism with the emphasis on reason and measurement to replace assertions of truth, moved to reductionism that promised knowledge of the whole, to determinism that offered change after discerning the causes, and finally to linearity that posited close relationships between the size of inputs and outputs. The authors argue that while such beliefs are embedded in scientific method, they have yet to be helpful in addressing the workings of the mind, processes of thought and abstraction, and the complexity of human adaption to the the world about them.

While respecting the freedom for researchers to develop novel methods in pursuit of their studies, there is no convincing reason to exempt them from being accountable to their colleagues, if not to society at large, for the logic of their undertakings and the methods they adopt to test them. Such post-modern developments led the Edinburgh and the Bath Schools of Sociology of Scientific Knowledge to open a vigorous area that would give free rein for scholars and experimenters to forge ahead with complete disregard for conventional standards of disputation[1] – as Andrew Sokal (2004) was able to demonstrate with the pretentious article that he concocted to embarrass them.

[1] http://en.wikipedia.org/wiki/Sociology_of_Scientific_Knowledge

Novices also need to be warned that venturing from the shelter of the somewhat controlled and artificial laboratory world into the maelstrom of real-life situations, is not made without considerable risk. For example, the study of terrorism – described as the ideology, recruitment, training, financial and organisational base of any faction seeking to change the balance of power – is fraught with difficulties of an intellectual, personal, and political kind (cf. Silke, 2003, pp. xv-xxi). Intellectually, the topic brings more than the usual insecurity of applied research in which the occurrence of events and the extent of their consequences are not always under the researcher's control, and there are few attested protocols ready on hand for researchers to adopt.. Personally, researchers will find their motives for dealing with such a contentious topic arousing suspicion, and have aspersions cast about their political affiliations - because the authorities are more inclined to move swiftly to retaliate against terrorists than to promote studies of the complex causes of terrorism and apply the remedies.[2] The textbooks in social science never promised an easy life for the venturesome – in fact they give little warning of the dangers ahead of novitiates.

CONCEPTUAL CONSIDERATIONS

While bearing the hazards of applied research in mind, it has to be said that it is more important for behavioural scientists to entertain the concept of justice than to be sidetracked into an endless discussion about its precise identification, measurement, and place in any particular theoretical framework. Such distractions led the early theologians to debate the number of angels dancing on the head of a pin, without giving thought to the application of their intellectual endeavours. Therefore to avoid the pedantry, because the online version of the *OED* (2004) gives no less than 14 slightly different definitions of the the word, 'need' is taken to mean 'the state or condition of lacking or requiring some necessary thing'. More precisely, following Thrash and Elliott (2001) and consistent with the concept as advanced originally by Henry Murray in 1938, the concept of 'need' is accepted as an

> 'hypothetical force that operates homeostatically, arising either when the organism experiences a hedonically negative state associated with an undesirable stimulus situation and dissipating when a change in the situation produces a satisfying hedonic state, or indicating a potentiality or readiness to respond towards a particular end under particular stimulus conditions'.

In short, needs are mainsprings of action that curiously are energised by depletion and tranquillised by repletion[3]. As such they have attracted the attention of philosophers and scholars since the dawn of history[4], and they have provided a fruitful field of inquiry for psychologists from the establishment of their subject as an academic discipline early last century. Pioneers like William James, Sigmund Freud, William McDougall, and Abraham

---

[2] Bongar, Beutler, Zimbardo, Brown, and Breckenridge (in press) might go some way to rectifying the omission.

[3] The point was acknowledged to some extent by the philosopher Moore (1993) when explanaining the historical emergence of social injustice.

[4] Historians and theologians can be excused a wry smile at the late awakening of behaviour scientists to the phenomenon of justice, their own disciplines having been concerned with it consistently from the times of the early Greeks – witness the place of justice as one of the seven heavenly virtues, and the corresponding seven consequent corporal works of mercy (http://www.deadlysins.com/virtues.html)

Maslow used a combination of clinical insights, introspection, empiricism, and experiential methods to lay tracks through the field of human motivation to identify and articulate human needs. Almost in parallel, a stream of animal and child experimenters led by Pavlov, Watson, Mowrer, Hull, Spence, Tolman, Skinner, and Bandura, made considerable advances in detailing the systems of reward under which needs could be satisfied and the laws of learning be established.

Yet another flow of researchers under the influence of Henry Murray and David McClelland made substantial progress by developing psychometrically robust rating scales and applying factor-analytic procedures to unravel some of the complexities of the topic, particularly as they applied to motivation and leadership in business and industry (cf. Steers, Porter, and, Bigley, 1987). In their latest managerial handbook the latter took advantage of developments in social psychology to refer to justice as it reflects a) the fair distribution of rewards and penalties in an employment setting, b) the fairness of the processes through which the distributions are made, and c) the fairness of the interpersonal consequences (Porter, Bigley, and, Steers, 2003, ch.2)

However, as mentioned in chapter 1, none of the early authorities, including the recent reviewer of motivational studies Wong (2000), was concerned with justice *per se*. Neither was Apter (1982; 1989; 2005), with his innovative and refreshing Reversal Theory that offered a systematic framework for the study of subjective phenomena. He construed human behaviour primarily as the outcome of four pairs of contrasting needs – viz. either for achievement or gratification, conformity or resistance, giving or taking, self-centrism or altruism. He regarded personality as deriving more from the constant reversal of reactions along each of the four polar opposites than from any somewhat consistent pattern. But commendable as might be the emphasis Apter placed on the capacity of individuals to defy categorisation in the display of ever-changing sequence of behaviour to gratify their immediate personal needs[5], it is difficult to see how communities could function without individuals making some more persistent adaptive concessions to each other. Therefore although Reversal Theory gives a healthy reminder that everyone is capable of excess, it has little to say about justice – in fact the words justice, law, and morality do not appear in the index of the expository texts.

To some extent Hauser, Young, and Cushman (in press) are an exception among recent motivation researchers in at least considering morality as an important component of the human psyche. Like Jose (chapter 4 in the present volume) they regard the development of morality as a biological phenomenon that depends on the complex interaction between innate structures, maturational factors, and environmental inputs. But they go so far as to postulate a moral faculty within individuals that smacks of the early 19th century phrenology promoted by Gall and Spurzheim, and they use explanatory terms reminiscent of those used in linguistics and traumatic memory that were either 'expressive' (i.e. accessible and declaratory) or 'operative' (i.e. relatively inaccessible and non-declaratory) (cf. van der Kolk, 1996). They accept that 'the principles underlying adult competence are phenomenally complex, abstract, and inaccessible to conscious awareness', and declare that their work is still in its infancy, but they confidently present their 'strong hunch' that once they have begun to uncover the principles underlying moral judgments the outcome will impact on theories of

[5] Perhaps unwittingly endorsing Edward Hoch's observation (1849-1925) that' there is so much good in the worst of us, and so much bad in the best of us, that it hardly becomes any of us to talk about the rest of us'.

behaviour. Accordingly they constructed a Moral Sense Test with four variations of a dilemma for obtaining empirical data about the underlying moral systems by which human beings operate, and they are collecting data over the Internet[6]. Their results will be worth attention.

As hinted earlier, of all the motivational researchers and theorists appraised, Abraham Maslow (1908-1970) was the only one to have come close to nominating justice as an important component of personal and social development, when

- in a footnote giving the very first intimation of his theory, Maslow (1943a) described security needs for 'a world that does not threaten and that is not dangerous', and he described the final stage of self-actualization 'in which the individual will tend to want to strive for all the conditions which make these satisfactions possible, e.g. freedom, full information, *justice,* order, etc.'[7]
- in the first article outlining his theory, Maslow (1943b) said that the 'healthy, normal, fortunate adult in our culture is largely satisfied in his safety needs. The peaceful, smoothly running, 'good' society ordinarily makes its members feel safe enough from wild animals, extremes of temperature, criminals, assault and murder, tyranny, etc… (*But*) the need for safety is seen as an active and dominant moiblizer of the organism's resources only in emergencies, *e.g.*, war, disease, natural catastropohes, crime waves, societal disorganization, neurosis, brain injury, chronically bad situation'
- in the same publication, Maslow (1943b) emphasised a number of safety needs, such as 'the child's need for some kind of undisrupted routine or rhythm…a predictable, orderly world' (*adding that*) '*injustice,* unfairness, or inconsistency in the parents seems to make a child feel anxious and unsafe' that subsequently he repeated verbatim his first major publication (1954, p.86)
- similarly Maslow warned of the consequences of *injustice*, the evidence for which would be seen in the 'neurotic or near-neurotic individuals' who had been endangered as well as 'the economic and social underdogs' (*who*) behave 'as if a great catastrophe were almost always impending, i.e. (*they are*) usually always responding as if to an emergency. (*Their*) safety needs often find specific expression in a search for a protector, or a stronger person on whom (*they*) may depend, perhaps a Fuhrer' (Maslow, 1943b; 1954, pp. 87-88)[8], and
- he also made reference to certain freedoms, including justice the denial of whioch could have serious consequences - viz.: 'Freedom to speak, freedom to do what one wishes so long as no harm is done to others, freedom to express oneself, freedom to investigate and seek for information, freedom to defend oneself, *justice* fairness, honesty, orderliness in the group…Thwarting in these freedoms will be reacted to with a threat or an emergency response. These ends are not ends in themselves but they are *almost* (sic) so since they are so closely related to the basic needs, which

[6] The Moral Sense Test can be accessed from http://wjh1.wjh.harvard.edu/~moral/test.html

[7] Although subsequently he resiled from the emphasis on the self-actualised to go beyond self-interest, as will be discussed below.

[8] But in setting out his theory Maslow made scant reference to the devastating effects of such external social forces on human behaviour – although he did happen to mention in an appendix that 'it would have been a blessing, not a curse, if Hitler or Mussolini had broken down with obvious schizophrenia' (1954, p.371).

are apparently the only ends in themselves. (*He went on to say that*)...without them the basic satisfactions are quite impossible, or at least, severely endangered' (Maslow 1943b;1954, p.92).

Maslow's strong if slender thread relating to justice aroused my keen interest. It led me to explore its emergence in some detail in both the 1954 and 1970 editions of his *Motivation and personality* that were published during his lifetime, and in the 1987 edition with new material by Ruth Cox and Robert Frager that was published long after his death[9]. Initially I wanted to see what consideration Maslow had given to justice in matters of individual safety and social belonging. After that, because of the apparent preoccupation with themselves of those fortunate enough to have reached the highest stage of personality development that Maslow postulated, I turned to all three editions of Maslow's parallel publication entitled *Towards a psychology of being* that focussed almost exclusively on self-actualisation. I had in mind Aristotle's saying that although the wise man does not expose himself needlessly to danger, since there are few things for which he cares sufficiently; he is willing, in great crises, to give even his life-knowing that under certain conditions it is not worth-while to live – but I wanted to find out whether Maslow had given it much thought. Then with doubts remaining, I found answers in Hoffman's (1988) biodraphy of Maslow.

In fairness to Maslow and his followers, the winding path has to be described, tendentious as at times it might appear.

MASLOW'S THEORY OF HUMAN MOTIVATION

In his seminal volume Maslow (1954) postulated a hierarchy of basic needs that ran through five levels from the physiological through security, belonging, and self-esteem to those that would allow for the ultimate fulfilment of life through the expression of creativity (Figure 1). He regarded the lower needs as deficiency needs (the so-called D needs) that for children had to be met by parent-figures, and the higher needs (the so-called B needs or Being and growth needs) as developing later through 'inner states of being' to the ideal stage of self-actualisation. He 'put forward as a thesis for further investigation that satisfying a person's basic needs... improves the individual not only in character structure but as a citizen on the national and international scene as well as in face-to-face relationships...(*saying that*) The possible implications for political, economic, educational, historical, and sociological theory are both tremendous and obvious...' (Maslow, 1954, p.117). In particular he warned of the 'danger of thwarting or actual thwarting of basic needs (including self-actualization), or the conditions upon which they rest, threat to life itself, threat to the integrity of the organism, threat to the integration of the organism, and threat to the organism's basic mastery of the world' (Maslow, 1954, p.162).

In chapter 12 of the same 1954 publication, Maslow applied the term 'self-actualization' to describe the heights of human development that in his opinion very few people were ever

[9] For the *aficianados*, it is interesting that although Maslow (1962, p.vii) himself described *Towards a psychology of being* as a continuation of his 1954 *Motivation and personality*, and also he referred to it in his 1970 edition of the latter, the editors of the revised 1987 edition presented 'to highlight Maslow's creative thinking and emphasize his far-reaching concepts', made no mention of either the 1962 or the 1968 editions of the companion volumes. Similarly Hoffman (1988) made no mention of the revised 1987 edition.

able to reach. He derived the concept from his 'global and holistic' impressions of a very small group of highly selected subjects within his immediate orbit who were far from preoccupied with themselves, were spontaneous, 'problem-centered', remote and unruffled, relatively independent of their physical and social environments, highly selective in their friendships, democratic in orientation, strongly ethical, and unlike 'any jungle denizen (their world is not) dominated and organised by the lower needs, especially the creature needs and the safety needs' (p. 232).

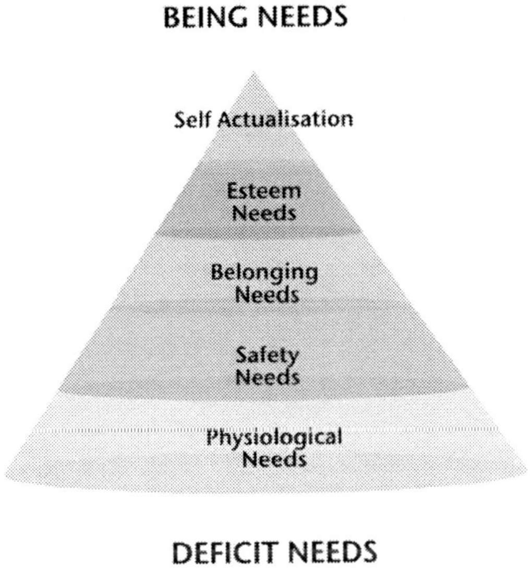

Figure 1. Maslow's Motivational Hierarchy

Later in an appendix, Maslow (1954, p.374) admitted that his sample of self-actualized subjects was somewhat limited – saying that people with a 'sense of duty, of loyalty, obligation to society, responsibility, the social conscience…The crusader. The fighter for principle, for justice, for freedom, for equality' had yet to be studied. Then, having declared that 'the behaviour of the healthy person is less determined by anxiety, fear, insecurity, guilt, shame, and more by truth, logic, justice reality, fairness, fitness, beauty, rightness, etc.', Maslow put the rhetorical question 'What produces the socially desirable characteristics of kindliness, social conscience, helpfulness, neighbourliness, identification, tolerance, friendliness, desire for justice, righteous indignation? (p. 377) - (again my emphasis in bold face).

Turning to the two subsequent editions of his *Motivation and personality*, Maslow affirmed the importance of human rights in the 1970 preface (p. xiii), when he asserted that 'In order to be fully human, these needs and meta needs gratifications are necessary, and may therefore be considered to be natural rights'. Then Robert Frager in his editorial preface to the third and posthumous edition of the same work (Maslow, 1987, p. xiii), reiterated that for Maslow ' a good society is one in which good relations are fostered and encouraged, (*and that*) psychological health (*is linked*) to the process of self-actualization and to the gratification of the other inherent needs of his need hierarchy'.

To add to the intellectual confusion about the meaning and significance of justice, or the 'semantic swamp' as Maslow (1968, p.85) called a similar clash over the meaning of his concept of peak experience, Maslow nominated justice specifically as # 4 in his list of 14 values essential for 'Being', and he alluded to the concept as a component of five other values (i.e. # 2 'perfection', # 3 'completion', # 7 'simplicity', # 9 'goodness', and # 13 'truth', and included 'living by its own laws' as elements of # 14 (Maslow, 1968, p.83). Finally Richard Lowry perpetuated the dilemma in his introduction to the posthumous third edition of *Towards a psychology of being* (Maslow, 1999, p.vi), by saying that throughout his life Maslow proclaimed 'the deeply moral nature of mankind', although being 'well aware that the pages of human history (*were*) stained with blood. He saw as clearly as anyone the indisputable evidence that human nature is capable of every conceivable kind of violence, viciousness, and cruelty. He was from his youth a very astute observer of those evils of everyday life that surface routinely in social interaction: belittlement, slander, guile, deception, manipulation, extortion.. (*and*) oppression'. Richard Lowry, was also the first Maslovian to list 'justice' in an index of one of the pioneer's books (1999, p.266),.

A Shortcoming of Maslow's Conceptualisation

However, the state of self-actualisation or psychological perfection that Maslow outlined, was supremely self-centered, despite the underlying recognition it gave to justice, natural rights, and good relationships. It placed no obligation on the psychologically most healthy to intercede on behalf of others suffering injustice, nor for them to take part in restorative activities to put matter right[10]. On this point I agree with Wong (2000, ch. 6) that the social motivation of attachment and altruism must come into consideration, but unlike him I was not convinced that it was manifestly 'something akin to self actualization' as construed by Maslow (Wong, 2000, p.216).

To seek clarification I turned to the different editions of Maslow's concurrent treatise *Towards a psychology of being*, and was disappointed. From comments in the preface of the first edition (1962, reprinted 1968, p.vi), it was apparent that others had entertained similar doubts about the self-actualised as I, and they must have expressed them directly to Masow, because he began by admitting that his description of the self-actualiser was 'proven to have the unforseen shortcomings of appearing a) to imply selfishness rather than altruism, b) to slur the aspect of duty and dedication to life tasks, c) to neglect the ties to other people and to society, and the dependence of individual fulfillment upon a 'good society'… and f) to stress, by implication passivity rather than passivity or receptivity'.

Yet in the preface to the second edition of the same work, and having established Humanistic Psychology as a 'third viable alternative to objectivistic, behaviouristic (mechanomophic) psychology and to orthodox Freudianism', Maslow (1968, pp. iii-iv) made clear that his work was 'a preparation for a still *higher* Fourth Psychology, transpersonal, transhuman, centered in the cosmos rather than in human needs and interests, going beyond

[10] Apart from the allusion to Aristotle given on page 6 above, my personal commitment to social justice was inspired a) by an adaptation of the Old Testament saying of the prophet *Micah,* 6,8 that to do justly, to love mercy, and to walk humbly were the requirements of God, and b) by the aphorism attributed to the Irish philosopher Edmund Burke (1729-1797) that the only thing necessary for the triumph of evil is for good men to do nothing. My intellectual commitment came more recently after reading Segerstråle, (2001).

humanness, identity, self-actualisation and the like'. Then later in the same text, in another swing back to a concern for addressing reality, Maslow (1968, p. 162) said that in the healthier person, 'anger is reactive (to a present situation) rather than a characterological reservoir from the past...it is a realistic effective response to something real in the present, for instance to injustice or exploitation or attack...it takes the form of decisiveness self-affirmation, self-protection, justified indignation fighting against evil and the like. And such a person is apt to be *more* effective fighter, for justice for example, than the average person' .

In the very same volume Maslow (1968, ch.6) vacillated on the point once more, this time by describing the self-actualised in ethereal terms, showing a benign indifference to the outer world of reality while fostering internally a state of Nirvana of sublime spirituality[11]. However, to my mind, such a state of existential withdrawal might conceivably be the only option for people in extreme circumstances, like the psychiatrist Viktor Frankl (1959) as a prisoner in Auschwitz. Otherwise it cannot be construed as anything but a major symptom of avoidance, inadequacy, and selfishness that is uncharacteristic of mature people.

Here other people come to mind whose circumstances enabled them to react against Nazism. They include the German psychiatrist John Rittmeister (1898-1944) who was executed for condemning the 'horrible torture and atrocities that he was witnessing', and Karsten Jasperson who protested to Hitler and to the Archbishop of Münster about doctors murdering their patients in mental hospitals in pursuit of racial purity (Meyer-Lindenberg, 1991). There is also the remarkable if eccentric Kurt Gerstein from an influential family who joined the SS to see for himself the extent of the atrocities his government was perpetrating in the extermination camps, before he secured a bureaucratic position that enabled him to reject certain consignments of lethal gas on the pretence of it being below standard (Joffroy, 1971).

For me, Maslow's apparent ambivalence about the moral concern of highly developed individuals to address injustice remained a conundrum. It raised questions about the attention he personally might have paid to the extreme forms of injustice that occurred during his lifetime - his era having included the holocaust in war-time Nazi Germany, the McCarthy era of anti-Communist oppression in the 1950's in the United States, and the abuse of civil rights and the major protests in that country against the Vietnam War that culminated in massive student protests in the 1960's (Taylor, 1970). I wondered why in his 1943b article Maslow had high expectations of the self-actualised to engage in worldly issues, but later he had changed his view.

Here Hoffman's (1988) biography of the man put my mind at rest, because it showed that Maslow was indeed sensible of the strains and stresses in society about him, and he was concerned enough to try to remedy some of them. In brief, Maslow was the eldest American born child of poor Russian Jewish immigrants who encountered anti-Semitism first in his neighbourhood and then later in academia when seeking a permanent teaching appointment (Hoffman, 1988, pp. 2-6, and 47-48). In his family life as a child he also suffered the constant biting criticism from his mother, and he had an absentee father, the effect of both perhaps making him emphasise the need for love over that of belonging (Hoffman, 1988, ch.1). He went so far as to describe his mother as a 'cruel, ignorant, and hostile figure, one so unloving

[11] At this point I found support in an article by Brownstein (2004) – an authority on meditation - saying 'Those of us who are spiritually involved must also have the courage to engage the world's confusion, demonstrating commitment that comes from political awareness. We must risk activating our compassion. Without this engagement our 'personal growth' will remain sterile and dry, and the status quo will only perpetuate itself. We cannot forsake our brothers and sisters who are needlessly suffering'.

as to induce madness in her children'. He never forgave her treatment of him, and he refused to attend her funeral (Hoffman, 1988, p.7).

Later when he became a father himself, he became aware of the tremendous student ferment of the 1960's in which one of his daughters Ellen participated and one of his students Abie Hoffman was a prominent activist (cf. Hoffman, 1988, ch. 16). In his teaching he strove to apply the research findings of psychology to promote social harmony and justice (p.158), and scholars who were trying to account for the authoritarian personality syndrome that featured in the rise of dictatorships in Europe before World War 2 sought his opinion (cf. Adorno, Frenkel-Brunswick, Levinson, and Sanford, 1950, p.231). In particular he deplored the '*jungle outlook*' (sic), and is quoted from his diaries as saying that 'If the world is actually jungle-like for an individual, and if human beings have behaved to him like wild animals behave, then the authoritarian is perfectly justified in all his suspicions, hostilities, and anxieties' (Hoffman, 1988, p. 159).

The biographer also revealed Maslow as being somewhat critical of university students and staff for being self-centred, and being impatient with members of encounter groups at the Esalen Institute in California for their emotional self-indulgence. In fact after an uncharacteristic outburst at one seminar there, Maslow declared that he had 'the feeling of historical urgency…that there's a fire that we have to put out. The world is burning up. It's literally possible there (will be) atom bombs next week' (Hoffman, 1988, p.293). After another such seminar Maslow wrote that he 'really did not care much about helping a privileged few to lead happier lives on the edge of catastrophe' (p.302). Finally in 1968, as President of the American Psychological Association, he declared his hand as one of 19 eminent Psychologists for Social Involvement who circulated a letter to all members to support fthe finding of a National Commission that the widespread riots on the streets of America 'resulted largely from conditions of discrimination, poverty, and unemployment, …(*that*) have their roots in racial prejudice', …(*and who went on to say*) 'strongly urge that direct action be taken to combat these unjust conditions' (p. 308)[12].

It is not for me to try to explain Maslow's reluctance to give justice its full due[13], but from the leads available from his own writing, and from those provided by his biographer, it would seem that the recognition of justice would not be inconsistent with his theory as a whole. Were it to be given, the recognition might also restore the obligation of the psychologically mature to address injustice.

PREVIOUS MODIFICATIONS OF MASLOW'S THEORY

Before advocating the firm incorporation of justice into Maslow's theory of motivation, I turned to three modifications that other psychologists had made of his theory, all of which

[12] In fact Maslow was saddened by the moral dissolution that had corrupted the Blackfoot tribe of Indians in Canada with whom he had done fieldwork as a student (Hoffman, 1988, ch.7; pp.299-300).

[13] The key might lie in Maslow's 'transpersonal, transhuman, cosmos-centered' focus already mentioned, together with his rejection of Aristotelian logic in favour of ambiguous 'holistic' definitions when describing the concept (Maslow, 1968, p.174). Although ambiguity is no defence against inconsistency and it cannot be used to explain Maslow's curious reliance on social injustice to rationalise what he termed 'biological injustice' when asking 'If only nature is there to blame, what will this mean for the self-esteem of the individual 'unfairly' treated by nature itself?' (Maslow, 1970, p.xvii).

happen to have been developed in response to employee/managerial situations[14] rather than to the broader and more fundamental issues raised in this book. The first modification was by Clayton Alderfer (1972), the second by Deci and Ryan (2000), and the third by Zohar and Marshall (2004). Alderfer (1972) adopted Maslow's conception of basic human needs, but reduced their cluster of levels from five to three and renamed them as 'existence', 'relatedness', and 'growth'. He also placed less emphasis on the progressive satisfaction of the needs from the lower to the higher levels, but allowed for the satiation of needs at higher levels to compensate for the deprivation of others below, and vice versa (as also had Maslow originally in 1943b!), and he recognised that basic needs could operate at different levels simultaneously. Then, unlike Maslow, Alderfer went further to devise an 88-item measure of satisfactions and a 16-item scale of desire, and then to verify them in an extensively documented series of psychometric analyses.

Certainly the scope, the application, and the validation of Alderfer's revision had some appeal, but it made no mention of matters pertaining to justice that arose outside offices and workshops[15]. Not that the importance of its area of application should be minimised, because as Wahba and Bridwell (1973/1987) have shown, and Porter, Bigley, and Steers, (2003, pp.6-9) continue to emphasise, variations of Maslovian theory underpin good employee/management relations. Moreover as shown in the present volume, the implications of injustice from industrial policies extend far beyond the factory floor.

Deci and Ryan (2000) provided another modification of Maslow' theory - albeit while ignoring Alderfer completely and referring only to an early article by the pioneer (Maslow, 1943b) rather than to any of his later and more substantial works. Like Alderfer, these researchers introduced a three-factor cluster theory of self-determination of innate needs that they called competence, autonomy, and relatedness, on the satisfaction of which they claimed psychological health depended. Like Maslow they focussed more on the individual generation of needs rather than on any environmental forces that might inhibit the 'fundamental human trajectory towards vitality, integration, and health'. Like Maslow they were also silent about any moral obligations that the more fortunate members of society might have for correcting matters that impinge adversely upon others. But as Lynne Eccleston and Tony Ward suggest in their chapter in the present book, their articulation of goal-seeking behaviour is useful to bear in mind when helping offenders to change their directions in life.

Zohar and Marshall (2004), on the other hand, expanded rather than contracted Maslow's categories, and they gave priority to the peak experience of individuals regardless of any adverse environmental circumstances that might confront them. By way of illustration they inverted the familiar triangle of Maslow's needs to reflect their stand (pp.16/17), but somewhat inconsistently they reverted to Maslow's original presentation when constructing a scale of motivations that allocated negative scores for specific unsatisfied deficiency needs and positive scores for satisfied higher needs (p.39). Their hope was that individuals might reflect on the personal significance of various items on the scale derived from their responses and then consider what adjustments they might make subsequently to bring about

[14] Maslow applied his own theory in the management of a factory in California owned by his brothers when he sought a spell of relief from academia, and when he acted as a consultant in the business and commercial world (Hoffman, 1988, ch.15).

[15] Similarly, Hoffman (1988) made no reference to Alderfer. Evidently, unlike the person from whom they drew inspiration, the disciples all preferred to work independently.

improvements – quoting Carl Jung's assertion that 'it is only in our most private and subjective lives that we make the epoch'.

Of particular interest for the present chapter, was Zohar and Marshall's concept of 'spiritual capital' with which individuals might balance their intellectual abilities and emotional behaviour: - defined as 'wealth that makes our communities and organizations function effectively for the common good' (p.5). The authors were at pains to point out that their use of the word spiritual had no necessary connection with organised religion, but it described a link with the innate capacity of certain unspecified structures in the brain that provide the basic ability to form meanings, values, and beliefs in the first place (p.65). They argued that individuals were able to access that primary base by exercising their 'spiritual intelligence', much as they might use rational intelligence for accessing thoughts, and emotional intelligence for accessing feelings. In their view, all three spiritual, rational, and emotional 'intelligences' are essential attributes for the prolongation of community life. Their emphasis on spirituality led them to focus on its application to business, because, in their view, 'business is the dominant instruments through which capitalist values have permeated our society'...(and it) has the money and the power to make very significant difference in the way that wealth of all kinds is generated and used to benefit society at large'. (p.6). They were not uncritical of capitalism, but they argued that 'the trick is not to reject capitalism but to transform it (because of) its rich potential to generate, within a wider framework, even more wealth and value, some of which can be used for the common good of humanity' (p.6). Apparently, and unlike Robert Jackall (1988), they did not consider the avarice of corporate managers beyond redemption, and they made no mention of corporate malfeasance that seemed endemic (and to which reference was made on page 6 above)..

However, aside from Zohar and Marshall's assertion that business is the best agency through which substantial change for the better might be brought about in the community, and apart from any reservation about the use of naked introspection alone in Zohar and Marshall's construction of theory, and their assertion that business is the best agency through which substantial change for the better might be brought about in the community, their emphasis on value-systems and their application to all of mankind was refreshing. But sadly, they too made no specific mention of justice as it might apply either to the business elite whom they described as 'knights, or to those whom they called 'masters' who embedded the new culture within the practice of the organisation – much less to the poor mortals on whom they advocated the imposition of the new value systems. Yet, regardless of their autocratic assumptions, they did affirm that values in general could be accommodated conveniently within Maslow's theory of motivation.

The Placement

Despite the specific neglect of justice *per se* by all three groups of latter-day Maslovians, in what Deci and Ryan described as 'this vigorous new field', it seemed appropriate to suggest that were justice to be given full status as a basic human need, it could be placed appropriately among Maslow's second level of safety needs that 'may serve as the almost exclusive organizers of behaviour, recruiting all the capacities of the organism in their service' (Maslow, 1970, pp. 39-42)[16].

Positioned there among the security needs, the need for justice would seem to be consistent with the need for people at all stages of life to be treated fairly, and hence with a better chance of being able to thrive cognitively, emotionally, and socially. Further, if placed there, it would:

- give tacit recognition to the neo-Kohlbergian theory that the young inculcate cognitive systems of right and wrong with which ultimately to moderate their own behaviour
- acknowledge the growth of reciprocal patterns of concern, and the part they come to play in framing and applying laws wisely between family members, neighbours, and wider communities (cf. Rest, Narvarez, Bebau, and Thoma, 1999)
- make clear the obligations of families and communities to ensure that they also met basic needs of all their vulnerable members such as the young, the sick, the elderly, and the disadvantaged
- be consistent with the philosophical, religious, developmental, and social aspects of justice enunciated earlier in the present book by Charles Tolman, Chris Marshall, Paul Jose, Ronald Fischer and Linda Skitka that underpin the restorative and therapeutic judicial processes raised by Lynne Eccleston and Tony Ward, Gaye Maxwell and Allison Morris, and David Wexler, and
- restore the essential social cohesion that economic injustice and totalitarian societies ignore, challenge the systems that condone the abuse, torture, and destruction of minority groups highlighted by Reg Orovwuje, Jeffrey Sluka, and Paul Burns, and endorse Andrew Ladley's view of the dialectic between the extremes individuality and community in the recognition and fulfilment of human rights for all.

Like the deprivation of any other basic need, conceivably the shattering of secure expectations would bring the need for justice to the fore, with the victims yearning to restore the status quo – either by asserting themselves or appealing for help until justice, or it approximation, once again might prevail. However, this time the victims should not expect their appeals fall on deaf ears, because the self-actualised will not be expected to be lacking in compassion and altruism. He it seemed appropriate to include justice with the safety needs, and to redraw Maslow's familiar triangular figure in the form of a three-legged stool, on which the precarious nature of the basic Deficiency needsl on which the development of Being needs depend (Figure 2). One leg upholds the familiar physiological needs for the maintenance of life, the second for security needs that now include justice, and the thid upholds the need for belonging that contributes both to a sense of wellbeing and to a sense of community. Only on such a stable base can needs for self-esteem and self actualization develop, with an obligation for individuals to help each other in difficult times.

[16] To quote from the last edition of the book with which Maslow personally was involved.

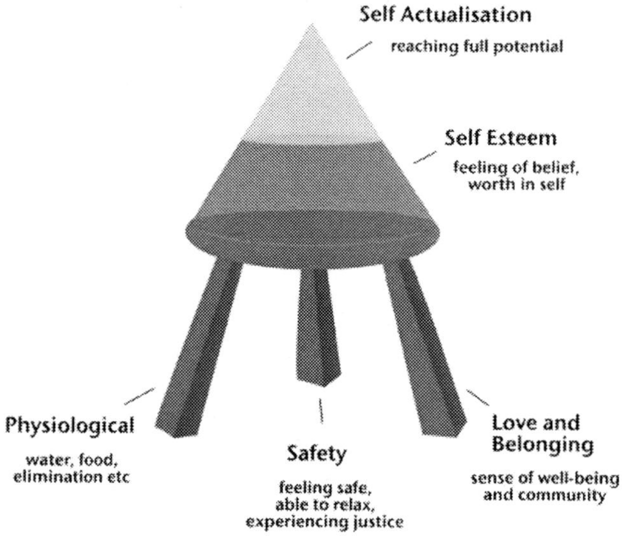

Figure 2. Maslow's schema refigured to include justice as a basic human need

VALIDATION

The question then arises as to how the proposition of justice might be incorporated firmly within the ranks of basic needs instead of being left outside, and then to validate it with methods having some acceptable degree of independence. Here Maslow gave no lead. As a humanist with an experiential and introspective orientation not unacquainted with both experimental and empirical methods[17], he admitted that his theory lacked experimental validation and support, and he made a plea for critics to avoid 'unreal perfectionism' in testing his claims (Maslow, 1954, p. xix; and p. xxvii). He argued that this 'kind of research is in principle so different – involving as it does a kind of lifting oneself by one's axiological bootstraps – that if we were to wait for conventionally reliable data, we should have to wait for ever. It seems that the only manly thing to do is not to fear mistakes, plunge in, to do the best one can, hoping to learn enough from blunders to correct them eventually' (Maslow 1954, p.199). Essentially he was reliant on 'the slow global development of a global or holistic impression of the sort that we make of our friends and acquaintances' (Maslow, 1954, p.203).

He made much the same stand later, in his preface to the first edition of his *Towards a psychology of being* (1962/1968 reprint, p.v111), viz:

> 'This book, like my previous one, is full of affirmations which are based on pilot researches, bits of evidence, on personal observation, on theoretical deduction and sheer hunch. These are generally phrased so that they can be proven true or false. That is, they are hypotheses, i.e.

[17] Not surprisingly, as a student with a focus on personal relationships. Maslow was repelled by E.B. Tichener's narrow psychophysical focus, inspired by J.B. Watson's promise of a science of psychology through behaviourism. He was also impressed by Harry Harlow's 'controlled objective observation' of animal behaviour, by Ruth Benedict's ethno-=psychological fieldwork, and by Kurt Goldstein's neuropsychiatry (Hoffman, 1988, pp. 26-31; 49-55; 138-139).

presented for testing rather than for final belief. They are also obviously relevant and pertinent, i.e. their possible correctness or incorrectness is important to other branches of psychology…They should therefore generate research.... For these reasons I consider this book to be in the realm of science or pre-science, rather than of exhortation, or of personal philosophy, or literary expression'.

Certainly many researchers accepted Maslow's pleading, and in the 30 years or so until the publication of the third edition of his 1954 volume, they contributed to a 'rich harvest' of some 1 580 citations of his theory (Maslow, Frager, and Fadiman 1987, p.365). None-the-less it is no longer acceptable for social scientists to accept propositions without testing their foundations thoroughly, especially when trying a) to make scientific contribution to the advancement of knowledge, b) to establish a sound base from which to embark on comparable studies, and c) to recommend changes in social policy to improve the circumstances of individuals and their communities. At issue is the need for theorists of social policy to test their hypotheses and propositions with rigour, but not to the point of rigor mortis, and then to consider the ethical implications of the policies they recommend. Witness the horrendous consequences of the application of eugenics campaigns in the 20th century that many of the leading scientists supported (Nuffield Council on Bioethics (2002, ch. 2), to say nothing of their part in the development of nuclear weaponry (Gellhorn, 1986), and now the suggestion that pioneers in behavioural science were involved in determining the precise techniques of torture for people with particular types of personality (Hodge and Cooper, 2004).

However, a few sympathetic researchers have used standard psychometric procedures with some success in seeking the essential prerequisites for healthy living that Maslow proposed, while still promoting the narrow scientist-practitioner model that he opposed: In fact four of such studies happened also to have had a bearing on the theme of the present chapter. First there was Harlow and Newcomb (1990) who surveyed young adults to identify their social, political, or religious beliefs that conceivably might be thought of relating to justice. They found that 'Peer Relationships, Intimate Relationships, Family Relationships, Purpose in Life, Perceived Opportunity, Work Satisfaction, and Health Satisfaction' were the primary positive factors in a hierarchy of satisfactions, but 'Meaninglessness' and 'Powerlessness' were to the contrary. Soon afterwards Ronen (1994) found substantial support across the board for Maslow's hierarchy when applying a fresh non-metric multidimensional scaling technique to international sets of motivational data on work experience. Then Slone, Kaminer, and Durrheim (2000) used a Political Life Event Scale to measure the reactions of 540 South African adolescents to the racial policy of apartheid, and they confirmed the interaction between innate personality variables and external social stressors. Finally Tepper (2001) documented the adverse health effects of injustice from organisational matters that arose with employees during the course of their work.

Indicative as they are, such studies highlight the importance, and the difficulty, of making the subjective objective in psychological research. Clearly, if justice were brought more into mainstream academic studies, alongside other well-researched topics, it would have its subjective elements exposed to more extensive empirical scrutiny.

The Prospect

Were justice to be given full recognition as a motivating force, as is suggested, many challenging topics would open to entice more researchers to develop and apply their skills. In general psychology, cognitive psychologists might be impelled to examine Kohlberg's theory of moral development in relation to children from underprivileged and criminal families. Their colleagues in cross-cultural psychology might open up topics in the long dormant but currently burgeoning field of justice in child-rearing practices, community development, and conflict resolution. They could see whether Triandis and Suh's (2002) 'allocentrics' and 'idiocentrics' are to be found in different proportions in all cultures, and whether collectivists prefer methods of conflict resolution that do not destroy relationships, as distinct from individualists who go to the bitter end in the settlement of disputes – or whether people in each group are flexible in 'frame-switching' their cultural belief-systems according to the significance of the particular situations they face (cf. Lehman, Chiu, and Schaller, 2004). They might also be inclined to design empirical techniques for examining the suggestion of the same authors that 'evolutionary processes have shaped culturally shared conceptions of morality pertaining to a broad set of behavioural domains, including obedience, reciprocity, interpersonal helping, social responsibility and group solidarity', and that mutually supportive behaviour is beneficial, both for survival and sexual reproduction.

Clinical researchers concerned with justice might consider the pathological proclivities of the sadists and masochists found at different ends of the cruelty spectrum, as well as those of the borderline unstable who satisfy their immaturity by simulating scenes of injustice sometimes to the point of making video-tapes of violence. They might also study the socialised psychopaths in position of responsibility who perpetrate injustice of the non-criminal kind (cf. McCormick and Burch, 2005).. More than that, they could bring legal, philosophical, and theological dimensions into their analysis of human behaviour. Already Francis (1999) has given a helpful lead with his guide to ethics for psychologists, and an extension is called for with regard to clinical practice and research.

In the general sphere of criminal justice, the restorative justice movement is beginning to conceptualise its endeavours in researchable form (cf. McCold, and Wachtel, 2003), and it is generating an enthusiastic inter-professional and interdisciplinary body of 'collective intelligence' with far reaching global implications at all levels from primitive village to complex city life (cf. Seidler, and Allena, 2004). As a result, researchers might be impelled to consider the effect of differential access to the judicial system for both victims and offenders, and the appropriateness of formal judicial procedures that operate in the Courts (cf. NZ Law Commission, 2004). They might also consider the impact of corrupt judiciaries on local communities[18], pay more attention to the determination of guilt of the accused beyond reasonable doubt in capital cases[19], and question the moral implications of the State having the power to impose the death penalty[20].

Similarly, in the domain of civil justice, researchers might find issues of micro- and macro-conflict ripe for study in which racism and xenophobia feature[21], as well as the

---

18 See http://www.unodc.org/unodc/corruption.html
19 See http://www.violettespage.com/released.html
20 See http://www.911justicephadp.org/Archive_death_penalty_articles.htm
21 See http://www.un.org/apps/news/story.asp?NewsID=10156&Cr=racism&Cr11=

multitude of global issues to which the United Nations (2004) has drawn attention. Then in the area of social justice far beyond that which obtains in management theory, there are the effects to be considered of policies for drastically reducing extreme poverty and hunger, for substantially improving the health and education of the most disadvantaged, and for ensuring for environmental sustainability under a developmental scheme for such countries to attain global partnership by the year 2015 that 189 countries endorsed in the year 2000 at the United Nations Millennium Assembly[22]. Blazer, Sachs-Ericsson, and Hybels (2005) for example, have shown that unmet basic needs relating to the adequacy of income, quality of housing, and neighbourhood safety perceived by the elderly, is a significant predictor variable of their mortality. It is therefore conceivable that less adverse effects from unmet needs might be found among other vulnerable sectors of the population.

Such research might go some way towards redressing the problems behind the wars, massacres and atrocities of the twentieth century that have left bitter legacies[23], to say nothing of the continuing feuds that have driven millions of people from their homes - either as displaced persons within their own countries, refugees seeking sanctuary abroad, or asylum-seekers in fear of losing their lives (UNHCR. 2002: *International review of the Red Cross*, 2003-No. 851).[24] It might induce more social anthropologists to follow Sluka (2000; present volume), rather than Brown (1991) who in an otherwise authoritative appraisal of universal human needs seems to have overlooked those of justice and security. Certainly, Eugene Brody (2005), in his firm concluding chapter to a series of authoritative contributions in the *Project 1 billion: Book of best practices: Trauma and the role of mental health in post-conflict recovery* (Mollica, Guerra, Bhasin & Lavelle, 2005), makes a loud appeal for such matters to be taken into consideration.

To his credit the diplomat/social scientist John W. Burton (1990; 1996, 1997; 2001: Mitchell, 2001) was on the right track when he argued that 'provention' – i.e. active prevention through meeting human needs – offered more promise in resolving bitter conflict between historical enemies than a continuation of the spiral of dominance and suppression. His early social casework studies led him through Maslow's (1954) holistic work to focus on identifying the deprivation of basic needs behind conflict. However, like Maslow he too was hesitant about the significance of justice - saying at one time that '*justice* (sic) can be given a universal meaning only insofar as it reflects the satisfaction of human needs, which by definition are universal' (Burton, 1996, p.32) but in a further volume on the same topic omitting the reference altogether (Burton, 1997). But it would only be a short step for him to recognise justice in the way suggested in this text. The same could be said for Offer and Sabshin (1991) who used Maslow's theory to underpin their work on normal growth and development, and for Young (1994/2004 update, ch.1) who used Maslow's existing theory to advantage as a framework in her authoritative handbook on psycho-social interventions after various types of catastrophe.

Further research should also go some way towards addressing the current phenomenon of complex international terrorism that is creating a fortress mentality in which in the name of

---

[22] See http://www.interaction.org/library/detail.php

[23] See. http://users.erols.com/m.white28/war-1900.htm

[24] Readers can take heart from Archbishop Desmond Tutu's revelation in his foreword to *The Human Security Report* (2005, p.iii) that 'Over the last 30 years the collapse of some 60 dictatorships has freed countless millions from repressive rule. The number of democracies has soared, interstate wars have become increasingly rare, and all wars have become less deadly'.

justice and self-protection the authoritarians are able to impose primitive policies of deterrence, retribution, and revenge in so-called 'pre-emptive strikes' on suspected targets abroad – albeit with sophisticated weaponry and explosive power of a kind hardly imaginable (M. Burton, 2004: Taylor, in press). Perhaps in that connection researchers at the Centre for the Study of Terrorism at the University of Maryland might be inspired to go beyond the defensive 'prediction and prevention of terrorist attacks and terrorist behaviours' to consider non-belligerent proactive remedies[25]. Certainly the World Commission on the Social Dimension of Globalization (WCSDG) (2004) has declared 'fairness (to be) a notion which is deeply felt and clearly recognized by people in every country', and to say that a 'fairer and more prosperous world is the key to a more secure world. Terror often exploits poverty, injustice and desperation to gain public legitimacy. The existence of such conditions is an obstacle in the fight against terrorism' (WCSDG, 2004, p.8). Subsequently the United Nations General Assembly (2005) endorsed the theme and urged member countries to give it priority to avoid catastrophe.

Inevitably any study of terrorism will raise larger political questions about the ability of democracies to respond quickly and robustly against those that would directly or indirectly destroy them, while in the process preserving the liberal traditions for which their forebears have fought long and hard. Here the paper by US Chaplain Maloney (1981) for the moral guidance of the military comes to mind, after what have been called 'the moral quakes' of Hiroshima, My Lai, and Watergate – and now Al Ghraib, as also does the United Nations (1982) paper on ethical principles affecting the role health professionals who might in some way be accomplices to the systematic abuse of prisoners and detainees.[26] Similarly the role, function, selection, and training of UN military peacekeepers is a topic demanding urgent attention, especially because they often find themselves in uncompromising situations between two hostile forces, neither of which is intent on establishing peace, much less on maintaining it (Taylor, 2004).

Yet to gain real momentum is the non-governmental peace and conflict resolution movement, despite the untiring efforts of individuals like John Burton (mentioned above) and John Galtung[27], and the ambitious plan of the World Council of Churches in nominating the years 2001-2010 as the Decade to Overcome Violence[28]. Collectively, these peacemakers, as distinct from peacekeepers, are not so optimistic as to think they can stop all violence, but their aim is to reduce the conditions under which violence appears. In the process, the ecumenical body formed in the years of apartheid identified four major themes, one of which concerns the resolution of immediate issues of justice, and the others concern the spirit and logic of violence (including anthropological and cultural legitimisations), the use, misuse, and abuse of power, and the crucial role of religious identities – all of which happen to happen to be covered to some extent in the contents of the present book. However, the one topic that cries out desperately for attention, is the place of justice in comparative religions. Presently injustice, ignorance, and bigotry abounds in that area, with the likelihood of bloodthirsty carnage between warring groups on the ground, and conflict between asymmetrical forces, one of which has the technological sophistication to slaughter the other from afar..

---

[25] 'Birth of a terrorist –US scholars seek clues' - http://www.rsnz.org/news/print.php?view=56580.

[26] See Borchelt and Pross (2005, pp. 45-47), Lucas and Pross (2004), and Pope and Garcia-Peltoniemi (2004).

[27] See courses at www.aspr.ac.at

[28] See http://overcomingviolence.org/dov.nsf/f2b3c6f6c91ade2ec1256bea0002bc786/4d

From all this, it can be said with confidence that no matter the particular field scholars and researchers choose to explore in the validation of justice, it will give them a chance to make worthwhile contributions to the resolution of critical individual and social issues. In the process they will enjoy the rare benefit of cooperating with members of related academic and professional groups and the public at large, while contributing to beneficial social policy-making. Most certainly their activities will be in accord with the formal aims and objectives of the major professional bodies to which they belong, i.e. of serving society as well as extending the boundaries of knowledge. It remains for them to get on with the job and put the proposition to the test.

REFERENCES

Adorno, T.W., Frenkel-Brunswick, E., Levinson, D.J., and Sanford, N. (1950). *The authoritarian personality.* New York: Harper and Row.

Alderfer, C. (1972). *Existence, relatedness and growth: Human needs in organisational settings.* New York: Free Press.

Apter, M.J. (1982). *The experience of motivation: the theory of psychological reversals.* London: Academic Press.

Apter, M.J. (1989). *Reversal theory: Motivation, emotion and personality.* London: Routledge.

Apter, M.J. (2005). Reversal Theory Society: Dancers not statues. – accessed May 7, 2005 from http://www.reversaltheory.org/RT_TheoryIntro.htm

Blazer, D.G., Sachs-Ericsson, N., and Hybel, C.F. (2005). Perception of unmet needs as a predictor of mortality among community-dwelling older adults. *American Journal of Public Health*, 95, 2, 299-305.

Bongar, B., Beutler, L., Zimbardo, P., Brown, L.M., & Breckenridge. J.N. (Eds). *The psychology of terrorism.* Oxford University Press.

Borchelt, A, G., and Pross, C. (Eds.). *Break them down: Systematic use of psychological torture by US Forces.* Cambridge MA: Physicians for Human Rights.

Brody, E.B. (2005). Human rights and mental health in post-conflict recovery. In R.F. Mollica, R. Guerra, R. Bhasin, & J.L. Lavelle. (Eds). *Project 1 billion: Book of best practices: Trauma and the role of mental health in post-conflict recovery.*(Ch. 17). - accessed 2 May 2005 from http://www.news.harvard.edu/prerss/pressdoc/supplements/

Brown. D.E. (1991). *Human universals.* New York: McGraw-Hill.

Brownstein, M. (2004). Activism is a spiritual path: Meditation. *Resurgence*, 225, July, 20-22.

Burton, J.W. (Ed.). (1990). *Conflict: Human needs theory.* New York: St Martin's Press.

Burton, J. (1996). *Conflict resolution: Its language and processes.* London: Scarecrow Press.

Burton, J. (1997). *Violence explained: The sources of conflict, violence and crime and their provention.* Manchester University Press.

Burton, J.W. (2001). Conflict provention as a political system. *International Journal of Peace Studies*, 6, 1, - accessed 22 June 2005 from
http://ww.gmu.edu/academic/ijps/vol6_1/Burton2.htm

Burton, M. (2004). Viva Nácho!: Liberating psychology in Latin America. *The Psychologist*, 17, 10, 584-587.

Cox, R. (1987). Afterword: The rich harvest of Abraham Maslow. In A. Maslow (1954/1987). *Motivation and personality*. (3rd. edn. rev.). (pp. 245-271). New York: Harper and Row.

Cox, S. (2002). Tools and techniques for evaluating psychological debriefing. In N. Tehrani. (coordinator).*Professional Practice Working Party: Psychological debriefing* (ch.3). Leicester: British Psychological Society. pp. 76.

Deci, E.L., and Ryan, R.M. (2000). Target article: The 'what' and 'why' of goal pursuits: Human needs and the self-determination of behavior. *Psychological Inquiry*, 11, 4, 227-268.

Efklides, A., Kuhl, J., and Sorrentino, R.M. (Eds.). (2001). *Trends and prospects in motivation research*. Dordrecht/Boston/London: Kluwer.

Forsyth, D.R. (1980). A taxonomy of ethical ideologies. *Journal of Personality and Social Psychology*, 39, 1, 175-184.

Forsyth, D.R. (2005). Studies in moral thought, emotions, and action. – accessed 2 June from http://ww.has.vcu.edu/psy/faculty/fors/ethics.html

Francis, R.D. (1999). *Ethics for psychologists: A handbook. Leicester:* British Psychological Society.

Frankl, V.E. (1959). *Man's search for meaning*. New York: Washington Square Press.

Gellhorn, (1986). *The face of war*. London: Virago Press.

Harlow, L.L. and Newcomb, M.D. (1990). Towards a general hierarchical model of meaning and satisfaction in life. *Multivariate Behavioural Research*, 25, 3, 387-405.

Hauser, M., Young, L., and Cushman, F. (in press). Reviving Rawls' linguistic analogy: Operative principles and the causal structure of moral action. In W. Sinott-Armstrong. (Ed.). *Moral psychology and biology*. New York: Oxford University Press.

Hayes, N. (Ed.). (1997). *Doing qualitative analysis in psychology*. Hove: Psychology Press.

Hodge, J., and Cooper, L. (2004). Roots of Abu Ghraib in CIA techniques: 50 years of refining, teaching, torture found in interrogation manuals. *National Catholic Reporter*, 3 November, available online at
http://ncronline.org/NCR_Online/archives2/2004d/110504/110504a.php

Hoffman, ER. (1988). *The right to be human: A biography of Abraham Maslow*. Los Angeles: Tarcher.

International review of the Red Cross 2003-No. 851. Special issue: Victims after war – humanitarian action, reparation and justice. -accessed 20 March 2004 from http://www.icrc.org/Web/eng/siteengo.nsf/html/section_review_2003_851?OpenDocu

Jackall, R. (1988). Moral mazes: The world of corporate managers. Oxford University Press.

Joffroy, P. (1971). *A spy for God: The ordeal of Kurt Gerstein*. (trans. Norman Kenny). London. Collins.

Jones, W., and Hughes, S.H. (2003). Complexity, conflict resolution, and how the mind works. *Conflict Resolution Quarterly*, 20, 4, 485-494.

King, P.M., and Mayhew, M.J. (2002). Moral judgment development in higher education; Insights from the 'Defining Issues Test'. *Journal of Moral Education*, 31, 3, 1-24.

Lehman, D.R., Chiu, C., and Schaller, M. (2004). Psychology and culture. *Annual Review of Psychology*, 55, 689-714.

Litz, B., Gray, M., Bryant, R., and Adler, A. (2002). *Early intervention for trauma: Current status and future directions.* National Center for PTSD. - accessed 27 August 2002 from http://www.ncptsd.org/facts/disasters/fs_earlyint disaster.html

Lucas, T., and Pross, C. (2004). Caught between conscience and complicity: Human rights violations and the health professions. – accessed 13 August 2004 from http://www.ippnw.org/MGS/V2N2Lucas.html

Maloney, S.D. (1981). Ethics theory for the military professional. Accessed 14 August 2004 from http://www.airpower.maxwell.af.mil/airchronicles/aureview/1981/mar-apr/maloney.htm

Marx, M.H., and Cronan-Hillix, W.A. (1987). *Systems and theories in psychology* (4th edn.). New York: McGraw-Hill.

Maslow, A.H. (1943a). A preface to motivational theory. *Psychosomatic Medicine,* 5, 83-92.

Maslow, A.H. (1943b). A theory of motivation. *Psychological Review*, 50, 370 – 396.

Maslow, A.H. (1954). *Motivation and personality.* New York: Harper and Row.

Maslow, A.H. (1962/1968). *Towards a psychology of being.* (2nd edn.). New York: Van Nostrand.

Maslow, A.H. (1970). *Motivation and personality.* (2nd edn.). New York: Harper and Row.

Maslow, A. H. (1999). *Towards a psychology of being.* (3rd edn.). New York: Wiley.

Maslow, A.H., Frager, R., and Fadiman, J. (1987). *Motivation and personality.* (3rd edn. rev.). New York: Harper and Row.

McClelland, D. C. (1985). How motives, skills and values determine what people do. *American Psychologist*, 40, 812-825.

McCold, P.and Wachtel, T. (2003). In pursuit of a paradigm: A theory of restorative justice. *Institute for Restorative Practices*, August 12 – retrieved from http://www.restorativepractices.org

McCormic, I., and Burch, G. (2005). Snakes in suits: Fear and loathing in corporate clothing. *Management*, November, pp. 34-35.

Meyer-Lindenberg, J. (1991). The holocaust and German psychiatry. *British Journal of Psychiatry*, 159, 7-11.

Milgram, S. (1974). *Obedience to authority.* London: Tavistock.

Mitchell, C. (Ed.) (2001). A special theme issue in honor of John Burton. *International Journal of Peace Studies*, 6, 1, - accessed 22 June 2005 from http://ww.gmu.edu/academic/ijps/vol6_1/cover6_1.htm

Mollica, R.F., Guerra, R., Bhasin, R. & Lavelle,J.L.. (Eds). *Project 1 billion: Book of best practices: Trauma and the role of mental health in post-conflict recovery.*(Ch. 17). - accessed 2 May 2005 from http://www.news.harvard.edu/prerss/pressdoc/supplements/

Moore, B. (1993). Inevitability and the sense of injustice. In M. Fisk (Ed.). *Justice.* (ch.4). Atlantic NJ: Humanities Press.

Murray, H.A. (1938). *Explorations in personality.* Oxford University Press.

NZ Law Commission. (NZLC R85). (2004). *Delivering Justice For All: A Vision for New Zealand Courts and Tribunals.* Wellington: Law Commission.

Nuffield Council on Bioethics. (2002). *Genetics and Human Behaviour: The ethical context.* London: authors.

NZ Law Commission. (NZLC R85). (2004). *Delivering Justice For All: A Vision for New Zealand Courts and Tribunals.* Wellington: Law Commission.

Offer, D., and Sabshin, M. (Eds.). (1991). *The diversity of normal behaviour: Further contributions to normatology.* New York: Basic Books.

Pope, K.S. and Garcia-Peltoniemi, R.E. (2004). *Resources for torture survivors, refugees, asylum seekers, and people affected by war: Responding to victims of torture: Clinical issues, professional responsibilities, and useful resources.* – accessed 14 August 2004 from http://kspope.com/torvic/torturel.php

Porter, L.W., Bigley, G.A., and Steers, R.M. (Eds.). (2003). *Motivation and work behaviour.* 7th edn. New York: McGraw-Hill.

Rest, J., Narvaez, D., Bebau, M.J., and Thoma, S.J. (1999). A neo-Kohlbergian approach: The DIT and schema theory. *Education Psychology Review,* 11, 291-324.

Ronen, S. (1994). An underlying structure of motivational need taxonomies: A cross-cultural confirmation. In H.C. Triandis, M.D. Dunette, and L.M. Hough. (Eds.). *Handbook of industrial and organizational psychology.* Vol.4. (ch.5). Palo Alto CA: Consulting Psychologists Press.

Segerstråle, U. (2001). *Defenders of the truth: The sociology debate.* Oxford University Press.

Seidler, M. and Allena, T. (2004). Mapping the restorative universe: A plenary process to promote a global alliance. *International Institute for Restorative Practices* Conference paper – accessed 9/08/2004 from http:/iirp.org/bc04/

Silke, A. (Ed.). (2003). *Terrorists, victims and society: Psychological perspectives on terrorism and its consequences.* New York: Wiley.

Slone, M., Kaminer, D., and Durrheim, K. (2000). The contribution of political life events to psychological distress among South African adolescents. *Political Psychology,* 21, 3, 465-487.

Sluka, J.A. (2000). *Death squads: The anthropology of state terror.* University of Pennsylvania Press.

Sokal, A. (2004). A physicist experiments with cultural studies – accessed 1 November 2004 from http://www.physics.nyu.edu/faculty/sokal/trasgfnrgress_v2_singlefile.html).

Steers, R.M., Porter, L.W. and Bigley, G.A. (Eds.). (1987). *Motivation and work behaviour.* (4th. Edn.). (Ch.2). New York: McGraw-Hill.

Taylor, A.J.W. (1970). Counselling and student unrest in universities abroad. *New Zealand Journal of Social Work*, 6, 3, 47-55.

Taylor, A.J.W. (2004). Occupational stress and peacekeeping. *Australasian Journal of Stress and Trauma Studies* accessed from http://www.massey.ac.nz/~trauma/issues/2004-1/taylor.htm

Taylor, A.J.W. (in press). Defusing terrorism of terror. In B. Bongar, L. Beutler, P. Zimbardo, L.M. Brown, and J.N. Breckenridge. (Eds). *The psychology of terrorism.* (ch. 10). Oxford University Press.

Tepper, B.J. (2001). Health consequences of organizational injustice: Tests of main and interactive effects. *Organizational Behaviour and Human Decision Processes*, 86, 2, 197-215.

Thrash, T. M., and Elliot, A.J. (2001). Delimiting and integrating achievement motive and goal constructs. In A. Efklides, J. Kuhl, and R.M. Sorrentino. (Eds.). *Trends and prospects in motivation research.* (ch.1). Dordrecht/Boston/London: Kluwer.

Triandis, H.C., and Suh, E.M. (2002). Cultural influences on personality. *Annual Review of Psychology*, 53, 133-160.

UNHCR. (2002). *Statistics on asylum-seekers, refugees and others of concern to the UNHCR.* - accessed 20 March 2004 from http://www.unhcr.ch/cgi-bin/texis/vtx/template/+jwLFqY5BwBo5Boq5eUh5cTPeUz

United Nations. (1982). *Principles of medical ethics relevant to the role of health personnel, particularly physicians, in the protection of prisoners and detainees against torture and other cruel, inhuman or degrading treatment or punishment.* Adopted by General Assembly resolution 37/194 of 18 December – accessed 14 August 2004 from http://www.unhcr.ch/html/menu3/b/h_compo40.htm

United Nations. (2004). Global issues of the twenty-first century: United Nations Challenges: Non-State actor: business, media, NGO, civil society roles. - accessed 20 March 2004, from http://www.global-challenges.org/14extra-state-actors.html

United Nations (2005). *In larger freedom: Towards development, security, and human rights for all. Report of the Secretary-General.* A/59/2005. New York.pp.62.

van der Kolk, B.A. (1996). The body keeps the score: Approaches to the psychobiology of post-traumatic stress disorder. In van der Kolk, B.A., McFarlane, A.C., and Weisaeth, L. (Eds.). *Traumatic stress: The effects of overwhelming experience on mind, body, and society.* (ch.10). New York: The Guilford Press.

Wahba, M.A., and Bridwell, L.G. (1973/1987). Maslow reconsidered: A review of research on the need hierarchy theory. In R.M., Steers, L.W. Porter, and G.A. Bigley. (Eds.). *Motivation and work behaviour.* (4th. Edn.). (Ch.2). New York: McGraw-Hill.

Wong, R. (2000). *Motivation: A biobehavioural approach.* Cambridge University Press.

World Commission on the Social Dimension of Globalization. (2004). *A fair globalization: Creating opportunities for all.* Geneva: International Labour Office.

Young, M.A. (1994/ 2004 update). *The Community Crisis Response Team training manual.* (2nd edn.). Washington DC: National Organization for Victim Assistance.

Zohar, D. and Marshal, I. (2004). *Spiritual capital: The wealth we can live by.* San Francisco: Berrett-Koehler.

INDEX

B

C

D

E

F

G

H

I

J

K

N

O

P

Q

R

S

$ 210.00